History Of The Second Regiment West Virginia Cavalry Volunteers, During The War Of The Rebellion

Joseph J. Sutton

W. Va.
Sut

Very Truly
George Crook

HISTORY

—: OF THE :—

Second Regiment

WEST VIRGINIA CAVALRY VOLUNTEERS,

— DURING THE —

WAR OF THE REBELLION

BY J. J. SUTTON,

LATE PRIVATE OF THE REGIMENT.

PORTSMOUTH, OHIO,

1892.

Introductory. * *

If it is true that he is a benefactor who causes two blades of grass to grow where only one grew before, then it may be said that he who causes two facts to stand out in bold relief where only one fact appeared before, is a friend to truth and a conservator of history; and if he brings a multitude of facts that otherwise would have been lost to sight, surely he is to be commended, and his motives not to be misconstrued. The author of this work needs not to apologize for bringing it forth. He has put upon record a multitude of facts that might have passed into oblivion, as far as the memory of man is concerned, had he not taken occasion to fix them on paper as he himself remembered them, and as hundreds of others will attest, for the perusal of the future historian.

Already the general results of the war are well known to every student of history, for the late war has now passed into history; but the thousands of incidents that appeared then to be of no importance have yet proved to be the pivotal points upon which many an engagement turned, and they are set forth in the light in which they appeared to the observant soldier, whose duty was to go and to come at the bidding of his superior officer. It was not his privilege to say yea or nay, but simply to obey. By no means was the American volunteer soldier a machine. Often was it the case that he who simply wore the blue, without insignia of office of any kind, was possessed of an insight as penetrating into the events that were passing about him as was that of those whose duty it was to direct the issues of the campaign. This may be said truthfully of the American volunteer, that, taken collectively, they rarely ever arrived at a wrong conclusion in the movement that was being made, and this without communication with their superior officers. They conversed freely with each other while around the picket fire, and intelligently forecasted the operations of their superiors, and not infrequently were pungent criticisms indulged in that would have cost them their hope of preferment; for every soldier hoped that in some way his services would be recognized, and that he might be able to go back to his people, if not with the insignia of promotion, at least with the commendation of his superior officers, that would enable him to look the whole world in the face.

The author of this book has made the various situations from 1861 to 1865 a careful study, and having been continually at the front during all that period, and having been a close student of all that was going on about him, he possesses a vantage ground from which he can take a broad survey of all the events of that period. Much of the time his opportunities for obtaining information were of the best, and while it was his duty to serve with closed lips, his ear was alert for everything that would tend to enlighten him upon what was going on. Often entrusted with the execution of important orders, his opportunities for observation were enlarged, and, being careful to keep a record of the daily doings of the army with which he was connected, he created a fund of information that for usefulness far surpassed anything that he then suspected, for when he conceived the idea of writing up the annals of his regiment, he found himself possessed of a vast amount of material that was like a reflected image, for it was the record of the hour and the place. But that was not all. His experience had prepared him to bring to his assistance the best testimony that could be obtained concerning the various campaigns in which his regiment was engaged. He has procured documents that emanated in the hour of engagement, under the showers of shot and shell, amidst the roar of battle, the huzzahs of victory, or in sight of the panic, it may be, that almost invariably attended defeat. Some of these documents are of more than ordinary interest, as they throw a strong light upon the motives that actuated the authorities on either side. Some have been prepared by the survivors of the war, who occupied prominent positions and wielded great influence, and the testimony will be of particular interest to all who participated in the battles described as reflecting the intention that was behind each movement. Letters have been written embracing events that would have faded from memory, and as they are thus brought to mind, they will find corroboration in the minds of many who participated in the actions described.

This volume will prove to be of great value to the student of the late war; first, because no pains have been spared to secure accuracy, and second, every form of exaggeration or laudation has been carefully excluded.

E. E. EWING,
Lieutenant 91st O. V. I.

ROSTER OF

Field, Staff and Company Officers of the Regiment,

Showing the changes therein from the date of original erganization to the date of muster out, June 30, 1865.

Date of Commission.	Names and Rank.	Com	Remarks.
	Colonels.		
Sept. 16, '61.	Wm. M. Bolles		Res. June 25, '62
July 18, '62.	John C. Paxton		Res. May 7, '63
May 18, '63.	Wm. H. Powell		Pro. to Brig. Gen
	Lt. Colonels.		
Sept. 16, '61.	John C. Paxton		Pro. to Colonel
Aug. 19, '62.	Rollin L. Curtis		Res. Oct. 25, '62
Dec. 5, '62.	Wm. H. Powell		Pro. to Colonel
May 18, '63.	David Dove		Res. July 5, '64
July 14, '64.	John J. Hoffman		Mus. out exp. term service.
Nov. 26, '64.	James Allen		Mus. out close of war
	Majors.		
Oct. 2, 61.	Rollin L. Curtis		Pro. to Lt Colonel
Oct. 2, 61.	John J. Hoffman		Pro. to Lt Colonel
Feb. 5, '62.	Henry Steinback		Mus. out Feb. 23, '64
Aug. 19, '62.	Wm. H. Powell		Pro. to Lt Colonel
Jan. 2, '63.	John McMahon		Mus. out Apr. 25, '64
Apr. 29, '64.	James Allen		Pro. to Lt Col
July 14, '64.	Chas. E. Hambleton		Mus. out exp. term service
Nov. 26, '64.	Edwin S. Morgan		Mus. out close war
	1st Lt. and Ad'jt.		
Oct. 25, '61.	John P. Merrill		Res. June 5, '62
Nov. 5, '62.	Elijah F. Gillen		Res. Sept. 7, '64
Nov. 12, '61.	Earl A. Cranston		Res. June 2, '62
Oct. 25, '61.	Geo. Downing		Res. May 1, '62
	1st Lt. & R. Q. M.		
Oct. 2, '61.	Sayres G. Paxton		Mus. out exp. term service
Oct. 23, '61.	Wm. Holden		Res. March 13, '62
	1st Lt. and R. C. S.		
Jan. 2, '63.	Geo. S. South		Mus. out exp. term service
	Surgeons.		
Oct. 25, '61.	Thos. Neal		Res. Feb. 9, '63
Jan. 17, '63.	Matthew McEwen		
	Assistant Surgeons		
Nov. 6, '61.	Lucius L. Comstock		Pro. to Surg., 8 W. Va. Inf.
Nov. 6, '63.	Ozias Nellis		Mus. out exp. term service
May 18, '63.	Edward L. Gilliam		
	Chaplain.		
Oct. 2, '61.	Chas. M. Bethauser		Res. Oct. 12, '62

Date of Commission.	Names and Rank.	Com	Remarks.
	Captains.		
Oct. 19, '61.	Jas. L. Waller	A	Dis. Apr. 25, '64
Apr. 29, '64.	Wm. V. Johnson	A	Mus. out exp. term service
Nov. 26,'64.	Alberto Campbell	A	
Nov. 22,'61.	Wm. H. Powell	B	Pro. to Major
Oct. 9, '62.	Chas. E. Hambleton	B	Pro. to Major
July 14, '64.	Israel B. Murdock	B	Mus. out exp. term service
Jan. 7, '65.	Will S. Merrill	B	Res. June 14, '65
Nov. 22,'61.	Thomas Neal	C	Res. July 22, '62
June 26,'62.	James Allen	C	Pro. to Major
Apr. 29,'64.	James A Morrison	C	Mus. out exp. term service
Nov. 5, '62.	Edwin S. Morgan	C	Pro. to Major
Jan. 7, '65.	Ebenezer E. Wilson	C	Mus. out close war
Oct. 19, '61.	Henry S. Hamilton	D	Res. date not known
May 18, '63.	Alex. H. Ricker	D	Tran. to Co. H Mar. 1 '64
Nov. 24,'63.	Jas. A. Umpleby	D	Mus. out exp. term service
Nov. 26,'64.	John McNally	D	Mus. out close of war
Nov. 22,'61.	Andrew Scott	E	Res. Jan. 12, '62
Jan. 27, '63.	Jeremiah Davidson	E	Pro. to Maj. 79 O. V. I. Sept. 14, '64
May 18, '63.	Joseph Ankrom	E	Mus. out close of war
Nov. 22,'61.	Arthur D. Eells	F	Res. May 6, '62
June 26,'62.	Oliver H. P. Scott	F	Res. Dec. 23, '62
Apr. 1, '63.	Geo. Millard	F	Mus. out exp. term service
Nov. 26,'64.	Henry S. Swentzel	F	Mus. out close of war
Oct. 19, '61.	John McMahon	G	Pro. to Major
Jan. 2, '63.	Jasper A. Smith	G	Res. May 14, '63
May 18, '63.	Joseph Ankrom	G	Tran. to Co. E.
Nov. 2, '64.	Jasper A. Smith	G	Mus. out close of war
Nov. 22,'61.	David Dove	H	Pro. to Lt Col.
Nov. 24,'63.	James A. Umpleby	H	Tran. to Co. D
May 18, '63.	Alex. H. Ricker	H	Mus. out exp. term service
Nov. 22,'61.	Newton J. Behan	I	Res. Oct. 23, '62
Nov. 5, '62.	Wm. M. Fortescue	I	Mus. out exp. term service
Nov. 22,'61.	Silas H. Emmons	K	Res. Oct. 17, '62
Nov. 5, '62.	Edwin S. Morgan	K	Tran. to Co. C.
Oct. 16, '61.	George W. Gilmore	L	Mus. rut exp. term service
Nov. 2, '64.	Jasper A. Smith	M	Tran. to Co. G
	First Lieutenants,		
Oct. 19,'61.	Lewis E. Campbell,	A	Res. Feb. 28, 1863.
May 18,'63.	Alexander Ward,	A	Mustered out ex term service.
Nov. 26,'64.	Elihu D. Robinson,	A	Mus. out close war.
Nov. 22,'61.	Chas. E. Hambleton,	B	Pro. to Capt.
July 31,'62.	P. F. Roherbacker,	B	Res. Feb. 24' 1863.

Date of Commission.	Names and Rank.	Com	Remarks.
May 18, '63.	Israel B. Murdock,	B	Pro. to Capt.
July 14, '64.	Edwin A. Rosser,	B	Mustered out.
Nov. 22, '61.	Jeremiah M. Boyd,	C	Killed Sept. '64.
Nov. 26, '61.	Ebenezer E. Wilson,	C	Pro. to Capt.
Jan. 7, '65.	Abijah B. Farmer,	C	Wounded at Sailor's Creek Apr. 6, '65.
Oct. 19, '61.	Geo. W. Snyder,	D	Res. Feb. 24, '63.
May 18, '63.	James M. Merrell,	D	Trans. to Co. K.
Nov. 5, '62.	John McNally,	D	Pro. to Capt.
Nov. 26, '64.	Samuel McVey,	D	Mus. out close war.
Nov. 22, '61.	Andrew A. Fouts,	E	Dis. Feb. 26, '62.
May 29, '62.	Jasper A. Smith,	E	Pro. to Capt. Co. G.
Jan. 2, '63.	Jeremiah Davidson,	E	Pro. to Capt.
Jan. 27, '63.	Joseph Ankrom,	E	Pro. to Capt. Co. G.
May 18, '63.	John D. Barber,	E	Killed near Winchester July 27, '63.
July 12, '64.	Wm. S. Merrell,	E	Pro. to Capt. Co. B.
Jan. 7, '65.	James W. Hicks,	E	Mus. out close war.
Nov. 22, '61.	Oliver H. P. Scott,	F	Pro. to Capt.
June 26, '62.	Wm. M. Fortescue,	F	Pro. to Capt. Co. I.
Nov. 5, '62.	Geo. Millard,	F	Pro. to Capt.
April 1, '62.	Lloyd B. Stephens,	F	Res. July 13, '64.
Nov. 26, '64.	Charles C. Clise,	F	Mus. out close war.
Oct. 19, '61.	Geo. B. Montgomery,	G	Res. Feb 24, '63.
May 18, '63.	John J. Medlicott,	G	Honorably discharged Sept. 27, 1864.
Nov. 2, '64.	Milton McMillin,	G	Mus. out close war.
Nov. 22, '61.	John Walden,	H	Res. Oct. 22, 1863.
Nov. 5, '62.	James A. Umpleby,	H	Pro. to Capt.
Apr. 29, '64.	James W. Ricker,	H	Mustered out ex term service
Nov. 22, '61.	John W. Neal,	I	Res. May 5, 1862.
June 26, '62.	Geo. K. Weir,	I	Killed at Fayetteville Sept. 12, 1862.
Oct. 9, '62.	Wm. V. Johnson,	I	Pro. to Capt. Co. A.
Apr. 29, '64.	Samuel S. Hawk,	I	Mustered out ex term service.
Nov. 22, '61.	Wm. Yard,	K	Res. Sept. 30, '62.
Nov. 5, '62.	John McNally,	K	Trans. Apr. 7, '63.
May 18, '63.	James M. Merrell,	K	Mustered out ex term service.
Oct. 16, '61.	James Abraham,	L	Mustered out ex term service.
Sept. 26, '64.	Jasper A. Smith,	M	Pro. to Capt.
Nov. 2, '64.	Milton McMillin,	M	Trans, to Co G.
	Sec. Lieutenants.		
Oct. 19, '61.	Charles A. Hudson,	A	Res. Sept. 30, '62.
Oct. 9, '62.	Alexander Ward,	A	Pro. to 1st. Lt.
May 18, '63.	James W. Ricker,	A	Pro. to 1st. Lieut. Co. H.
Apr. 29, '64.	Ebenezer E. Wilson,	A	Pro. to 1st. Lieut ·Co. C.
Nov. 26, '64.	Abijah B. Farmer,	A	Pro. to 1st. Lieut· Co. C.

Date of Commission.	Names and Rank.	Com	Remarks.
Jan. 7,'65.	Emerson McMillin,	A	Mus. out close war.
Nov. 22,'61.	James Allen,	B	Pro. to Capt. Co. C.
June 26,'62.	Israel B. Murdock,	B	Pro. to 1st Lt.
May 18,'63.	Jas. A. Morrison.	B	Pro. to Capt. Co. C.
Apr. 29,'64.	Wm. S. Merrill,	B	Pro. to 1st. Lieut. Co. E.
Nov. 26,'64.	Martin Kramer.	B	Mus. out close war.
Nov. 22,'61.	Wm. Church,	C	Res. Sept. 30, '62.
Oct. 9,'62.	Harvey J. Fulmer.	C	Mustered out ex term service.
Nov. 26,'64.	Geo. Freeman,	C	Mus. out close war.
Oct. 19,'61.	Edwin S. Morgan.	D	Pro. to Capt. Co. K.
Jan. 2,'63.	James A. Hoover,	D	Mustered out ex term service.
Nov. 26,'64.	W. S. Clannahan,	D	Mus. out close war.
Nov. 22,'61.	Joseph Ankrom,	E	Promoted to 1st Lt.
Jan. 27,'63.	Henry F. Swentzel,	E	Pro. to Capt. Co. F.
Nov. 26,'64.	James W. Hicks,	E	Pro. to 1st. Lt.
May 18,'63.	Alberto Campbell,	E	Pro. to Capt. Co. A.
Jan. 7,'65.	John M. Corns,	E	Mus. out close war.
Nov. 27,'61.	Wm. M. Fortescue,	F	Pro. to 1st. Lt.
June 26,'62.	George Millard,	F	" " " "
Nov. 5,'62.	Lloyd B. Stephens,	F	" " " "
Apr. 1, 63.	Oliver C. Ong,	F	Prisoner of war.
Nov. 26,'64.	Elisha T. Fisher,	F	Mus. out close war.
Oct. 19,'61.	Jeremiah Davidson,	G	Pro. te 1st. Lieut. Co. E.
Jan. 2,'63.	John J. Medlicott,	G	Pro. to 1st. Lt.
May 18,'63.	Alberto Campebll,	G	Trans. to Co. E.
Sept. 30,'64.	Wm. J. Kirkendall,	G	Mus. out close war.
Nov. 22,'61.	James A. Umpleby,	H	Pro. to 1st Lt.
Nov 5,'62.	Geo. W. Shoemaker,	H	Killed May 2, '63.
Oct. 24,'63.	Charles C. Clice,	H	Pro. to 1st. Lieut. Co. F.
May 22,'61.	John A. Lowe,	I	Res. Sept. 30. '62.
Oct. 9,'62.	Jonathan B. Carlisle,	I	Mustered out March 21, '65.
Nov. 22,'61.	John McNally,	K	Pro. to 1st. Lt.
Nov. 5,'62.	Walter Christopher.	K	Prisoner of war captured at Fayetteville July 4, '63.
Aug. 22,'61.	Lewis M. Dawson,	L	Dis. Oct. 31, '61.
Oct. 22,'61.	Isaac N. Fordyce,	L	Dis. Nov. 19, '62.
Sept. 30,'64.	Wm. J. Kirkendall,	M	Trans. to Co. G.

NON-COMMISSIONED STAFF.

Names.	Rank.	Age	When mustered into service.	Remarks.
Sam'l B. Murdock,	Sgt Maj.	29	Nov. 8, 61	Pro 2nd Lt. Co. B
James M. Merrell,	"	44	"	Pro. 1st Lt. Co. K
Ed. A. Thomas,	"		Oct. 10, 62	Killed near Winchester July 24, 1864.
Abijah B. Farmer,	"	36	July 24,61	Pro. 2nd Lt. Vet.
J. S. Duke,	"	33	Nov. 8, 61	Vet.
Jas. A. Hoover,	Q M S	22	"	Pro. 2d Lt. Co. G
Thos. A. Lyttle,	"	24	"	Mustered out ex-service.
E. McMillin,	"	18	"	Pro. 2nd Lt.
Jno. J. Medlicot,	Com Sgt	40	"	Pro. 2d Lt. Co. G
Rich'd W. Sayres,	"	20	"	Mustered out ex-service.
Martin Cramer,	"	24	"	Vet. Pro. 2nd Lt.
John M. Corns,	"	23	"	" "
John R. James,	H. S.		"	Died Sept. 4, 62
Dan'l W. Higgins,	"		"	Vet
Geo. DeBussey,	"	21	"	"
G. W. Tinkham,	Sadd'r		"	"
Jac. H. Emmons,	Chief Bugler	22	"	Trans. to Co. K
Thos. James,	"	24	"	Mustered out ex-service.
Rob't Mitchell,	V. Sgn	32	"	" "

Stand Up, Second West Virginia Cavalry, and Be Counted!

Roster of the Second West Virgiuia Volunteer Cavalry, showing the changes in said regiment from the date of organization to the date of first muster out on the 28th day of November, 1864.

COMPANY A.

Names.	Rank.	Age	When mustered into service.	Remarks.
Wallar, James L.	Cap't	40	Nov. 8, 61	Dis. Apr. 24, 64
Johnston, Wm. V.	"	25	"	Not mustered out.
Campbell, L. E.	1st Lt	21	"	" "
Ward, Alexander,	"	28	"	Pro. from 1st Sgt.
Henderson, C. A.	2d Lt	24	"	" " "
Ricker, Jas. W.	"	21	"	Pro. from 1st Sgt. Co. H.
Wilson, E. E.	"	23	"	Pro. from 1st Sgt. Co. C.
Gilmore, Jos. H.	Corp'l	23	"	Not mustered out.
Shindle, Samuel	Sadd'r	23	"	" "
Jones, Charles	Priv.	19	"	" "
Recruits.				" "
McIntosh, Alex. R.	Segt	23	Mch 14, 62	Not mustered out
Stevens, William	Black-smith	30	Jan. 15, 64	" "
Alkin, John	Priv	22	"	" "
Calhoun Noble A.	"	18	"	" "
Davis, Henry	"	41	"	" "
Dye, Andrew	"	20	"	" "
Forrest, Florentine	"	19	"	" "
Fultz, Gco. W.	"	18	"	" "
Frost, Truman	"	19	"	" "
Gilkey, Ira H.	"	19	"	Prisoner of war
Graham, Abner	"	18	"	Not mustered out.
Graves, Daniel	"	40	"	" "
Green, Alonzo J.	"	18	"	Prisoner of war.
Grimes, Joseph W.	"	18	"	Not mustered out.
Hysell, Oren	"	18	"	" "
Hysell, Wilson	"	18	"	" "
Hughes, Thos. C.	"	19	"	" "
Humphrey, J. M.	"	21	Dec. 29, 64	" "
Humphrey, Selden	"	29	"	" "
Hunt, Alonzo	"	19	Jan. 15, 64	" "
Ihle, Christopher	"	18	"	" "
Knapp, Henry	"	36	"	" "
Love' Arthur C.	"	23	"	" "
Martin, W. B.	"	18	"	" "
McClure, Henry	"	25	"	" "
McMasters, Thos.	"	18	"	" "

Names.	Rank.	Age	When mustered into service.	Remarks.
Newman, Jos. B.	Priv.	19	"	Not mustered out.
Parr, Peter	"	18	"	" "
Pierce, Amos	"	19	Jan. 14, 64	" "
Pieree, Elmore	"	42	Jan. 15, 64	" "
Price, B. F.	"	19	"	" "
Plummer W. S.	"	18	"	" "
Rupe, John C.	"	18	"	" "
Russell, Sheffield	"	22	Dec 29, 63	" "
Russell, Chas. R.	"	18	Jan. 15, 64	" "
Rutherford, M. J.	"	18	Dec. 29, 63	" "
Sansbury, Isaac	"	18	Jan 15, 64	" "
Scott, Austin	"	27	"	" "
Searls, William	"	18	"	" "
Smith, David C.	"	24	"	" "
Stout, Geo, P.	"	19	"	" "
Tedrow, William	"	23	"	" "
Welker, David	"	31	"	" "
Welker, Samuel	"	19	"	" "
Woodard, Geo. W.	"	29	"	" "
Veterans.				
Robinson Elihu	1st Sgt	21	Nov. 8, 61	Re-enlisted Nov. 20, 1863.
Cornwell, Jno. G.	"	22	"	" "
Sanders, Ezra	"	23	"	" "
Crouser, John A.	Segt	22	"	" "
Ollvin, Isaac W.	"	27	"	" "
Nease, Lewis S.	"	27	"	" "
Smith, Clark B.	"	24	"	" "
Sanders, Emerson,	Corp'l	20	"	" "
Campbell, Chas. B.	"	20	"	" "
Sipon, David	"	21	"	" "
Chappell, B. M.	"	19	"	" "
Simms, W. H. H.	"	21	"	" "
Crooks, John L.	"	20	"	" "
Merrill, Robert	"	38	Feb. 26,62	" "
Day, Simeon	Bugler	20	Nov. 8, 61	" "
Krofoot, Geo. M.	Black-smith	20	"	" "
Garner, James	"	19	"	" "
Dubois, Levi	Wag'r	27	"	" "
Barker, Leand'r R.	Priv.	18	"	" "
Biggs, Alex. T.	"	18	"	" "
Boling Joseph R.	"	22	"	" "
Calhoun, Thos. J.	"	19	"	" "
Cartwright, G. T.	"	18	"	" "
Hysell, Sampson	"	29	"	" "

Names.	Rank.	Age	When mustered into service.	Remarks.
Hysell, Sam'l P.	Priv.	21	Nov. 8, 61	Re-enlisted Nov. 20, 1863.
Hysell, Lewis	"	18	"	" "
Jones, Andrew P.	"	19	"	" "
Kennedy, A. M.	"	21	"	" "
Lewis, John L.	"	41	"	" "
Loomis, Sam'l C.	"	21	"	" "
Lyman, Rush R.	"	18	"	Not mus. out.
Morgan, Gran.	"	18	"	" "
Peck, A. J.	"	19	"	" "
Quickle, Alex. K.	"	23	"	" "
Richards, Morgan	"	18	"	Re-enlisted Nov. 20, '63.
Robertson, J. W.	"	18	"	" "
Roush, Wm.	"	18	"	" "
Rutherford M. W.	"	20	"	" "
Schilling, Stephen.	"	18	"	" "
Sprague, Saml S.	"	21	"	" "
Stephenson, T. W.	"	29	"	" "
Sanders, Wm. G.	"	18	"	" "
Webster, Benj.	"	23	"	" "
Discharged.				
Goddard, Pearley.	"	18	Jan. 15, '64.	At Gallipolis, O., date unknown.
Garner, Silas.	"	18	Nov. 8, '61.	At Pt. Pleasant, Va, date unknown
Giles, Wm. H.	"	21	"	At Gallipolis, O, date unknown
Gerolman, Peter.	"	14	"	At Pt Pleasant, Va, date unknown
Lanhead, Silas A.	"	22	"	Gallipolis, O.
Murray, Wm.	"	18	Jan. 15, '64.	" "
Sanders, Danl. W.	"	19	Nov. 8, '61.	" "
Skinner, Jas. D.	"	18	"	" "
Died.				
Singer, Thos. A.	Bugler.	21	Nov. 8, '61.	See death roll.
Chase, Summer F.	Priv.	23	Jan. 15, '64.	" "
Bailey, David C.	"	21	Nov. 8, '61.	" "
King, Thos. B.	"	21	Jan. 16, '64.	" "
McCormick, J. W.	"	18	Nov. 8, '61.	" "
Reynolds, Wm. L.	"	21	"	" "
Radford, Joseph.	"	21	"	" "
Skiles, Thos. C.	"	18	"	" "
Transferred.				
Campbell, Alberto.	1st Serg't.	24	"	Com and assigned to Co G
Shoemaker, G. W.	Segt.	21	"	Com and assigned to Co H
Atkinson, James.	Priv.	19	"	To Co. E.
Brown, Leander.	"	18	Jan. 15, '64.	To Co. B.
Calhoun, Wm. W.	"	20	Jan. 2, '64.	To Co. K.
Chamberlain, J. M	"	18	Nov. 8, '61.	To Co. E.

Names.	Rank.	Age	When mustered into service.	Remarks
Crouser, Wm. H.	"	25	"	Trans. to Co. E.
Cornwell, Geo.	"	19	"	" " E.
Dickens, H.	"	22	Aug. 30, '63.	" " K.
DeBussey, Geo.	"	21	Jan. 1, '62.	Pro hospital stewart
Harley, Wm. H.	"	20	June 30, '63.	Trans. to Co. K.
Holmes, Barron.	"	18	"	" " K.
McCollom, F.	"	18	Jan. 15, 64	" " B.
McMasters, J. L.	"	18	Nov. 8, 61	" " E.
Monroe, James M.	"	18	Jan. 15, 64	" " B.
Mathew, James P.	"	23	Nov. 8, 61	Pro to Lt in 3rd Va calvary
McClain, Chas.	"	19	"	Trans. to Co. E.
McCollough, John.	"	20	"	" "
McCollough H.	"	18	"	" "
McElhinny S. C.	"	18	Jan. 2, 63	" "
Newsome Edwin.	"	30	Aug 24,63	" "
Peck, Darius.	"	20	Nov. 8, 61	" "
Quickle, Nial A.	"	20	"	" "
Romines, T. S.	"	18	Jan 15, 64	" " B.
Sias, Isaac.	"	24	June 30,63	" " K.
Sprague, Thos. J.	"	22	Nov. 8, 61	Pro to 1st Lt 4th W Va calvary
Scott, Charles.	"	39	"	Trans. to Co. K.
Sisson, Nat.	"	18	Jan. 2, 63	" " K.
Thomas, John W.	"	23	Nov. 8, 61	" " E.
Thompson, H. M.	"	22	"	" " K.
Winters, Wm. A.	"	22	"	Trans. V. R. C.
Weaver, Geo.	"	18	"	" " E.
Wilcoxen, J. C.	"	22	"	" " K.
Deserted.				
Halsey, Alfred.	"	20	Mar. 4, 62	Nov. 18, 63.
Richard, Groner.	"	19	Nov 15, 61	Oct 8, 62, at Pt Pleasant
Robinson, Lewis.	"	27	Jan. 15, 64	At Williamsport, Md
Ummensetta, J. B.	"	21	Nov. 8, 61	Oct 27, 62 at Seary, Va

Aggregate,..151 men

Names.	Rank.	Age	When mustered into service.	Remarks
Powell, Wm. H.	Capt.	36	Nov. 8, 61	Pro. to Maj.
Hambleton, C. E.	"		Nov 22, 61	Pro. to Maj.
Murdock, I B.	"	29	"	Pro. to 1st Lt.
Roherback, P. F.	1st Lt.		"	Res Feb 24, 53
Rosser, Edwin A.	"	22	Nov. 8, 61	Pro from Co. I.
Allen, James.	2nd. Lt.		"	Pro Capt Co. C.
Morrison, Jas. A.	"	26	"	Pro. from Sergt.
Merrill, Wm. S.	"	18	"	Pro. from Sergt.
Ferguson, W. W.	Com. Sergt.	24	"	Pro. from Priv.
Clark, Samuel.	Qm. Sergt.	41	"	Not mus. out.
Able Jesse.	Sergt.	27	"	Not. mus. out.
Kirker Richard A.	"	18	"	Pris. of war.
Hopkins, D. W.	Corp.	21	"	Mustered out.
Parker, Wm. H·	"	22	"	" "
Blankenship, Wm.		21	"	" "
Howard, Michael.	Black-smith.	44	"	" "
Booth, Nathaniel.	Priv.	19	"	" "
Burch, Wayne.	"	21	"	" "
Henry, Wm. K.	"	31	"	" "
Hopkins, Wm. G.	"	33	"	" "
Hopkins, H. G.	"	18	"	" "
Lewis, Richard.	"	22	"	" "
Morgan, Mordeci	"	36	"	" "
Millard, Richard.	"	18	"	" "
Monroe, R. M.	"	18	"	" "
Morris Jefferson.	"	34	"	" "
Pugh, John.	"	19	"	" "
Ridout George	"	27	"	" "
Swartenalter H. A.	"	24	"	" "
Starlin Abraham	"	23	"	" "
Stinson Albion B.	"	24	"	" "
Sanders Oscar W.	"	18	"	" "
Todd Alfred	"	44	"	" "
Williams Thomas	"	34	"	" "
Recruits.				
Kirker Casey L	Bugle.	18	Oct. 2, '63	Missing in action at Newtown
Brown Leander	Priv.	18	Jan. 15, 64	Not mustered out
Carmichael John	"	19	Oct. 10, 62	" "
Caruthers Wm. L.	"	23	"	" "
Drake Stephen P.	"	44	"	" "
Eakins Emory A.	"	19	Dec. 23, "	" "
Hafflich Frank	"	19	Aug. 23, 63	" "
Kirker Robt.	"	18	Nov. 24, 62	" "
Kirk Eli E	"	18	Mar. 29, 64	" "

Names.	Rank.	Age	When mustered into service.	Remarks
Morris Chas. E.	"	23	Oct. 10,62	Not mustered out
Morris Chas. L.	"	19	"	" "
Morris James A.	"	19	Nov.27,63	" "
Mitchell Wm.	"	20	Oct. 10,63	" "
Monroe James M.	"	18	Jan. 15,64	" "
Parker John S.	"	18	Oct. 10,62	" "
Tinkerman Elias	"	21	Dec. 2, 63	" "
Pifer George	"	18	Aug.28,63	" "
Romine Thaddeus	"	18	Jan. 15,64	" "
Sanders John	"	20	Oct. 10,62	" "
Spencer Elias C.	"	24	Jan. 15,64	" "
Tracks Joseph	"	18	Aug.23,63	" "
Windel John R.	"	18	Feb. 27,64	" "
Veterans.				
Duke John S.	1st Sgt	30	Nov. 8, 61	Re-enl. Jan.1, 64
Corns John M.	"	23	"	" "
Boynton Henry B.	"	20	"	" "
Sanders E. N.	"	28	"	" "
Kippenger Wm. J	Corp.	25	"	" "
Verbeck A. J.	"	20	"	" "
Messer Jacob	"	27	"	" "
Dempsey John H.	"	20	"	" "
Hurn Mills C.	Blacksmith	25	"	" "
Irwin, John	Wag'r	27	"	" "
Boynton, Chas. C.	Priv.	24	"	" "
Blankenship, Jos.	"	18	"	" "
Carr, Jeremiah	"	40	"	" "
Carr, Cornélius	"	18	"	" "
Cally, Wm. L.	"	21	"	" "
Daniels, John	"	30	"	" "
Evans, Evan	"	22	"	" "
Ginheimer, Fred	"	22	"	" "
Gates, Stephen P.	"	29	"	" "
Kimball, Joseph	"	18	"	" "
Lloyd, David	"	18	Nov.17,61	" "
McCoy, Alfred	"	18	Nov. 8, 61	" "
Murphy, Horace	"	21	"	" "
Pine, James	"	22	"	" "
Staten, Wm. H.	"	18	"	" "
Slack, John	"	21	"	" "
Todd, Geo. B.	"	18	"	" "
Vandervort, E T.		19	"	" "
Discharged.				
Burkett, David K.	Qm. Sgt	33	"	Apr. 7, 62

Names.	Rank.	Age	When mustered into service.	Remarks.
Blankenship, John	Priv.	25	"	For dis. Oct.15 62
Bertram,Chester P	"	20	"	For dis. Oct.18 62
Evans John	"	34	"	For dis. Jan. 7,63
Hamilton, Wm.	"	44	"	For dis. Oct.14,62
Johnson, Hiram	"	19	"	For dis. Oct.16,62
Patton, Wash.	"	27	"	Fordis. July21,64
Millard, Geo.	1st Sgt	25	"	Pro. 2nd Lt Co. F
Died.				
Stewart, John N.	Com Sgt	27	"	See death roll
VanEvery, Martin	Sgt	41	"	" "
Thomas, Ed. A.	"	28	Oct. 10,62	" "
Reeves,Braxton P.	"	34	Nov. 8, 61	" "
Hailey, Irwin R.	Corp.	21	"	" "
Mitchell, Edward	Blacksmith	38	"	" "
Tomlinson,Thos H	Bugle	25	"	" "
Butler, James H.	Priv.	23	Dec. 11,61	" "
Blankenship, E.	"	27	Nov. 8,61	" "
Conway, Lewis	"	31	Oct. 10, 62	" "
Davis, Edmond	"	44	Nov. 8, 61	" "
Henshaw, H. H.	"	20	Oct. 10,62	" "
Hoffman, Geo.	"	18	Nov. 8, 61	" "
Jones, Henry	"	19	"	" "
McKee, Amos	"	23	"	" "
Transferred.				
James, Thomas	Bugle	24	Nov. 8, 61	Pro. Chief Buglar
Carlisle, Jno. B.	Sgt	18	"	Pro. 2nd Lt Co. I.
Brammer, Sydney	Priv.	19	Oct. 10,62	To V. R. C.
Skelton, John C.	"	23	"	" "
Mitchell, Robt.	"	32	Nov. 7, 61	To Vet Surgeon
Deserted.				
McCollum, Frank.	"	18	Dec. 15,61	At Charleston June 28, 64
Foler, Emanuel	"	17	Mar. 27---	Apr. 28, 64

Aggregate, less received from other Co's....111 men.

J. J. SUTTON, The Author.

J. J. SUTTON,

Names.	Rank.	Age	When mustered into service.	Remarks.
Neal, Thomas	Capt.		Nov. 8, 61	Res. July 2, 62
Allen, James	"		"	Promoted Major
Morrison, Jas. A.	"	26	"	Mustered out
Boyd, Jeremiah	1st Lt	49	"	" "
Church, Wm.	2d Lt	47	"	" "
Fulmer, Harry J.	"	21	"	" "
Harn, Thomas	Segt	41	"	" "
Burrows, Wm.	"	22	"	" "
Penn, Columbus	"	19	"	" "
Long, Richard S.	"	24	"	Wounded Sept. 19, 64
Mitchell, Rosebery	Corp.	43	"	Mustered out
Adams, Thomas	"	26	"	" "
Holland, Wm. H.	Sdlr.	26	Dec. 2, 61	" "
Barker, Noah	Priv.	20	Nov. 8, 61	" "
Bontrigger, H.	"	20	"	" "
Bliss, Samuel	"	21	"	Wounded at Raleigh July 14, 63
Cohen, Burnett	"	18	"	Mustered out
Eikey, Charles	"	18	"	" "
Gault, Andrew	"	44	Sept. 7, 61	" "
Goosman, Israel	"	18	Nov. 8, 61	Wounded at Raleigh July 14, 63
Hoffman, Jacob M.	"	28	"	Mustered out
Hubbs, Solomon	"	38	"	" "
Hoffman, R. M.	"	24	"	" "
Hisson, John	"	18	"	" "
Lorey, John	"	18	"	Wounded at Raleigh July 14, 63
Lorey, Conrad	"	19	"	Mustered out
Miller, James G.	"	21	"	Wounded at Winchester Sept. 5, 64
McMillen, Richard	"	20	"	Mustered out
Porter, Alvin	"	19	"	" "
Ridgway, Sam'l	"	22	"	" "
Smith, Sam'l	"	42	"	" "
Winton, Clark	"	25	"	" "
Recruits.				
Burris, John A.	"	19	Mar 24, 64	Not mustered out
Burns, John M.	"	40	"	" "
Drake, Benjamin	"	25	Dec 22, 62	" "
Dorff, Rueben	"	18	Dec 22, 63	" "
Ehman, Lagans	"	18	"	" "
Ellswick, Geo. W.	"	42	Apr. 2, 64	" "
Fields, John C.	"	19	Dec. 7, 63	" "
Johnson, Wm. L.	"	35	Jan. 4, 64	" "
Mitchel, Jas. B.	"	34	Aug 28, 63	" "
Miner, Harper	"	40	Mar 30, 64	" "

Names.	Rank.	Age	When mustered into service.	Remarks.
Miner, Geo. W.	"	19	Apr. 5, 64	" "
Reed, Benjamin	"	35	Jan. 4, 64	
Shell, John H.	"	18	Mar 24, 64	Wounded and prisoner
Truax, William	"	22	Mar. 4, 62	Not mustered out
Weisend, George	"	18	Jan. 4, 64	" "
Veterans.				
Freeman, George	1st Sgt	22	Nov. 8, 61	Re-enlisted March 9, 64
Larcomb, Chas.	Qm. Sgt	22	"	Re-enlisted Nov. 20, 63
Young, Silas E.	Com. Sgt	20	"	" "
Barnes, Griffith C.	Sgt	22	"	" "
Ullom, Frank	Corp.	26	"	" "
McAllister James	"	19	"	" "
Dodds, Joseph	"	19	"	" "
Kimball, Joseph	"	25	"	" "
Gamlin, George	"	21	"	" "
Hamilton, Thos.	Black-smith	43	"	" "
Switzer, Chas.	"	22	"	" "
Stewart, Elias	Wgr	21	Dec. 2, 61	" "
Brown, James W.	Priv.	18	Nov. 8, 61	re-enl. Mar. 9, 64
Brown, John	"	23	"	re-enl. Nov. 20, 63
Barker, Ezra	"	22	Dec. 2, 61	Wounded and prisoner
Bottomfield, Wm.	"	37	Nov 8, 61	Re-enlisted Nov. 20, 63
Bottomffeld, Isaac	"	30	"	Re-enlisted March 9, 64
Coldbaugh, John	"	18	"	" "
Dye, Enoch L.	"	18	"	Re-enlisted Nov. 20, 63
Dennis, Joseph	"	18	"	" "
Darff, Charles,	"	20	"	" "
Drake, John	"	22	"	" "
Drake, Thomas	"	22	"	Re-enlisted March 9, 64
Dorr, John T.	"	21	Mar. 4, 62	Re-enlisted Nov. 20, 63
Gatton, Robert	"	20	Nov. 8, 61	" "
Hartshorn, Wm.	"	22	"	" "
Hamilton, A. J.	"	22	"	" "
Hoffman, R.	"	22	"	" "
Hern, Granville	"	34	"	Re-enlisted March 9, 64
Hobaugh, Jas. M.	"	18	Mar. 4, 62	Re-enlisted Nov. 20, 63
Myers, John	"	27	Nov. 8, 61	Re-enlisted March 9, 64
McKaig, John B.	"	20	"	Re-enlisted Nov. 20, 63
Petty, Samuel	"	25	"	" "
Steele, Jabez	"	35	"	" "
Steele, Adam	"	21	Mar. 4, 62	Wounded and prisoner
Sole, Isaac	"	18	Dec. 2, 61	Re-enlisted Nov. 20, 63
Stout, Jacob	"	19	Mar. 9, 62	Re-enlisted Mar. 9, 64

Names.	Rank.	Age	When mustered into service.	Remarks
Young, David	"	18	Feb 13, 62	Re-enlisted Nov. 20, 63
Discharged.				
Barrens, F. A.	"	18	Nov. 8, 61	For dis. Oct. 6, 62
Boyd, Henry	"	19	"	" "
Foutz, Thos. B.	"	23	"	For dis. Oct 14, 62
Lynch, Geo. B.	"	43	"	For dis Oct. 8, 62
Thompson, Orville	"	18	"	At Pt. Pleasant Nov. 25, 63
Slack, Robt S.	"	21	"	At Gallipolis Oct. 16, 62
Woods, Simon	"	30	"	" "
Wilson, J. M.	"	25	"	Dis. at enlistment
Died.				
Dye, Enoch L.	Sgt	22	Nov. 8, 61	See death roll
Swallow, John W.	Corp.	20	"	" "
Cox, Baldwin	Priv.	22	"	" "
Hamilton, S. B.	"	20	"	" "
Hoskins, Hudson	"	21	"	" "
Leonard, A. W.	"	19	"	" "
McMillin, Marion	"	19	Dec. 1, 63	" "
Shreves, Jas. H.	"	20	Nov. 8, 61	" "
Smith, William	"	18	"	" "
Ullum, Stephen	"	44	"	" "
Transferred.				
Barber, John B.	1st Sgt	23	Nov. 8, 61	Pro. 1st Lt. Co. E
Johnston, W. V.	"	25	"	Pro. 1st Lt. Co. I
Smith, Geo. S.	Bugler	23	"	Pro. 1st Lt. Co. –
Wilson, E. E.	1st Sgt	22	"	Pro. 2d Lt. Co· A.
Deserted.				
Barker, Elisha	Priv.	22	Dec. 2, 61	Sept. 17, 62
Batton, Jas. O.	"	18	"	At Charleston Jan. 5, 64
McMillin, Levi	"	16	Nov. 8, 61	At Parkersburg July 19, 64
Switzer, Fred	"	24	June 2, 61	Sept. 16, 62

Aggregate,..111 men

Names.	Rank.	Age	When mustered into service.	Remarks.
Hamilton, H. S.	Capt.	30	Nov. 8, 61	Resigned date unknown
Ricker, Alex H.	"	38		Assigned to Co. H
Umpleby, James A.	"	28	Nov. 8, 61	Not mustered out
Snyder, Geo. W.	1st Lt.	23	"	Resigned date unknown
McNally, John	"	26	"	Pro. to captain
Morgan, Edwin S.	2d Lt.	27	"	" "
Hoover, James A.	"	22	"	Not mustered out
Ward, Alexander	1st Sgt	27	"	Pro. 1st Lt. Co A
Lowry, Grafton	Sgt	21	"	Wounded at Winchester Sept. 19, 64
Shry, Sylvester	Corp.	21	"	Mustered out
Dowd, Homer C.	"	18	"	" "
Barthoff, James	Priv.	18	"	" "
Carpenter, B. F.	"	21	"	" "
Chidester Z.	"	22	"	" "
Dunkle, Henry	"	22	"	" "
Emigh, Joshua	"	32	"	" "
Fout, George W.	"	32	"	" "
Harbarger, John	"	36	"	" "
Joseph, James	"	26	"	" "
Moore, Jesse	"	44	"	" "
Millbeck, Wm.	"	32	"	" "
McAllister, Allen	"	23	"	" "
Schwarp, Andrew	"	25	"	Prisoner of war.
Recruits.				
Armstrong, James	"	18	Aug 28,63	Not mus. out.
Bush, Samuel	"	18	"	" "
Bess, Charles	"	20	Feb. 20,64	" "
Bower, Leonard	"	40	"	" "
Coulter, Benj.	"	18	Jun. 30,63	" "
Cook, Paris	"	19	Nov. 18,63	" "
Davis, John	"	21	Mar. 6, 64	" "
Davis, Benj.	"	21	"	" "
Gore, John H.	"	18	Jun. 30, 63	" "
Herndon, Wm.	"	21	"	" "
Huggins, Wm.	"	24	Feb. 20,64	" "
Jones, Granville	"	20	Nov. 18,63	mis'g May 15, 63
Jones, Emanuel	"	18	May 1, 64	not mustered out.
Johnson, Elmer A.	"	20	Dec. 2, 62	" "
Miller, And'rs'nT.	"	21	Mar.25,64	" "
Oiler, John A.	"	21	Feb. 20,64	" "
Oiler, Geo. R.	"	29	Mar. 24,64	" "
Partlow, Morgan	"	18	Jun.30, 63	" "
Reach, Peter N.	"	21	Dec. 19,62	G. C. M.

Name.	Rank.	Age	When mustered into service.	Remarks.
Simmons, Henry	Priv.	21	Aug.28,63	Not mustered out.
Soulsby, Edward	"	21	Mar. 6, 64	" "
Thomas, David C.	"	20	Aug.28,63	" "
Wills, David T.	"	18	"	" "
Workman, Rob't	"	44	Dec. 2, 63	" "
Workman, David	"	41	"	" "
Veterans.				
M'Clannahan, W S	1stSegt	24	Mar.25, 62	re-enl. Mar. 25,64
Frazee, Jekhiel	2d Segt	18	Nov. 8, 61	woun'd Sep. 22,64
Davis, Samuel	C. Sgt	24	"	re-enl. Jan. 1, 64
Shaw, James	Segt.	21	"	" "
Andrews, Jos. W.	"	18	"	" "
Dunkle, Perley	"	19	"	" "
Steele, James S.	"	20	"	" "
Jarvis, Emanuel	Corp.	28	"	" "
Hawks, John L.	"	18	"	" "
Nunnemaker, Jno.	"	21	"	" "
McConnell, Wm.	"	23	"	W'nded and pris.
Smith, Silas	"	23	"	Re-enl. Jan. 1, 64
Shuster, John S.	"	19	"	" "
Coulter, Jos. C.	Bugler	19	"	" "
Cooper, Isaac N.	Saddl'r	22	"	" "
Myers, Fred	Bl'k	32	"	" "
Blackford, Thos.	Wag'r	24	"	" "
Black, Geo. N.	Priv.	18	"	" "
Boyer, Geo. W.	"	19	"	" "
Bobo, Arvi J.	"	19	"	Re-enl. Mar.25,64
Brown, James N.	"	21	"	Re-enl. Jan. 1, 64
Cable, John	"	19	"	Wounded and prisoner, July 24, '64.
Dixon, Henry	"	18	"	Wounded and prisoner May 10, '64.
David, F. M.	"	20	"	Re-enl. Jan. 1, 64
Eby, Philander	"	18	"	" "
Erwin, Wm. D.	"	25	"	" "
Herrold, Chas. P.	"	18	"	Wounded and prisoner May 10, '64.
Hileman, H. H.	"	21	"	Re-enl. Jan 1, 64
Hannah, S. P.	"	23	"	" "
Hays, Christopher	"	18	"	" "
Hanning, John	"	21	"	Wounded and prisoner May 10, '64.
Jurock, Prosper	"	27	"	Re-enl. Jan. 1, 64
Keeton, J. M.	"	19	"	" "
Kale, John	"	20	"	" "
Lowry, Thomas	"	35	"	" "
McQuaid, L. M.	"	18	"	" "

Name.	Rank.	Age	When mustered into service.	Remarks,
McQuaid, C. W.	Priv.	19	"	Re-enl. Jan. 1, 64
Morgan, Morgan	"	40	"	" "
McGaby, W.	"	22	"	" "
McElheny, John	"	29	"	" "
Nixon, Isiah	"	18	"	Wounded May 10, '64.
O'Donnell, D.	"	35	"	Re-enl. Jan. 1, 64
Shry, Jacob	"	18	"	" "
Stephens, Benj.	"	21	"	Wounded May 10, '64.
Latman, John W.	"	20	"	Re-enl. Jan. 1, 64
Tomlinson, J. F.	"	21	"	" "
Watkins, Samuel	"	21	"	" "
Wyatt, John W.	"	20	"	" "
Welsh, James	"	22	"	" "
Discharged.				
Herrold John	"	22	"	For Dis. Oct. 16, '62.
Nixon, John	"	27	"	For Dis. Oct. 24, '62'
Ebys, Andrew	"	42	"	For Dis. Oct. 14, '63
Transferred				
Ward, Alexander	1st Sgt	27	"	Pro. 2nd Lt. Co A
Morgan, Edward	2nd Lt.	27	"	Pro. to Capt. Co. K.
Died.				
Black, Benj. F.	Priv.	43	"	See death roll.
Bobo, G. C.	"	18	"	" "
Lowry, David C.	Corp.	22	"	" "
Lowry, Courtney	Priv.	21	"	" "
Burgess, Wm. T.	"	37	Aug. 28, 63	" "
Remy, William	"	18	June 30, 63	" "
Jackson, John J.	"	21	Mar. 6, 64	" "
Deserted.				
Keeton, John J.	"	22	Nov. 8, 61	Camp Piat, Dec. 8. '62.
Powers, Dan'l V.	"	22	Dec. 23, 62	Camp Piatt, Jan. 6' '63.
Barthoff, Azariah	"	32	Nov. 8, 61	Camp Piatt, Mar. 3, '63.
Peckenpaugh, R.	"	18	Aug. 28, 63	Camp Toland, Dec. 28, '63.
Mullens, John H.	"	26	Dec. 2, 63	Camp Toland, Feb. 28, '64.
Boyer, Ashel	"	18	Nov. 8, 61	Parkersburg, July 18, '64.
Ratliff, Darius	"	21	Feb 20, 64	Blacksburg, May, 13, '64.
Null, Francis M.	"	21	Nov. 8, 61	Parkersburg, July 13, '64.
Dunkle, Amos	"	19	"	Camp Toland, July 8, '64.

Aggregate..117 men.

Names.	Rank.	Age	When mustered into service.	Remarks
Scott, Andrew	Capt.	48	Nov. 8, 61	Res. Jan. 12, '62
Davidson, J.	"	27	"	Pro. Maj. 79th O. V. I.
Fout, Andrew A.	1st Lt.	22	"	Cashiered Feb 26, '62.
Smith, Jasper A.	"		"	Pro. Capt. Co. G.
Ankrom, Joseph	"	29	"	" " "
Barber, John D.	"		"	Killed July 27, '64.
Swentzel, H. F.	2nd Lt		"	Prc. from 9th Penn. Inf.
Rush, Asa C.	1st Sergt.	42	"	Mustered out.
Craig, Henry C.	Com Sgt	28	"	" "
Martin, Geo. P.	Sgt	19	"	
Hedges, Warren	"	20	"	" "
Crisman, Thomas	"	18	"	" "
Davis, Chris.	Corp.	20	"	" "
Dickerson, J. L.	Bugle	26	"	" "
Fouts, Benj.	Blacksmith	38	"	" "
Rush, Joseph	"	27	"	" "
Porter, Wm. H.	Sadd'r	27	"	" "
Ankrom, David	Priv.	32	"	" "
Ankrom, Linz	"	31	"	" "
Becket, Jessie M.	"	23	"	" "
Cross, Monroe	"	18	"	" "
Carder, Martin	"	18	"	" "
Callihan, C. M.	"	25	"	" "
Chamberlain, J. N	"	21	"	" "
Crowser, H. W.	"	27	"	" "
Carwell, George	"	21	"	" "
Grubb, Archibald	"	26	"	" "
Herron, James U.	"	26	"	" "
Hadley, Richard	"	39	"	" "
Hardway, H. M. D	"	22	"	" "
Henry, Robt. M.	"	27	"	" "
Jackson, Saml C.	"	19	"	" "
Knight, J.	"	28	"	" "
Lighthizer, W. T.	"	24	"	" "
Mosgrove, T.	"	30	"	" "
McCullough, J.	"	20	"	" "
McCullough, H.	"	18	"	" "
McClain, Charles	"	18	"	" "
McMasters, J. L.	"	18	"	" "
Patton, Henry W.	"	28	"	" "
Peck, Dairus D.	"	20	"	" "
Quickle, Nial A.	"	20	"	" "
Robinett, Thomas	"	28	"	" "

Names.	Rank.	Age	When mustered into service.	Remarks
Shoemaker, J. H.	Priv	40	"	Mustered out.
Stephens, Jos. R.	"	19	"	.. ..
Thomas, John W.	"	23	"	.. ..
Wickersham, P.	"	18	"	.. ..
Weaver George	"	18	"	.. ..
Recruits.				
Alberry, Richard	"	26	Jan. 5, 64	Not mus. out.
Alberry, A.	"	18		.. ..
Alberry, Joseph	"	18	Nov.20,64	.. ..
DeMasters, J. A.	"	21	Mar. 2, 64	.. ..
Hill, Samuel	"	21	Jan. 5, 64	.. ..
Kellison, M.	"	18	June30,63	.. ..
Livingston, J. D.	"	18	Feb 26,64	.. ..
Martin, A. T.	"	18	Sept 14,63	.. ..
McGraw, Wm.	"	18	Dec. 23,62	.. ..
Morris, Philip	"	38	Jan. 5, 64	.. ..
McElheny, S. C.	"	18	June2, 63	.. ..
Nixon, William	"	29	Jan. 5, 64	.. ..
Newsome, E. M.	"	27	Sept. 1, 63	.. ..
Palmer, Geo. B.	"	23	Dec. 31,63	.. ..
Rollin, Franklin	"	20	June30,63	.. ..
Rollins, Joseph	"	22		.. ..
Trout, James H.	"	29	Mar 31,64	.. ..
Vincent, Wm. J.	"	33	Jan. 4, 64	.. .
Veterans.				
Fisher, Elisha	Q M S	18	Nov. 8, 61	Re-enl. Jan. 6, 64
Burrows, James	Sgt	35	"	Re-enlNov. 20,63
Boyd, James	"	44	"	.. ..
Vansickle, A.	Corp.	26	"	.. ..
Rolen, Daniel	"	24	"	.. ..
Alberry, John	"	19	"	.. ..
Coburn, R. L.	"	22	"	.. ..
McCarty, Wm. H.	"	20	"	.. ..
Robinson, Justice	"	20	"	Re-enl. Jan. 6, 64
Hooker, Wm. H.	Wagn'r.	20	"	.. ..
Gilbert, Robt. H.	Priv.	18	"	.. ..
Hayes, Oliver	"	18	"	Re-enl Nov.20,63
King, Martin, S.	"	19	"	.. ..
McGrath, George	"	19	"	.. ..
Oliver, Alex.	"	19	"	.. ..
Phillips, Richard	"	22	"	.. ..
Ross, Thomas	"	18	"	Re-enl. Jan 6, 64
Shafer, John	"	18	"	.. ..

Names.	Rank.	Age	When mustered into service.	Remarks.
Smith, John	Priv.	18	Nov. 8, 61	Re-enl Nov.20,63
Smith, Jacob	"	18	"	.. ..
Spencer, Geo. J. C.	"	19	"	.. Jan. 6, 64
Williams, Peter	"	23	"	.. Nov. 20, 63
Benson, Calvin	"	32	"	.. ..
Discharged.			"	
Ankrom, Joseph	"	42	"	Fordis. Sept16,62
Ankrom, Andrew	"	23	"	.. ..
Calwell, James	"	18	"	.. Aug. 62
Davis, George	"	44	"	.. Oct. 62
Graw, John W.	"	28	"	By G. C. M. Feb. 18, 62
Hart, Josiah M.	"	44	"	Fordis. Mar.10 63
Hallcraft, Elijah	"	42	"	.. Oct. 62
McQuaid, Eli	"	40	"	.. Sept 16, 63
McGwigan.Wm. E	"	36	"	.. Nov. 11, 62
Moore, John W.	"	18	"	Date and cause unknown.
Sweatland, Joel G.	"	46	"	For dis. June 62
Troyman, Joseph	"	28	"	.. Oct. 62
Woodyard, John E	"	26	"	.. ..
Woodyard, T. W.	"	19	"	.. ..
Died.				
Smith, Wm.	Corp		Nov. 8, 61	See death roll
Humpfield, Ed.	Bugler		"	.. ..
Burdett, Silas A.	Priv.		"	.. ..
Chaplin, John L.	"			.. ..
Durbin, Samuel A.	"		Nov. 8, 61	.. ..
Filkill, Wm. H.	"		"	.. ..
Hartford, Wm. M.	"		"	.. ..
Irwin, Justice	"		"	.. ..
Orr, Wm. W.	"		"	.. ..
Worman, Franklin	"		"	.. ..
Phillips, George	"		Apr. 5 64	
Transferred.				
Ong, Oliver C.	1st Sgt	20	Nov. 8, 61	Pro. 2nd Lt Co F
Deserted.				
Bradley, Patrick	"		"	Camp Piatt Feb. 9, 63.
Eades, Geo. W.	"			.. Jan. 5, 64
Parr, John J.	"		Nov. 8, 61	At Weston W. Va.
Hamilton, Isaac	"		Aug.28,63	Gallipolis June 17 64

Aggregate, less received from other Cos.......106 men.

Names.	Rank.	Age	When mustered into service.	Remarks.
Eells, Arthur D.	Capt	24	Nov. 19 61	Res'd May 5, 62
Scott, Oliver H. P.	"		Nov. 8 61	.. Dec. 23, 62
Millard, George	1st Lt		"	Pro. Capt.
Fortescue, Wm. M.	"	29	"	Pro. Capt. I
Stephens, Lloyd B.	"	29	"	Res'd date unknown
Ong, Oliver C.	2nd Lt	21	"	Pris. May 12, 62
Bunnington, H. H.	Sgt	23	Nov. 19 61	Mustered out
Sharp, Thomas	"	21	"	Pris. Nov. 10, 63
Jenkins, Samuel	Corp	27	"	Mustered out
Brooke, Henry R.	"	28	"	.. ..
Bucey, Wm. T.	Priv	23	"	Wn'd May 10, 64
Ellson, Isiah	"	24	"	Mustered out
Gray, Joshua	"	18	"	.. ..
Hall, John	"	23	"	.. ..
Herman, Chas. A.	"	26	"	.. ..
Metcalf, Joseph	"	42	"	.. ..
Miller, Elbridge	"	19	"	.. ..
Smith, Wm. A.	"	24	"	.. ..
Strouse, Phillip	"	23	Sept. 20, 61	.. ..
Shuman, Samuel	"	23	Nov. 19, 61	Wn'd Sept. 6, 64
Weir, Wm. C.	"	25	"	Mustered out
Cassell, Wm. E.	"	20	"	Deserted from military prison.
Recruits.				
Barker, Josiah W.	"		July 8, 63	Not mustered out.
Ballenger, James	"	18	June 29, 63	.. ..
Cunningham, A. J.	"		Sept. 29, 62	.. ..
Deval, Samuel	"	19	Jan. 5, 64	.. ..
Gray, Thomas	"	21	Aug. 28, 63	.. ..
Hall, Leman	"	18	June 29, 63	.. ..
Hall, Isaac	"			.. ..
Hoffman, A. J.	"	21	Oct. 10, 62	.. ..
Hunt, Edwin	"	26	Feb. 20, 64	.. ..
Langley, Nicholas	"	18	June 29 63	.. ..
Light, Henry	"	22	Oct. 10, 62	.. ..
Lilly, Pleasant H.	"	21	Dec. 28, 62	.. ..
Lilly, Geo. W.	"	20	June 29, 63	.. ..
Lane, John P.	"	20	Dec. 28, 52	.. ..
Monnett, George	"	22	Oct. 10, 63	.. ..
Murphy, John	"	29	Oct. 10, 63	.. ..
Meadows, Creed T.	"	18	Aug 28, 63	.. ..
Meadows, Wm.	"	18	Aug 28, 63	.. ..
Maron, Horatio	"	29	Dec. 28, 63	.. ..
Nichols, William	"	20	Oct. 10, 62	.: ..

Names.	Rank.	Age	When mustered into service.	Remarks.	
Ormsby, James	Priv	19	Oct. 1, 62	..	..
Ray, Samuel	"	19	..	..	..
Smith, Jacob	"		Sept 29,63	..	..
Stryers, Jehu	"	19	June 29,63	..	..
Spooner, Cyrus M.	"	31	Jan. 5, 64	..	..
Walters, Geo. R.	"		Sept 29,62	..	..
Whitehill, Resin	"		..	..	..
Vickery, Azell R.	"	28	Aug. 28 63	..	..
Veterans.					
McVey, Samuel	1st Sgt		Nov. 8 61	Re-enl. Jan. 1, 64	
Dearner, John F.	2m Sgt	38	Nov. 19 61	..	..
Eckleberry, M.	Com S	20	..	..	..
Harris, Samuel	Segt	24	..	..	..
Wilson, Wm.	"	21	..	..	..
Sanford, Geo. P.	Corp'l	20	..	..	..
Nickel, James B.	"	24	..	..	..
Wright, Amos	"	21	..	..	..
Alton, Milton	"		..	..	..
Ellis, Lindlay F.	"	21	..	..	..
Leasure, Ephraim	"	21	..	..	..
Jenvey, Geo. K.	Bugler	18	..	..	..
Morgarage, D. J.	"	19	..	..	..
Stutes, David	Black-smith	30	..	..	..
Dyer, Charles	"	18	..	..	..
Papp, John	Sadd'r	33	..	.,	..
Walker, Andrew	Wag'r	35	..	..	..
Andrews, Marcel	Priv		..	..	..
Brooks, Joseph	"		..	..	..
Biggers, Wilson S	"		..	..	..
Bartlett, Calvin	"	28	..	..	..
Byers, James F.	"	20	..	..	..
Byers, William A.	"	18	..	..	..
Clifford, Samuel	"		..	..	..
Cronley, Paul F.	"	23	..	..	..
Cowce, Seneca A.	"	21	..	..	..
Darby, Thomas	"	21	..	..	..
Dyer, John	"	21	..	..	..
Freek, John F.	"	22	..	..	..
Goodwin, John A.	"	22	..	..	..
Hankinson, H. J.	"	19	..	..	..
Hall, Jonathan	"	22	..	..	..
Hays, James M.	"		..	..	..
King, John	"	21	..	..	..

Names.	Rank.	Age	When mustered into service.	Remarks.
Laughery, Thorn.	Priv.	18	Nov. 19, 61	Re-enl. Jan. 1, 64
Love, Solomon	"	18	..	.. ..
Lucas, Jacob	"		..	.. ..
Mains, Simon	"	20	..	.. ..
Mains, Elijah	"	22	..	.. ..
McAtee, Wm.	"	20	..	.. ..
McDeiel, John J.	"	29	..	.. ..
Mallory Johnson	"		..	.. ..
Prindle, Martin	"	18	..	.. ..
Pyle, Geo. D.	"	18	..	.. ..
Rogers, George	"	22	..	.. ..
Rarden, Wm. H.	"	22	..	.. ..
Rarden, W. H. H.	"	22	..	.. ..
Ross, Daniel	"	19	..	.. ..
Rink, Geo. W.	"	21	..	.. ..
Whyde, James	"	19	..	.. ..
Colvon, Edward	"	18	"	.. ..
Discharged.				
Perry Armstrong	Corp.	23	"	For disability.
Byers, John A.	Priv.	22	..	.. ..
Bell, James R.	"	20	..	.. ..
Bushon Joseph	"	22	..	.. ..
Cornelius, George	"		..	.. ..
Dozer, Lyman	"	21	"	.. ..
Fisher, Joshua	"		..	.. ..
Gardner, James	"	27	..	.. ..
Rarden, Jacob C.	"	24	..	.. ..
Stoddard, Milton	"	33	..	.. ..
Signor, Thomas	"	45	..	.. ..
Warner, Geo. P.	"	38	..	.. ..
Henderson, Wm.	"	38	..	.. ..
Died.				
Bolen, Joseph M.	"			See death roll.
Fitzpatrick, John	"	20	Nov. 19, 61	.. ..
Howell, Isaac	"	19	Dec 23, 62	.. ..
Perry, James W.	"	21	Aug 28, 63	.. ..
Scott, Freeman	"	18		.. ..
Taylor, Joseph P.	"	38	Nov. 19, 61	.. ..
Pathers, Chas. J.	"	32	..	.. ..
Transferred.				
Weir, Geo. K.	1st Sgt	21	Nov 19, 61	Pro. 1st Lt. Co. I
Clise, Chas. C.	Segt	25	..	Pro. 2nd Lt. Co. H
Medlicott, John	Priv.	20	..	Pro. 2nd Lt. Co. G

Names.	Rank.	Age	When mustered into service.	Remarks.
Deserted.	Priv.			
Alchier, William	"	20	Oct. 10, 62	At Camp Piatt
Baaz, Samuel	"			" "
Snodgrass, Joseph	"	18	Nov.19, 61	" "
Langley, Harvey	"	18	"	At Charleston
Lowery Alvin	"	27	"	" "

Aggregate...129 men.

COMPANY G.

Names.	Rank.	Age	When mustered into service.	Remarks.
McMahon, John	Capt.	48	Nov. 8, 61	Pro. Maj. Dec. 31, '62.
Smith, Jasper A	"	27	..	Res'nd May14, 63
Ankrom, Joseph	"	29	..	Trans. from Co. E
Montgomery, Geo.	1st Lt.	22	..	Res'nd Feb. 24,63
Medlicott, John J.	"	20	..	Dis. Sept. 27, 64
Davidson, Jerm'h	2d Lt.	27	..	Pro. 1st Sgt Co E
Campbell, Alberto	"	23	..	Pro. from 1st Sgt. Co. A.
Zehring, Freder'k	1st Sgt	29	..	Mustered out
Arthur, Caleb	Q.M.S.	31	..	" "
Lunsford, Wm.	Sgt.	22	..	" "
McLaughlin, E.D.	"	36	"	" "
Absher, John	Priv.	27	"	" "
Anderson, Boyd	"	35	..	" "
Ashcroft, Smith	"	44	..	" "
Butler, James E.	"	43	..	" "
Barron, Thomas,	"	22	..	" "
Barron, Richard	"	20	..	wnd'd July 4, 63
Delancy, Edmund	"	20	..	Mustered out
Daley, John	"	19	..	Missing in Acton, Oct. 9 '64
Flynn, John	"	30	..	Mustered out
Farer, Daniel	"	18	..	Trans. from Co. H
Gardner, Samuel	"	23	..	Missing in action Dec. 11, 1863.
Golden, John	"	18	..	Missing in action Aug. 24, 1863.
Glenn, William	"	22	..	Trans. from Co. H
Hoaley, John	"	36	..	Missing in action May 8, 1863.
King, Mark	"	23	..	Mustered out
Lunsford, Levi	"	20	..	" "
Lunsford, Andrew	"	40	..	" "
McMahan, Jacks'n	"	27	..	" "
Riter, Phillip	"	19	..	" "
Ritchey, Geo. B.	"	34	..	" "

Names.	Rank.	Age	When mustered into service.	Remarks.
Sullivan, Jerry	Priv.	37	Nov. 8, 61	Mustered out
Throckmorton, B.	..	31	..	Trans. from Co. H. wounded July 24, 1864.
Whitt, George	..	28	..	Mustered out
Warneke, August	..	32	..	" "
Recruits.				
Doran. Nicholas	Corp'l	21	Jun. 2, 62	Not mustered out.
Atkins, Robert	Priv.	19	..	" "
Blankenship, Jas.	..	18	Feb. 27,64	" "
Christian Quincy	..	21	..	" "
Craig, Peter	..	18	Sept. 19,62	Trans. from Co.H
Elderkin, Jackson	..	18	Jun. 7, 64	Wnd'd Oct. 1, 64
Harris, David	..	23	Jun. 24,63	Missing in action Oct. 1, 1861.
Howell, Silas	..	18	Jun. 25,63	Missing in action July 4, 1863.
Johnston, James	..	25	Oct. 10, 62	Trans. Co. H
King, James	..	18	Jun. 25,63	Not mustered out.
King, John	..	18	Mar.27, 64	" "
Massey, James	..	18	June 8, 63	Trans from Co H
Mann, Caleb	..	23	July 22,63	" "
Osborn, James	..	20	Feb. 2, 63	" "
Rafferty, Thomas	..	18	Feb. 27,63	Not mustered out
Rousey, Samuel	..	26	Apr. 27,63	Trans from Co H
Smith, William	..	32	Sept. 1, 63	Not mustered out
Todd, James	..	20	Oct. 10, 62	Trans from Co H
Williams, Samuel	..	26	Nov. 8, 61	" "
Veterans.				
Ashcraft, Joshua	Q.M.S.	21	..	Wnd'd Oct 18, 64
Buck, James	Sgt.	32	..	Re-enl Dec 25, 63
Mandel, Fred	"	25	..	Re-enl Feb 6, 64
Lunsford, Thos.	Corp'l	20	..	Re-enl Dec 25, 63
Jones Joseph	..	21	..	" "
Waits, Conrad	..	20	..	" "
Kiner, Alex	..	21	..	Missing in action Oct. '64
Payne, James W.	..	18	..	Re-enl Feb 6, 64
Cave, Aquilla	..	28	..	Re-enl Jan 4, 64
Coates, George	Bugler	28	..	Re-enl Dec 25, 63
Fisher, August	Sadl'r	25	..	Missing Luray, Oct. '64
Doetz, John K.	Black-smith	27	..	Re-enl Jan 6, 64
Franck, John	..	20	..	Missing in action Oct. 2, 63
Breeding, James	Priv.	19	..	Re-enl Dec 25, 63
Burke, Thomas	..	35	..	" "
Briner, George	..	19	..	" "
Buck, Darius S.	..	30	..	" "
Barnhardt, James	..	18	..	" "

Names.	Rank.	Age	When mustered into service.	Remarks.
Doran, Wm.	Priv.	23	Nov. 8, 61	Re-enl Jan 4, 63
Delaney, Arthur	..	23	..	Re-enl Dec 25, 63
Dunfield, John	..	25	..	Re-enl Feb 6. 64
Dailey, James	..	22	..	Re-enl Dec 25, 63
Goodfellow, John	..	44	..	" "
Harman, White	..	18	..	Re-enl Feb 6, 64
Harvy, John	..	34	..	Re-enl Jan 4, 64
Hilburn, John	..	32	..	Re-enl Dec 25, 63
Morford, Julien R.	..	18	..	" "
Morford, John R.	..	19	..	" "
Marckel, James	..	18	..	.. ..
McCaslin, Geo.	..	28	..	.. ..
Patterson, James	..	24	..	.. ..
Sullivan, Dennis	..	18	..	.. ..
Sloan, Granville	..	30	..	Re-enl. Jan. 6, 64
Wood, William	..	18	..	Re-enl. Dec. 25,63
Yates, Biddle	..	24	..	.. ..
Discharged.				
Angel, Henry	..	23	..	Dis. Oct. 28, 63
Barrett, Michael	..	19	..	Dis. Dec. 25, 62
Beals, Wm.	..	37	..	Dis. June 15, 63
Beals, Isaac	..	28	..	Dis. June 25, 63
Evans, Edward	..	27	..	By order Sec. war
Green, Wm. D.	..	40	..	For disability
Sullivan, Jeremiah	..	43	..	For disability June 20, 63
Died.				
Lunsford, Pressley	Sgt.	20	..	See death roll
Dundan, John	..	21	..	.. ..
McConnell, James	Corp.	27	..	.. ..
Claybaugh, Jacob	Bugler	33	..	.. . ..
Dunfield, George	Priv.	21	..	.. ..
Doran, Edward	..	24	..	.. ..
Harvey, Albert	..	18	..	.. ..
Miller, Matthew	..	26	..	.. ..
Transferred.				
Hoover, James	Com. Sgt.	21	..	To Qm. Dept.
Deserted.				
McDonough, M.	Priv.	22	..	Camp Piatt Feb. 17, 63
Saunders, Patrick	..	21	..	.. ..
Syurs, James	..	23	..	Charleston, July 5, 64
Sheaver, John	..	18	Aug. 7, 63	Charleston, July 10, 64
Deerman, Wm.	..	17	Not mustered.	Lewisburg, June 28, 64
Mankins, Robt.	..	18	..	Martinsburg, July 21, 64

Aggregate less received from other Co's......101 men.

Names.	Rank.	Age	When mustered into service.	Remarks.
Dove. David	Capt.	22	Nov. 8, 61	Pro. Lt. Col.
Umpleby, Jas. A.	"	26	"	Trans. to Co. D
Ricker, Alex H.	"	39	May 18, 63	Mustered out
Walden, John	1st Lt.	23	Nov. 8, 61	Res. Oct 22, 64
Ricker, James W.	"	20	"	Pro. from 2nd Lt. Co. A
Shoemaker, G. W.	2d Lt.	22	"	Killed May 2, 63
Clice, Charles C.	"	23	"	Pro. from 1st Sgt. Co. F.
Louderback, A.	Qm. Sgt.	25	"	Mustered out
Weed, Columbus	Sgt.	28	"	" "
Pugh, George	"	28	"	" "
Tarr, Alonzo	Corp.	32	"	" "
Cherrington, D. W	Bugler	28	"	Wounded at Fisher's Hill Sept. 22, 64
Lovejoy, Paul M.	Black-smith	33	"	Mustered out
Grossman, A. A.	Priv.	25	"	" "
Lackey, Juguretha	"	30	"	" "
McMillin, Andrew	"	21	"	" "
Smith, Jonas	"	18	"	Prisoner since July 15, 63
Worman, Thomas	"	33	"	Mustered out
Recruits.				
Baxter, Felix J.	"	28	Aug. — 63	Not mustered out
Brown, Geo. W.	"	24	Oct. 10, 62	" "
Cutlip, James D.	"	23	July 22, 63	" "
Cutlip, A. E.	"	22	"	" "
Cooper, Balis	"	18	Mar. 21, 64	" "
Elswick, Rosdell	"	38	Oct. 10, 62	Wounded Sept. 5, 64
Ford, John	"	25	July 7, 63	Not mustered out
Hanna, Samuel	"	28	"	" "
Halfpenny, Lewis	"	22	"	" "
Hutchinson, J. A.	"	25	July 22, 63	Wounded Sept. 22, 63
Kady, William	"	37	Oct. 10, 62	Not mustered out
Kinnison, E. G.	"	22	Feb. 27, 64	" "
Kirk, James	"	18	Mar. 24, 64	" "
Lane, William H.	"	18	Dec. 23, 62	" "
Landers, Allen T.	"	18	Oct. 10, 62	" "
Morton, G. W. T.	"	29	"	" "
Morton, Paschal T.	"	18	"	" "
Massy, M.	"	13	Apr. 24, 63	" "
Mercer, Levi J.	"	24	Aug 12, 63	" "
Rapp, Joseph A.	"	24	Aug. 7, 62	" "
Smith, Gordon	"	30	Oct. 10, 62	" "
Smith, Elisha	"	18	Mar. 22, 64	" "
Stypes, Samuel	"	18	"	" "
Settle, Isaac J.	"	22	Oct. 10, 62	" "

Names.	Rank.	Age	When mustered into service.	Remarks.
Sutton, Joseph J.	..	20	Mar. 29,63	Not mus. out.
Williams, S. P.	..	29	Oct. 10, 62	.. ..
Williams, John	..	18	Apr. 24,63	.. ..
Williams, Henry	..	22	..	.. ..
Williams, Alfred	..	28	Mar. 24,64	.. ..
Woolwine, Jacob	..	25	Sept. 10,63	.. ..
Veterans.				
Kramer, Martin	Sgt.	24	Nov. 8, 61	Re-enlNov. 22,63
Marshman, H. H.	..	23	..	.. ..
McMillin, E.	..	18	..	.. ..
Hammons, R. T.	..	20	..	.. ..
Howe, Jefferson	..	24	..	.. ..
Nickle, Harrison	Corp.	20	..	.. ..
Stewart, Geo. A.	..	20	..	.. ..
Hull, Reuben E.	..	21	..	.. ..
Spurrier, Wm.	..	22	..	.. .
Philley, A. T.	..	20	..	.. ..
Bartoe, David	..	20	..	.. ..
Hoover, Nathaniel	Bugler	22	..	.. ..
Cherrington, D. W	..	22	..	.. ..
Branson, Chas. W.	Sadl'r	21	..	.. ..
Alton, John	Priv.	18	..	.. ..
Brunton, Wm.	..	20	..	.. ..
Ellis, Pierson V.	..	18	..	.. ..
Flowers, A. J.	..	18	..	.. ..
Fullerton, G. W.	..	30	..	.. ..
Garret, Albert B.	..	21	..	.. ..
Gardner, John I.	..	18	..	.. ..
Heniker, Gustave	..	35	..	.. ..
Helphenstine, J. F.	..	18	..	.. ..
Higgins, Dan'l W.	..	38	..	App Hospital steward.
McArron, Wm. J.	..	20	..	Re-enl Nov.22,63
McKeever, Thos.	..	21	..	.. ..
McMillin, Murray	..	19	..	.. ..
McCarty, M. D.	..	39	..	Pris. Aug. 64.
Myers, Joseph	..	20	..	Re-enlisted Nov. 22, 63
Miller, Thomas	..	24	..	.. ..
Milliken, James	..	19	..	Pris. Oct. 4, 64.
Owens, Thomas	..	24	..	Re-enlisted Nov. 22, 63.
Poor, John W. T.	..	27	..	.. ..
Poor, Gabriel T.	..	23	..	.. ..
Patton, John	..	23	..	.. ..
Radcliff, John M.	..	19	..	.. ..

Names.	Rank.	Age	When mustered into service.	Remarks.
Sutberland, M. O.	Priv	18	Nov. 8, 61	Re-enl Nov.22,63
Smith, David	"	22	"	Pris. Oct. 1, 64
Tucker, Wm. E.	"	22	"	Re-enl. Nov.22,63
Weed, Chas. M.	"	18	"	" "
Weed, Wm. H.	"	21	"	Woun'd Apr. 1,65
Willis, Cyrus H.	"	20	"	Pro. to corp'l
Discharged.				
Jones, David E. F.	Corp.	24	"	Date unknown.
Richbaugh John H.	Priv.	18	"	On writ habeus corpus.
Died.				
Shoemaker, G. W.	Lt.		"	See death roll.
Burnside, Wm. H.	Segt.	22	"	" "
Gard, Scott	Corp.	19	"	" "
Brooks, William	Priv.	21	"	" "
Claar, Samuel	"	19	"	" "
Faires, Cyrenus B.	"	18	"	" "
Garvin, Wm.	"	20	"	" "
Goddard, Peter	"	18	"	" "
Hale, Geo. W.	"	18	"	" "
Harding, Joseph J.	"	22	"	" "
James, John R.	"	25	"	" "
Millhoff, Jacob P.	"	18	"	" "
Morton, Thos. T.	"	23	Sept. 2, 63	" "
Moore, Isaac	"	34	Oct. 10, 62	" "
Prim, Benj.	"	23	Nov. 8, 61	" "
Simpson, Geo. W.	"	18	"	" "
Smith, James H.	"	20	"	" "
Weed, Andrew J.	"	20	"	" "
Worman, C.	"	35	"	" "
Woodram, James	"	25	Sept.11,63	" "
Baxter, J. M.	"	44	Oct. 10,62	" "
Transferred.				
Smith, Jasper A.	Sgt	27	Nov. 8, 61	Pro. 1st Lt. Co E
Hawk, Samuel S.	"	19	"	Pro. 1st Lt. Co.I.
Craig, Peter H.	Priv.	18	Oct. 10, 62	Trans to Co. G. Apr. 26, 64.
Farrer, Daniel S.	"	18	Nov. 8, 61	" "
Glenn, Wm. W.	"	22	"	" "
Hooley, John	"	36	"	" "
Johnston, J. W.	"	35	Oct. 10, 62	" "
Moore, M.	"	20	"	" "
Massey, James D.	"	18	Jun. 18,63	" "
Mann, Caleb M.	"	22	July22, 63	" "
Osborn, James H.	"	20	Feb. 26,63	" "

Names.	Rank.	Age	When mustered into service	Remarks.
Rousey, Samuel	Priv.	28	Apr.17, 63	" "
Throckmortin, B.	"	31	Nov. 8, 61	" "
Todd, James P.	"	20	Sept. 1, 63	" "
Williams, S. P.	"	26	Oct. 10, 62	" "
Deserted.				
Peppers, Geo. W.	"	21	Nov. 8, 61	Guyandotte, '62.
Stanton, Oscar C.	"	35	Dec 23, 62	Remount Camp, Oct. 13, 64,

Aggregate...129 men.

COMPANY I.

Names.	Rank.	Age	When mustered into service..	Remarks.
Behan, Newton J.	Capt.	22	Nov. 8, 61	Res. Oct. 23, 62
Fortescue, W. M.	"	28		Pro from 1st Lt Co F.
Neal, John W.	1st Lt.	34	"	Res. May 5, '62
Weir, Geo. K.	"	21	"	Killed Sept. 12, '62.
Johnston, Wm. V.	"	25	"	Pro to Capt Co A.
Hawk, Samuel S.	"	21	"	Pro. from 1st Sgt Co H.
Lowe, John A.	2d Lt.	30	"	Res Sept 30, '62.
Carlisle, J. B.	"	21	"	Pris Sept 14, 63.
Dudley, Daniel	Com Sgt.	46	"	Mustered out
Prescott, Charles	Sgt.	22	"	" "
Carr, A. W.	Corp.	21	"	Pris. Sept. 14, 63.
Hamilton, David	"	25	"	Mustered out
Cammell, Henry	Bugler.	21	"	" "
Allen, Lewis D.	Priv.	24	"	" "
Berry, T. P.	"	22	"	" "
Dawson, Wm.	"	24	"	Pris. Sept. 14, '63
Hawk, Vanson	"	24	"	Mustered out.
Jones, Junius M.	"	23	"	Pris. Sept. 14, 63.
Jobes, William	"	32	"	Mustered out
Leyshon, Wm.	"	23	"	Pris. Sept. 14, 63.
Lowes, John H.	"	19	"	" "
Lee, Harrison P.	"	27	"	Mustered out
Lowry, John	"	25	"	" "
Lowden, Geo. W.	"	23	"	" "
Lowden, Thomas	"	21	"	" "
Miller, Wm.	"	21	"	" "
Owens, William	"	43	"	" "
Rice, Lewis	"	24	"	" "
Terrill, John	"	25	"	" "

Names.	Rank.	Age	When mustered into service.	Remarks.
Thompson, Ed.	Priv.	29	Nov. 8, 61	Mustered out
Thompson, Jos.	"	26	"	" "
Wade, Enos	"	22	"	" "
Recruits.				" "
Lavender, John S.	Corp.	23	Apr. 24, 63	Not mustered out
Butler, William	Priv.	24	Oct. 10, 63	" "
Buchanan, James	"	19	Apr. 12, 63	" "
Bone, Wm. M.	"	25	Aug 28, 63	" "
Bone, Doctor H.	"	21	"	" "
Bobo, Francis M.	"	23	Oct. 10, 62	" "
Cline, Lemuel J.	"	19	Aug 28, 63	" "
Cornet, Reuben	"	25	June 30, 64	" "
Cornet, Jacob	"	23	"	" "
Carr, John C.	"	18	"	" "
Condry, Jacob A.	"	18	Mar 4, 64	" "
Dunbar, Theo.	"	24	Dec 23, 62	" "
Humphrey, Geo.	"	20	"	" "
House Robert	"	25	Oct. 10, 62	" "
Horden, Richard	"	19	Aug 28, 63	" "
Jacose, Wm.	"	38	Oct. 10, 62	" "
Lax, Thomas	"	19	Aug. 28, 63	" "
Long, Archibald	"	18	"	" "
Lowes Thomas	"	18	"	" "
Murrah, William	"	19	Dec. 23, 62	" "
McHenry, Robt.	"	19	Oct. 10, 62	" "
Mills, Anderson	"	28	"	" "
McCleary, J.	"	25	Aug. 28, 63	" "
Mahala, Jesse	"	24	"	" "
Mahala, Wm.	"	34	"	" "
Meadows, John C.	"	25	"	" "
Miller, Benj.	"	21	July 10, 63	" "
Miller, Jacob	"	18	Mar. 1, 63	" "
McCormick, Wm.	"	18	Apr. 24, 63	" "
Pressly, Wm.	"	19	Apr. 28, 63	" "
Price, Wm.	"	42	"	" "
Price, Thomas	"	33	"	" "
Price, David	"	33	Apr 30, 63	" "
Price, Moses	"	21	Nov. 1, 63	" "
Roark, Jesse	"	22	Aug. 28, 63	" "
Roark, Timothy	"	32	"	" "
Robson, Joseph	"	18	"	" "
Stewart, Chris.	"	21	Oct. 10, 63	" "
Swisher, Samuel	"	19	Oct. 18, 63	" "

Names.	Rank.	Age	When mustered into service.	Remarks.
Sellers, James W.	Priv.	22	Jun. 30, 63	" "
Stiff, Allen	"	19	Aug 28, 63	" "
Varran, Daniel	"	20	Jan. 1, 64	" "
Wiggins, Geo. W.	"	20	"	" "
Wills, Macron R.	"	22	Aug 28, 64	" "
Wilson, Charles	"	25	May 1, 64	" "
Young, S. H.	"	18	July 3, 64	" "
Veterans.				
Hicks, James W.	1st Sgt	24	Nov. 8, 61	Re-enl Nov. 20, 63
Fountain, W. H.	Qm, Sgt.	23	"	" "
Torrence, Alex. C.	Segt	24	"	" "
Yeager, Wm. V.	"	27	"	" "
Reed, Henry N.	"	24	"	" "
Fellows, Geo. W.	"	25	"	" "
Rawling, Richard	Corp.	20	"	" "
Spencer, Saulcer	"	28	"	" "
Curtis, Erastus	Black-smith	23	..	" "
Buckner, Wm H.	"	23	"	" "
Variana, Chas. G.	Sad'lr	26	"	" "
Bush, John E.	Priv.	20	"	" "
Collins, Joseph	"	21	"	" "
Glover, Charles	"	20	"	" "
Hawk, Solomon F.	"	20	"	" "
Hysell, Gaston	"	20	"	" "
Stanley, James	"	20	"	" "
Terrill, Isaac	"	22	"	" "
Tull, Wm.	"	22	"	" "
Townsend, Wm. E	"	20	"	" "
Vancleif, Dorsey	"	22	"	" "
Willis, John	"	35	"	" "
Woomar, John	"	20	"	" "
Discharged.				
Gilliam, David T.	Corp.	18	"	Sept. 12 63 for wounds
Jackson, Andrew	Black-smith.	38	"	Dis. Jan. 19, 63
Buckhee, James A.	Sad'lr	33	"	Dis. Oct. 19, 62
Bowen, Abednego	Priv.	23	"	Dis. Oct. 9, 62
Dennis, John	"	18	"	Dis. Jan. 9, 63
Flesher, William	"	21	"	Dis. Oct. 18, 62
Hanes, Shelton	"	18	"	Dis. Oct. 15, 62
Hicks, John	"	30	"	Dis. Oct. 15, 62
Lytton, James	"	38	"	Dis. Apr. 7, 62
Saddler, Lewis	"	23	"	Dis. July 24, 62
Tiplady, Edmond	"	32	"	Dis. Oct. 9, 62

Names.	Rank.	Age	When mustered into service.	Remarks
Calvert, Geo. W.	Priv.	21	"	Dis. Oct. 15, 62
Thompson, S.	"	26	"	Dis. Dec. 31, 62
Died.				
Hoover, John W.	Corp.	24	"	See death roll
O'Brien, Thomas	"	43	"	" "
Packard, Myron	"	20	"	" "
Crantz, Michael	Priv.	32	Sept. 18,62	" "
Dill, David	"	21	Nov. 8, 61	" "
Eggers, Isaac	"	20		" "
Harris, Cyrus	"	19	Nov. 8 61	" "
Hewitt, Casper	"	37	"	" "
Roberts, W.E.M.	"	30	July 22,63	" "
Sluder, David	"	21	Not mus.	In Libby prison
Robert, Byron	"	24	"	See death roll.
Robinson, Wm.	"	18	Nov. 8. 61	" "
Transferred.				
Fulmer, Henry J.	Sgt	24	"	Pro. 2nd Lt Sept. 1, 62
Gilliam, Ed. L.	Priv.	23	"	Pro. 2nd assist. Sg'n May 3, 63
Rosser, Edwin A.	"	24	"	Pro. 1Lt July 21, 64
Sayres, R. W.	Sgt	22	"	R. C. S. Nov. 63
Little, Thos. O.	"	27	"	Q. M. S. Nov. 63
Deserted				
Aikers, Adam	Priv.	32	Apr. 24,63	Charleston Sept 18, 63
Bradley, Silas	"	19	"	Charleston, July 16, 64
Chapman, Wm.	"	23	Nov. 8, 61	Meadow Bluff, June 12, 62
Congrove, George	"	19	"	" "
Lamb, John	"	22	"	" "
Mankin, Ashford	"	23	Sept.18,61	Camp Piatt, Mar. 4, '63.
Price, Timothy	"	19	Not mus.	At Charleston Nov. 63
Spicer, Henry T	"	27	Nov. 8, 61	Camp Piatt Mar. 4. '63.
Skinner, James	"	19	Sept.18,62	" "

Aggregate...140 men.

Names.	Rank.	Age	When mustered into service.	Remarks
Emmons, Silas H	Capt.		Nov. 8, 61	Res. Oct 17, 62
Morgan, E. S.	"	29	"	Pro. from 2nd Lt
Yard, William	1st Lt.		"	Res. Sept. 30, 63
McNally, John	"		"	Trans. to Co. D
Merrill, James M.	"	44	"	Pro. from 1st Sgt
Walter, Chris.	2d Lt.		"	Pris. July 63
Carr, Stephen	Com. Sgt.	26	"	Mustered out
Morse, John	Sgt.	28	"	Pris. July 29, 63
Ward, John	"	35	"	Mustered out
Hastings, John	"	19	"	" "
McMackin, John	"	34	"	Wn'd July 4, 63
Peni, James M.	Corp.	44	"	Mustered out
McMackin, Dan.	Sgt	26	"	" "
Calfer, Walter	Corp.	35	"	Wn'd July 29,63
Sterm, Wm. W.	"	29	"	Pris. July 29, 63
Emmons, Jacob H.	Bugler	22	"	Mustered out
Prince, John W.	Black-smith	34	"	" "
Bartler, Isaac K.	Sad'lr	25	"	" "
Clark, Henry	Priv.	41	"	Pris. July 64
Donaldson, A.P.	"	27	"	Mustered out
Friel, Edward	"	32	"	" "
Hall, John	"	23	"	" "
Kinkaird, James	"	32	"	" "
McGregor, M'chl	"	27	"	" "
Murphy, Robt.	"	42	"	" "
McGlone, Patrick	"	31	"	" "
Mooney, James	"	32	"	" "
Milhorne, James	"	35	"	Mustered out
Null, Andrew	"	38	"	" "
Quinn, Thomas	"	26	"	" "
Reed, Samuel	"	43	"	" "
Rush, Wm.	"	38	"	" "
Stafford, Matthew	"	18	"	" "
State, James	"	40	"	" "
Smith, P. M. C.	"	21	"	" "
Scott, Charles	"	39	"	" "
Thompson, H. M.	"	22	"	Pris. May 10, 64
Wangler, John	"	40	"	Mustered out
Wilcox, James C.	"	25	"	" "
Recruits.				
Wheeler, Alex.	Corp.		June 25, 62	Not mustered out
Sisson, Nathaniel	"	19	July 2, 63	" "
McKinney, N.	Bugler	32	Aug. 31,63	" "

Name.	Rank.	Age	When mustered into service.	Remarks.	
Addis, Benj.	Black-smith	18	Nov. 24, 63	"	"
Ashby, Azanah	Priv.	18	July 23, 64	"	"
Alderson, Geo. W.	"	18		"	"
Bunch, Isaac W.	"	19	Dec. 23, 63	"	"
Broyles, Simeon	"	44	Ang 31, 63	"	"
Cawley, John	"	19	Nov. 23 63	"	"
Calhoun, Wm. W.	"	20	Jan. 2, 63	"	"
Cotherin, Robert	"	37	Feb. 24, 64	"	"
Cotherin, James	"	18	"	"	"
Dickens, Harrison	"	21	June 3 63	"	"
Holliday, Samuel	"	27	June 25, 63	"	"
Haley, Wm. H.	"	20	June 3, 63	"	"
Holmes, Byron	"	18	Jun. 3, 63	"	"
Little, Daniel	"	18	Mar. 20, 64	"	"
Mullen, John W.	"	18	Feb. 20, 64	"	"
Sias, Isaac	"	27	June 3, 63	"	"
Yohn John L.	"		Feb. 20, 64	"	"
Veterans.					
Kiscadden, Geo.	1stSegt	33	Nov. 8, 61	Re-enl. Nov. 18, 63	
Sanders, Elisha	Corp.	22	"	"	"
Marks, Thomas	"	24	"	"	"
Davis, Barton	"	18	"	"	"
Dogget, Even	"	22	"	"	"
Romine, Steph'n M.	Black-smith.		"	"	"
Patterson Samuel	Wag'r	31	"	"	"
Angel, Robert	Priv.	21	"	"	"
Alderson, Samuel	"	34	"	"	"
Beach, Joseph	"	44	"	"	"
Donahue, Joseph	"	23	"	"	"
Donahue, Jacks'n	"	18	"	"	"
Fleming, Wash.	"	35	"	"	"
Goodman, Evan	"	18	"	"	"
Goodman, Martin	"	21	"	"	"
Guard, Noah	"	22	"	"	"
Golden, James	"	19	"	"	"
Ingles, William	"	35	"	"	"
Martin, Hugh	"	20	"	"	"
Martin, John	"	30	"	"	"
McGowan, James	"	36	"	"	"
Pine, William	"	18	"	"	"
Robinson, Joseph	"	27	"	"	"
Scott, Thomas	"	31	"	"	"
Shields, Barnard	"	28	"	"	"

Names.	Rank.	Age	When mustered into service.	Remarks.
Stewart, Sanford	Priv.		Nov. 8, 61	re-enl. Nov. 18,63
Shelton, Charles	"	20	"	" "
Spence, William	"	31	"	" "
Turner, Milan	"	42	"	" "
Torbert, Wm. B.	"	20	"	" "
Wilson, Thomas	"	18	"	" "
Webb, Pleasant	"	20	"	" "
Discharged.				
Cotheran, Abr'h'm	Corp.	34	"	Disability.
Hanthorn, Jas. W.	Blacck-smith.	40	"	" "
Barr, Samuel	Priv.	35	"	" "
Henry, Abr'h'mB.	"	35	"	From wounds.
Spears, Peter	"	27	"	Disability.
Died.				
Myers, Jacob A.	"	34	"	See death roll.
Chamberlain,Ruf's	"	18	Feb. 24,64	" "
Irwin, John	"	28	Nov. 8, 61	" "
Javens, John	"	21	"	" "
Martin, Edward	"	38	"	" "
O'Donald, Daniel	"	28	"	" "
Sweeny, James	"	21	"	" "
Transferred.				
Merrell, Will S.	1st Sgt	20	"	Pro. 1st Lt.
Deserted.				
Furr, Daniel	Corp.	19	"	July 1, 63
Dugan, Patrick	Priv.	22	"	Nov. 20, 63
Liney, Anthony	"	25	"	July 1, 63
Sias, Isaac	"	18	Jun. 30,64	At Charleston.

Aggregate less rec'd from other companies, 99 men.

Names.	Rank.	Age	When mustered into service.	Remarks.
Smith, Jasper A.	Capt.	30	Nov 23,64	Not mustered out
McMillin, Milton	1st Lt.	31		Com'd Nov. 2, 64
Kirdendall, W. J.	2nd Lt	35		Com'd Sept. 30,64
McMillin, J. H.	1st Sgt	28	Sept. 9, 64	Not mustered out
Sanders, John	Qm Sgt	35	Sept. 5, 64	" "
Dunlap, James	Com Sgt	36	Sept.27,64	" "
Hull, Reuben E.	Sgt	21	Nov. 8, 61	Trans. from Co.H
Stewart, G. A.	"	20	"	" "
Whetsel, Jacob A.	"	22	Aug 27,64	Not mustered out
McLaughlin, J.	"	36	"	" "
Dempsey, A. S.	"	23	Sept 2, 64	" "
Daran, Nicholas	Corp.	21	June 2, 62	Trans. from Co.G
Smith, Gordon	"	30	Oct 10, 62	Trans. from Co.H
Walden, Charles	"	19	Sept 30,64	Not mustered out.
Nichols, T. V.	"	20	Aug 27,64	" "
O'Rorick, M.	"	21	"	" "
Halterman, D.	"	24	"	" "
Bartlett, M. B.	"	18	Sept. 9, 64	" "
Hall, James	"	22	Oct. 14, 64	" "
Wiseman, Geo. L.	Bugle	23	Aug 27,64	" "
Zinn, George	"	18	"	" "
Lynch, Geo. W.	Black-smith	23	Oct. 6, 64	" "
McKinney, N.	"	32	Aug 31,63	Trans. from Co.G
Call, William	Wagn'r	27	Sept. 9, 64	Not mustered out
Springer, Wm.	Sadd'r	26	Oct. 6, 64	" "
Adkins, Robert	Priv.	19	Jan. 2, 64	Tans. from Co.G.
Baazzle, Wm.	"	25	Sept. 1, 64	Not mustered out
Beyron, Jacob H.	"	36	Sept 15,64	" "
Becket, Wm. B.	"	19	"	" "
Butler, William	"	27	Oct. 10,62	Trans. from Co. B
Brown, Geo. W.	"	24	"	" " H
Caruthers, W. L.	"	23	"	" " B
Carmichael, John	"	19	"	" " B
Craig, Peter	"	18	"	" " G
Carder, Thomas	"		Oct. 12,64	Not mustered out
Carrick, J. M.	"	22	Sept 27,64	" "
Compston, J. H.	"	28	Aug 27,64	" "
Collard, John	"	27	"	" "
Coon, James	"	28	"	" "
Dawson, Wm.	"	31	"	" "
Dasher, Jackson	"	25	"	" "
Edwards, Wm. H.	"	18	Sept. 1, 62	" "
Eakins, Emory A.	"	19	Dec 28, 62	Trans. from Co.B

Names.	Rank.	Age	When mustered into service.	Remarks
Elswick, Rosdell	"	28	Oct 10, 62	" " H
House Robert	"	39	Oct 10, 62	Trans. from Co. I
Humphrey, G.	"	20	Dec. 23,62	" " I
Hager, James S.	"	.	Oct. 8, 64	Not mustered out.
Hall, William	"	42	Sept 21,64	" "
Halterman, David	"	21	Aug 27,64	" "
Harmon, Wesley	"	20	"	" "
Hutchinson, W. B.	"	18	"	" "
Jeffries, Isiah C.	"	20	Sept 30,64	" "
Jacox, Wm. D.	"	30	Oct 10, 62	Trans. from Co. I
Johnston, James	"	25	"	" " G
Kady, William	"	37	"	" " H
Kisor, Benj. F.	"	19	Aug 27,62	Not mustered out.
Lott, Nathan B.	"	22	Sept.27,64	" "
Lane, William H.	"	18	Dec. 23,62	Trans. from Co.H
Landress, Allen F	"	18	Oct. 10,62	" " H
Light, Henry	"	22	"	" " F
Morton, Geo. W.T	"	27	"	" " H
Morton, Paschal	"	18	"	" " H
Mills, Anderson	"	26	"	" " I
Murray, Wm. F.	"	20	Dec. 23,62	" "
Morris, Chas. L.	"	19	Oct. 10,62	" " B
Morris, Chas. B.	"	23	"	" "
Mason, Thos. L.	"	23	Oct. 6, 64	
McKinley. Robert	"	20	Oct. 10,62	Trans. from Co. I
McKinmis, Milton	"	19	Sept.27,64	Not mustered out
Montgomery, Wm.	"	19	Sept.30,64	" "
Montgomery,G.W.	"	18	Sept.15,64	" "
Manning, A. J.	"	27	Sept. 9, 64	" "
Moreland, E. N.G.	"	18	Sept. 9, 64	" "
Maxwell, Bernard	"	27	Sept. I, 64	" "
Morrison, Robt.	"	35	Aug.27,64	" "
Palmer, Isaac	"	25	"	" "
Palmer, Levi	"	30	Sept. 5, 64	" "
Quimbly, Geo. A.	"	23	Sept.25 64	" "
Rexroad, Hezekiah	"	35	Sept. 9, 64	" "
Shinn, Ebert R.	"	17	"	" "
Spencer, Jacob E.	"	18	Sept.21,64	" "
Steele, Robt. M.	"	18	Sept.27,64	" "
Sanders, John	"	20	Oct. 10, 62	Trans. from Co. B
Swisher Samuel	"	20	Oct. 18 62	" " I
Settle, Isaac J.	"	22	Oct. 10,62	Trans. from Co. H
Williams, S. P.	"	29	"	" "

Names.	Rank.	Age	When mustered into service.	Remarks.
Williams, Samuel	"	25	"	Trans. from Co. H
Winding, Geo. W.	"	18	Sept. 21, 64	Not mustered out.
Wiseman Jos. N.	"	18	Sept. 5, 64	" "
West, Isaac F.	"	37	Aug. 27, 64	" "
Willey, Elam	"	18	"	" "
Wurts, James	"	28	"	" "
Wilson, John	"	22	Oct. 18, 64	" "
Weddle, Jacob H.	"	24	Dec. 5, 64	" "
Zinn, Griff	"	20	Aug. 27, 63	" "
Zinn, Harvey	"	24	Sept. 22, 64	" "

Aggregate, less received from other Co's.......64 men.

Captain Gilmore's company served with the regiment from July 14th, 1863, until September 1st, 1864, and were mustered out as Company L Second West Virginia Cavalry.   Their casualties are given in the death roll.

Total enlistments...............................1221 men.

PREFACE.

"About the man who fights on horseback the romance of war has always centered. From the first chronicled battle the horseman has been not only the most picturesque, but the most dramatic figure in warfare. Writers who have recorded the history of armed conflicts have found the most thrilling climaxes in the sweep of riding squadrons. Tennyson's "Charge of the Light Brigade" will be read when the stories of greater combats have been forgotten.

In the days of chivalry the mounted man was the main reliance in war. But gradually the more deadly musket became the chief instrument of death. Drill and discipline were reduced to a science. The art of war was revolutionized.

There have been still greater changes since. The duties of mounted men have greatly expanded. They not only rush upon the solid lines of infantry in battle array, but in a thousand minor ways lend aid and inspiration to great armies. They flash upon the flanks of the enemy, and make daring raids for the destruction of lines of communication for war supplies. They are the swift annoyance of the enemy, the restless messengers of defeat and death. The hoof-beats of the horseman falls through every gap in the lines, and the reckless charge marks the end of battle and the beginning of pursuit. The cavalry feels the enemy, and reports upon the condition and the presence of his armies. It is the resistless support of the infantry, in the horrible clash of steel, which forces the final decision. Such, in greater or less degree, has been its functions for many years. But in our late war it largely increased its usefulness, and won a broader recognition than ever before.

The cavalryman still retains his romantic pre-eminence. The poet who sings of battle instinctively makes the trooper his theme. Read "Paul Revere's Ride" to arouse the men of Middlesex, Tom Hood's "Wild Steed of the Plains," and a dozen other songs, where even a single trooper has made his cause famous. The rush of Murat's squadrons is heard through all the long story of Napoleon's struggle for existence. With us the record has been the same. The history of the Revolution was enriched by the exploits of Marion's horsemen. Blackhorse cavalry has ever been a conspicuous figure in the romance of all wars.

In our latest conflict, the music of battle comes to us laden with the blare of Sheridan's bugles, and the rush of Stewart's rough riders. Custer's resistless charges, Kilpatrick's raids, Torbett's, Wilson's, Merritt's, Averell's swift dashes by day and by night, are filled with the vigor of movement and the charm of success. Buford, Bayard, Grierson and a hundred other generals, knights of the saber and stirrup, fill in a wonderful picture of dashing heroism that will live in song and story as long as the records of war are read. These horsemen taught the world new lessons in the use of cavalry. The story of Brandy Station, Kilpatrick's raid on Richmond, the cavalry fight at Trevillian Station, the resistless charges at Winchester and Cedar Creek, and the rough experiences of Averell's battallions, give to all mankind a thrilling and instructive narrative.

To give the story of some of these horsemen, inspired to brave deeds by lofty patriotism, is the purpose of these pages." F. A. B.

COL. WM. M. BOLLES.

First Col. of the Regiment.

Flag of the free hearts' hope and home
   By angel hands to valor given,
Thy stars have lit the welkin dome,
   And all thy hues were born in heaven.
Forever float that standard sheet
   Where breathes the foe but falls before us,
With freedom's soil beneath our feet
   And freedom's banner streaming o'er us.

CHAPTER I.

INTRODUCTION AND ORGANIZATION.

In preparing this work, it has been my aim to present the history of the regiment, in as complete a form as possible. Many incidents worthy of note have no doubt escaped me, but the war has been over for near twenty eight years and many of these thrilling occurrences have passed from the memory of many of us. I have endeavored to admit of no matter that is not supported by records, or upon the statement of those whose privilege it was to know them. I have been compelled to give in part, an account of marches and battles that are familiar to all readers of war history. In such of these as I have given, the regiment bore a conspicuous part. The design of this little work originated in the belief, that the record of the regiment in a book form, would be acceptable to the survivors, and their families; as a memento of their sufferings, their privations, and their services in the war of the rebellion. And I hope that it will also serve as a slight tribute to the memory of those gallant and heroic members, who have sacrificed their lives upon their country's altar.

Under President Lincoln's call of July 2d, 1861, the formation of a regiment for the cavalry arm of the service was begun about August first, in Southern Ohio. Three companies were recruited in Lawrence county, two in Meigs, one in Jackson, one in Vinton, one in Washington and one in Morgan. The remainder of the regiment was composed largely of volunteers from Putnam and Monroe counties.

When this body was ready for muster and commission, application was made to Hon. William Dennison, Governor of Ohio, to complete the organization. This he declined to do, giving as a reason therefor that the governors of all the northern states had received instructions from the War Department to recruit no more cavalry, and that they were also advised that all cavalry in excess of forty regiments would be mustered out of service.

Application was then made to F. R. Pierrepont, provisional governor of that portion of Virginia, now known as West Virginia, the latter state not having been admitted into the Union until June 20th, 1863. Governor Pierrepont, with the consent of the Secretary of War, accepted the organization as cavalry, ordering the same into camp quarters at Parkersburg, where ten companies reported about the middle of September, 1861. As soon thereafter as practicable, the officers were commissioned, and all were mustered into the service of the United States as the Second Regiment cf Loyal Virginia Cavalry, at Parkersburg, Va. Nov. 8th, 1861.

The original organization of "Field and Staff" was as follows: Colonel, William M. Bolles; Lt. Colonel, John

C. Paxton; First Major, R. L. Curtis; Second Major, John J. Hoffman; Adjutant, Elijah F. Gilliam; Quartermaster, S. G. Paxton; Commissary, Geo. S. South; Surgeon, Thomas Neal; Assistant Surgeon, L. D. Comstock; Hospital Steward, Edward L. Gilliam.

The following were the original company officers:

	Captains.	1st. Lts.	2nd. Lts.
A	Jas. L. Waller	L. E. Campbell.	C. A. Henderson.
B	W. H. Powell.	C. E. Hambleton.	Jas. Allen.
C	Thos. Neal.	J. M. Boyd.	Wm. Church.
D	H. S. Hamilton.	Geo. W. Snyder.	E. S. Morgan.
E	Andrew Scott.	A. A. Fouts.	Jos. Ankrom.
F	E. D. Eells.	O. H. P. Scott.	W. M. Fortescue.
G	John McMahon.	G. B. Montgomery	J. Davidson.
H	David Dove.	John Walden.	J. A. Umpleby.
I	N. J. Behan.	John W. Neal.	John A. Lowe.
K	S. H. Emmons.	Wm. Yard.	John McNally.

On the 15th of December, after many vexatious delays which was unavoidable at the time, the regiment was armed and equipped. The arms were of a very inferior quality, and almost really totally unfit for effective service. Most of the fire arms consisted of huge and unwieldy horse-pistols, which, if used in action, would certainly endanger the lives of our own men quite as much as those of the enemy. A portion of the regiment was armed with short Enfield rifles, but being muzzle loaders they were very inconvenient for cavalry. The sabers were better, but in a mountainous country like western Virginia, they were more ornamental than useful. The horses were very good, and many of the companies succeeded in obtaining all of one color. This matter of color in horses was kept up for some time, but finally had to be given up.

At the date of muster in the war had been in progress about seven months, and many of the rank and file of the new organization had seen active service in the three months regiments. Company H was largely composed of a Jackson, O., company, that had served out their time in the 18th Ohio Infantry. The organization when mounted presented a fine appearance, and the officers had every reason to be proud of the fact that they had been chosen to command so fine a body of Ohio soldiery. Much could be reasonably expected of such volunteers, and how well that expectation was realized, those who read this little volume shall judge.

Many of us have always regretted that we were not allowed to be mustered in as, the 4th Ohio Cavalry, where we properly belonged; yet, neither during the progress of the war nor since its close, have we had the slightest cause to complain of our treatment at the hands of the little mountain state, born amid the throes of war, rocked and shaken with the roar of cannon, and whose soil drank the blood of many of her own loyal sons—West Virginia, the "Child of the Storm." All honor to our little neighbor across the river, and may the words inscribed on her escutcheon always characterize the patriotism and valor of her people "Montani Semper Liberi."

Soon after being mounted and equipped, the regiment was ordered into winter quarters at Guyandotte, Cabell county, West Virginia, for drill and discipline. How little we comprehended the demands and necessities of war while we were enjoying this early camp life. Like all new organizations situated some distance from actual hostilities, the boys were just spoiling for a fight.

On the 2d day of January, 1862, Col. Bolles received orders from Gen. Rosecrans, commanding this department, to move his command at once, and report to Col. Jas. A. Garfield, at Louisa, Ky. Col. Bolles, with the regiment, reported to Col. Garfield on the morning of January 7th. Proudly the new regiment took the advance, with orders to drive the enemy from the village of Paintsville. On reaching this point it was found the enemy had disappeared but a short time before our arrival. Col. Bolles at once moved his command forward up the north bank of Paint Creek to a point opposite the mouth of Jennett's Creek, where the rebel rear guard was discovered, prepared to resist our attack. Captain Powell's squadron, composed of Cos. B and C, was ordered to charge in col-

umn, to which order they responded with spirit, and succeeded in driving the enemy upon his main column at
dark.   They were fired upon by a force of rebel infantry
from an ambuscade on both sides of the road.   Here the
first blood of the regiment was spilled by the killing of
two men—Amos McKee of Co. B, and Albert Leonard of
Co. C, and the wounding of five others.   Three horses
were also killed.

Feeling sure that the main body of the enemy had
been overtaken, the little band fell back a short distance,
and at once informed Col. Garfield of the situation.
Early on the morning of the 8th, Col. Garfield with
1000 cavalry, composed of the 2nd Virginia, one
squadron of the 6th Kentucky, and one squadron
of Ohio cavalry, the latter under the command of
Major McLaughlin, and 150 infantry of the 42d Ohio, advanced upon the rebel position.   The enemy were found
to have fallen back again, burning many of their stores,
and in full retreat in the direction of Prestonburg.   Deem-
ing further pursuit unnecessary, the command returned to
Paintsville, the 2d Virginia taking the bodies of their
dead comrades with them, and forwarding them to their
friends in Ohio.

A few days after, the 2d Virginia returned to their winter quarters at Guyandotte.   The march, exposure and actual service in this first engagement afforded the regiment
its initial experience in war, and impressed upon its officers
and men the importance of drill and discipline for more
active service.

CHAPTER II.

ORDERED TO THE FRONT.   BATTLE OF LEWISBURG.

The regiment remained in winter quarters at Guyandotte, Va., on the Ohio river. Most of the time was occupied in drilling and fitting for active service. On the 6th of April, 1862, Col. Bolles received orders from General J. D. Cox, commading the Kanawha division, to send one battalion of his regiment to Flat Top Mountain, and to hold the balance in readiness to move. In accordance with these orders, the division of the regiment into battalions was made as follows: The first battalion was composed of Companies B, C, F, H and I; the second was composed of Companies A, D, E, G and K.

On the 8th of April, Lt. Col. John C. Paxton, with the second battalion, accompanied by Major Curtis, moved out from camp, and finally reported according to orders. On the 29th of April, Col. Bolles with the first battalion, and accompanied by Major Hoffman, left camp with orders to report to Col. L. S. Elliott, of the 47th Ohio Infantry, who was enroute to Meadow Bluff on the Lewisburg pike. The regiment thus divided performed important duty for Col. Geo. Crook in the vicinity of Meadow Bluff, Greenbriar county, and similar service for General J. D. Cox in Raleigh and adjoining counties, during the spring and summer campaign of 1862. On the 12th of May the first battallion surprised and routed a rebel command known as Edgar's battallion, and Captain White's company of rebel cavalry at early dawn, near Handley's farm, driving the enemy in utter rout through Lewisburg to White Sulphur Springs. Many prisoners were captured in this wild and exciting chase.

On May 16th, Col. Geo. Crook, of the 36th Ohio then

in command of the third brigade of the Kanawha division, composed of the 36th, 44th, and 47th O. V. I., and the first battallion of the 2nd Virginia Cavalry, and a battery of artillery, began a reconnaissance in force upon Jackson river depot, via Lewisburg, White Sulphur and Covington. In this expedition the 2d Virginia Cavalry had the advance, and succeeded in destroying several depots of supplies, bridges, etc., also capturing five captains and twenty-five men belonging to the "Moccasin Rangers," near Callahan station.

The command then returned to camp. On May 23d occurred the battle of Lewisburg, one of the best planned little engagements of the war. In brief, it was as follows: Col. Crook learned that Gen. Heth, a former class-mate of Crook, with a considerable body of infantry, was marching in the direction of Lewisburg, and like the true soldier that he was, he determined to try the mettle of his men in battle. It was eighteen miles back to Meadow Bluff, a natural position for defense, and where a few more troops were stationed. To be fully prepared for any emergency, Col. Crook had every pound of property of every kind loaded in the wagons, the teams hitched to them and headed in the direction of Meadow Bluff. Wishing to give the enemy a fair show, Col. Crook formed his line in the rear of the town, thus giving them the advantage of the inspiration they might receive from the presence of their enthusiastic friends in this hot rebel town. The infantry was placed on either side of the battery. with the cavalry on the left. Soon our pickets fell back through Lewisburg, amid the jeers of the inhabitants. The enemy made their appearance on the hill opposite, formed their line, and when all was ready their battery fired the first shot, to which ours responded. They came down the hill into the town amid the wildest enthusiasm, the entire population cheering them on and shouting, "Drive the Yankees to the Ohio river." As soon as the line of the enemy came in view ascending the hill on a charge, our infantry arose and poured a withering volley

into them.   Both infantry and cavalry joined in a charge,
completely routing the opposing force, killing seventy-two,
wounding over one hundred, taking one hundred and
fifty-seven prisoners, four cannon, three hundred stands of
arms and twenty-five horses.   The Union loss was thirteen killed, fifty wounded and six missing.   From the
time the first shot was fired until the last, was twenty-
seven minutes.

In this engagement the cavalry was highly compli-
mented for its gallantry by the Brigade Commander.
Col. Crook was wounded in the left foot.

The brigade remained here until April 29th, when it
fell back to Meadow Bluff for the purpose of shortening
the haul of supplies, which was obtained at Loup Creek
on the Kanawha river.   The battallion camped at Meadow
Bluff until August 14th.   In the meantime they had been
very active in scouting.   Several brisk engagements occurred with the rebel cavalry, among which might be
mentioned Alderson's Ferry, June 9; Wolf Creek, July
10; Lewis' Mills July 15; Blue Sulphur Springs, July 20;
Alderson's Ferry, July 23, Williamburg, July 28th.   In
these various engagements the enemy lost ten killed, six
wounded, and twenty prisoners, besides horses and arms.

The commanding officer, Col. Geo. Crook, growing tired
of camp life, thought it about time for another fight.   The
rebel Gen. Heth, with his command, was then at Salt Sulphur Springs; and as the two commanders had been class-
mates at West Point, and were very good friends, Col.
Crook concluded it would only be right and proper to return Gen. Heth's call of the 23rd of May.   According,
on June 22nd, Col. Crook, with his brigade (less a safe
camp guard) took up the line of march on the road via
Blue Sulphur Springs, Alderson's Ferry and Centreville
to Salt Sulphur Springs.   Camping at the mouth of Wolf
Creek and Centreville en route, the morning of the 24th
found the command at a point on the Centreville
and Salt Sulphur Springs road, within a distance of three
miles from General Heth's camping grounds.   That morn-

ing all arose early, ate a hearty breakfast of sow-belly,
hard tack and coffee, and assuring ourselves that our toilet
was just right, started on our early morning call.

We were under the impression that our commander's
distinguished friend and classmate would extend to his old
friend and comrades as warm a reception at least as Col.
Crook had given him thirty days before at Lewisburg. But
we were doomed to disappointment, as the cavalry soon
found that General Heth, apparently not caring to culti-
vate the further acquaintance of Col. Crook and his Yanks
in blue, had retired to the mountains the day before. The
brigade then returned to camp.

On June 15th, Col. Wm. M. Bolles tendered his resignation as Colonel of the 2d Loyal Virginia Cavalry, to
take effect immediately. The resignation of this officer was
accepted, and Lt. Col. John C. Paxton was promoted and
commissioned as Colonel, July 18th, 1862. Major R. L.
Curtis was promoted to the office of Lt. Colonel, and commissioned Aug. 19th, 1862. Capt. W. H. Powell was
promoted and commissioned as Major Aug. 19th, 1862.
The following changes, made necessary by these promo-
tions, occurred in the companies.

1st. Lt. Chas. E. Hambleton to rank and services as
Captain of Co. B, Capt. Thos. Neal having resigned as
Captain of Co. C, 2nd Lt. James Allen was promoted to
service as Captain of Co. C. Orderly Sergeant Geo.
Millard was promoted to 2nd Lt. Co. F, Lt. Eells having
resigned. Sergt. Major I. B. Murdock was promoted to
2nd Lt. of Co. B. 1st Sergt. J. B. Carlisle was promoted
to Sergeant Major.

From August 1st to 14th the infantry did but little
duty other than drill. The cavalry, however, was kept
busy almost night and day, scouring the country for supplies, and any stray rebel soldiers that might fall in their
way. The country around Meadow Bluff was well suited
to grass, the inhabitants seemed to be quite well to do,
and taking it all in all, this was the most pleasant season
we experienced during the war.

CHAPTER III.

LIGHTBURN'S RETREAT.

On August 14th the brigade consisting of the 44th O. V. I. and the 2nd Virginia Cavalry left Meadow Bluff under orders for Gauley Bridge. Genl. J. D. Cox commanding Kanawha Division, with Col. Crook and Scammon's brigade were ordered to Washington City. This left but a small force in the Kanawha Valley, under command of Col. J. A. J. Lightburn.

During the time in which the events already narrating here were transpiring with the first battallion under Col. Crook on the Lewisburg front, the second battallion under Lieutenant Colonel —— but now Col. J. C. Paxton, was actively engaged in scouting in the counties of Raleigh, Fayette and Wyoming. Of its movements no detailed account can be found. This is much regretted, as the battallion experienced lively and thrilling times in their many encounters with bush-whackers. Repeated letters to officers now living, have failed to secure the information necessary to enable me to place upon record the active work of the second battallion during this period.

If there was one thing more than another that the Second Virginia Cavalry hated, it was the detestable bush-whackers. We did not object to being shot at on general principles, but to have some unprincipled scoundrel who was too cowardly to join the army and fight as a man, sneak around like a thief in the night and shoot from behind a tree or from some inaccessible position, was more than we could patiently stand.

The service performed by the Regiment, beginning
May 1st and ending Aug. 14, 1862, was mostly rendered
by small details, rarely exceeding a company organization.
The character of the service being that of picket duty,
scouting and foraging, was in a mountainous country like
western Virginia, constantly exposed, hazardous and laborious, and last, but not least, to a good, faithful soldier,
thankless and unappreciated.

Much of the alleged inefficiency of the cavalry arm of
the service, so frequently talked of by the infantry, was
the result of the imperfect organization and application of
that branch of the service during the first and second years
of war. General Sheridan was the first officer in the
United States army to organize and efficiently utilize the
cavalry forces. Its unparalleled achievements attained
under him and his gallant division commanders, Torbett,
Wilson, Merrett, Averell, Custer and Powell, in the Shenandoah Valley in 1864 and 1865, fully demonstrated the
efficiency and possibilities of the mounted warrior, and
rendered the name and fame and service of Sheridan and
his cavalry immortal.

The cavalry of the confederacy was a famous and terrible weapon in the hands of its leaders for more than the
first half of the war period. The contempt of our organizers for this arm of the service, brought to the people who
deserved it not, a good deal of severe punishment. The
Southern leaders, certainly at first, understood the logistics
of the situation better than our own authorities. One reason of that is perhaps to be found in the fact that so many
of the confederate commanders—those from the regular
service especially—had been in the cavalry service. Jefferson Davis himself evidently appreciated this arm, as he
took especial pains while secretary of war, under Pierce,
in organizing four additional regiments to the regular
army, to procure the necessary legislation necessary to
equip them as cavalry, and then to officer them with those
who, it seemed to him, would best serve the South in the
contingencies likely to arise. The ex-cavalrymen among

commanding and leading generals of the Confederacy can be named by the score.

Among them might be mentioned J. E. B. Stuart, Fitzhugh Lee, Ewell Hill, Joseph E. Johnson and a hundred others who could be named, who were fine organizers of cavalry forces. The Confederates were not, also, without most gallant cavalry soldiers and leaders whose sabers carved their way from civil life to martial eminence. Among those still living are such men as Wade Hampton, Wheeler, Chalmers and Mosly. General Gordon himself has shown all the finest qualities of a cavalry commander. Of those who have passed away may be named with respect for soldierly qualities at least, Stuart, Forrest, Cleburne, Wickham, Gilmore, Ashby and many others. The planter was necessarily a horseman. His work of supervision was mainly done in the saddle. As a slave-holder owning many or few human chattels, he was more of a man on the back of his saddle horse, in the eyes of his slaves, than when on foot like any ordinary person. He knew how to both ride and shoot.

What gave the Confederate cavalry, then, its first form and usefulness was the rule of requiring each recruit to mount himself. Equipments were sometimes or in part provided, sufficient to give some uniformity. He was required, however, to remount himself. The endeavor to achieve this necessity was the source of much of the activity shown by Mosby, Morgan, Duke and other partisan leaders, in different parts of the large field of border operations. Such a condition applied to the raising of cavalry could only be made in an agricultural country. It was at first peculiarly adapted to the conditions of the South. The rich, slave-holding planters, like Wade Hampton; the ambitious and dashing leaders like Wheeler and Chalmers, then lawyers and planters with careers before them; the born horsemen like Forrest, Morgan, Mosby, the Ashbys and others, were able to bring together a mounted yeomanry, accustomed to their horses, and used, in the rude atmosphere of slavery to command. Yet, as it turned out, given time and occasion, the loyal states were able, in the long run, to mold and make a better cavalry force, to mount it far more effectively and handle it more efficiently for final victory. General Grant said, while the Southern soldiers may have possessed more dash and enthusiasm, yet the Union soldier had the staying qualities, which brought the final victory.

After the re-assembling of the regiment from Lewisburg and Flat Top Mountain in August, it always operated thereafter during the war in its regimental organization.

Early in September the camp was filled with rumors that a rebel force of 6,000 men under General Loring was advancing via Flat Top Mountain and Princeton, with the avowed purpose of driving the "Yanks," as 'twas said, out of the Kanawha Valley, and north of the Ohio river. Just previous to this advance of General Loring, Col. Lightburn received information that Col. A. G. Jenkins was moving his rebel cavalry force down the Guyandotte river towards Barboursville and the Ohio river. This was a considerable distance to the rear of the position of our army. Col. Lightburn seemed to treat the matter with such indifference that Col. J. C. Paxton begged for permission to be allowed to march and drive back this rebel invader. Permission being granted, two companies were left with the main force, and with the remaining eight companies, Col. Paxton moved down the west bank of the Kanawha river to a few miles below the city of Charleston, where the pike crosses through the country to Teaz Valley, thence to Barboursville and Guyandotte.

This route was pursued to the farm of Mr. Warren Reece, near where the town of Milton, W. Va. now stands, ten miles east of Barboursville. Major Powell had charge of the advance, with Capt. Hambleton's Company B. At the farm of Mr. Reece a halt was made for the purpose of feeding and resting the command. While we were enjoying our afternoon meal, the rebel cavalry appeared in our front, and fired at us at long range. Our troopers were soon in the saddle and marching to meet the enemy. As soon as they showed a disposition to make a stand, Capt. Hambleton, under orders, charged upon them, driving them toward Barboursville.

A halt was now made to ascertain the strength and location of Jenkins' force. Major Powell learned from the prisoners that the enemy's force consisted of between 1,000 and 1,200 cavalry under command of Col. Jenkins, and that they were in camp near Barboursville, and had been there twenty-four hours, resting and shoeing their horses. It was also learned that they were to move in the direction of Charleston the next morning, where they expected to meet the advance of the retreating army of Col. Lightburn, as he was driven back by General Loring.

It was dark when Col. Paxton with the regiment came up with the advance. After a short conference between Col. Paxton and Major Powell, the latter was ordered forward with Company B, Capt. Hambleton commanding. On nearing Barboursville, Major Powell, learning the exact location of Col. Jenkins' headquarters, which was in the house of Mr. Wm. Miller, determined to try to capture that officer. Upon nearing the house a charge was made upon it. It was found to be guarded by at least fifty confederate soldiers, which fact could not be observed by the charging column on account of the extreme darkness of the night. The rebel guard fired and fled, and while the house was being surrounded, Col. Jenkins and his staff escaped by the rear of the house through the garden. This caused the entire rebel force to abandon their camp and flee up the Guyan river, unexpectedly diverted from their proposed attack upon the Union forces the next day. This occurred on the night of September 8th, 1862.

In this charge upon Col. Jenkins' headquarters, Company B lost one of its bravest and best men—killed by the rebel guard. I refer to the death of 1st Duty Sergeant, Braxton P. Reeves, who lived at Buckhorn Furnace, Lawrence county, Ohio.

When Col. Paxton became satisfied that the rebel force was in full retreat up the Guyan Valley, he moved the regiment to Guyandotte, on the Ohio river, where the body of Sergeant Reeves was forwarded to his friends. The force remained here for twenty-four hours resting the horses, then returned by the same route via Teaz Valley to the mouth of Coal river—now St. Albans, W. Va. At Coalsmouth the government transports were met en route to Gallipolis, Ohio, and we received orders to guard them out of the Kanawha river. The cause of all this was, that the entire force under Col. Lightburn was being driven out of the valley. At Charleston Col. Lightburn left the Kanawha river and retreated to the Ohio river via Jackson C. H., W. Va. He crossed the Ohio river at Racine, Ohio, and moved down the north bank of the river to opposite Point Pleasant, thus almost literally fulfilling everything that had been told us by the prisoners at Barboursville.

But to our command. The 2nd Va. Cavalry guarded the transports to the mouth of Thirteen Mile Creek, where they were out of all danger; thence moved across the country to Letart Falls, on the Ohio river, and down the south bank to Point Pleasant. We were the only portion of the Lightburn command that determined to remain, and that did remain, on the sacred soil of Virginia. The defeat suffered by the Kanawha troops under Col. Lightburn, induced the ordering of General Q. A. Gilmore, U. S. A., who was then at Cincinnati, Ohio, to the command at Point Pleasant. General Gilmore was soon relieved by General Milroy, and in a few days he was in turn replaced by General J. D. Cox, the former commander of the Kanawha Division. General Cox re organized the command, and with the old, and some new troops, left Point Pleasant on the 20th of October, 1862, for the purpose of regaining the Kanawha Valley.

The rebel forces fell back before the Union forces without battle. In a few days the City of Charleston was reached. Here the infantry and artillery went into camp, and the 2d Va. cavalry went ten miles up the river to Camp Piatt and established winter quarters.

On the 16th of November, 1862, Col. Geo. Crook, having been promoted to the rank of Brigadier General U. S. Volunteers, returned to the Kanawha Valley with his brigade, being assigned to the command of the Kanawha Division, relieving General J. D. Cox. This was very gratifying to the officers and men, as all had the most implicit confidence in the leadership of General Crook.

John C. Paxton

CHAPTER IV.

SINKING CREEK RAID.

The regiment having virtually completed the active campaign work of 1862 as was supposed, was now enjoying the luxury of good winter quarters at Camp Piatt, on the classic banks of the Kanawha, ten miles above the present capital of West Virginia, when, much to the surprise and gratification of the boys, we were again in the saddle, in obedience to the following order:

Headquarters Kanawha Division ⎱
Charleston, Kanawha Co., W. Va., ⎰
            November 23, 1862.

Special order No.

Colonel John C. Paxton, commanding the 2nd Regiment Loyal Virginia Cavalry, will proceed with all the serviceable men of his command, tomorrow morning, Nov. 24, 1862, to Cold Knob Mountain in Greenbriar county, Virginia, via the Summerville and Lewisburg road, leaving the Kanawha river route at Cannelton. On Cold Knob Mountain he will overtake Colonel P. H. Lane, commanding the 11th O. V. I., ordered to that point to reinforce your command. From which position you will proceed against the camps of the 14th Virginia Rebel Cavalry Regiment, located in the Sinking Creek Valley, some two miles apart in winter quarters, recruiting. Break]up the organization if possible.

GEORGE CROOK,
Brigadier General commanding Kanawha Division.

This was the most business like document we had ever received, and the concluding sentence clearly implied that something must be done. However, at daylight on the 24th, we were on the road en route for Cannelton, where we left the river route and followed a narrow road over the mountain to the mouth of Twenty mile creek, where we struck the main Summerville road. We reached the latter place by 10 o'clock at night, and camped there on the night of the 24th, having marched sixty miles. Early on the morning of the 25th we broke camp, and twenty miles from Summerville went into camp again, preparing such shelter as was possible in that sparsely settled country. The weather was very cold, with indications of snow.

The only adventure experienced during the day was by Lieutenant Davidson, of the advance guard. This officer was ordered to select a place to camp. With a guide he left the main road to look for hay and soon came in sight of a log house where the guide said there was forage of that kind. When opposite the place, the officer heard the click of muskets and looking toward the house he saw five or six rebels with leveled muskets, commanding him to halt. Lieutenant Davidson was one of the coolest officers in the regiment, and one of the quickest to grasp a situation and act upon it; so, when he heard the summons, he promptly obeyed. The rebels asked him who he was and what he was doing there. The lieutenant told them he belonged to Colonel Jenkins' (rebel) regiment, and that the command was coming there to camp. This apparently satisfied them, "but," said they, "where did you get those blue clothes?" The lieutenant did not have to tell a story this time for he replied that he got them from the Yankees. Then he rode on, glad to get away.

About this time the advance came in sight, when the Johnnies realized that they had been duped, and all ran for the woods, but the advance guard captured most, if not all of them. Major Powell pursued and captured one, who proved to be a rebel lieutenant. The major has since told the writer that he often wondered why the fellow did not stop behind some tree and shoot him, when he saw that he was being pursued by only one man.

During the night of the 25th, a heavy snow had fallen, and it continued to snow on the 26th. The march

CAPT. JEREMIAH DAVIDSON.

See page 144..

was taken up early in the morning of that day, and at 10 o'clock a. m. we reached Cold Knob Mountain, where we found the 11th O. V. I., they having been there but a short time.

After a conference between Colonel Paxton and Colonel Lane of the infantry, the latter decided that the condition of his men, caused by exposure to the severe storm for the past eighteen hours rendered the continuation of the march impracticable and compelled him in justice to his men to return to camp at Summerville. Thereupon the infantry countermarched and returned.

The cavalry officers had no thought of returning from this point, for when the order to make the raid had been delivered by General Crook, he had confidentially charged Major Powell not to return to camp without good results. This was well understood, and has since been authenticated by General Crook.

The men had borne their sufferings without a murmur, and when they learned that they were within a few miles of the rebel camp, were full of enthusiasm and anxious to proceed. Preparations were at once made to descend the mountain and attack the camp.

Cold Knob Mountain towers over the surrounding hills and valleys like a sentinel. From its summit where we stood that dreary day it is said one could see into the state of North Carolina. It is so bald and bleak and barren that no grass can secure and maintain a foot hold in its soil, and no trees grow near its summit. As we stood there on that day with the howling storm about us, and the mercury in the thermometer---if there had been one there----crawling down to the bottom, the marrow in our bones nearly freezing, we were convinced that the spot had been appropriately named.

Major Powell was placed in charge of the advance, which consisted of Lieutenant Davidson and twenty men of Company G. It was early in the afternoon when the command started down the mountain for the Sinking Creek Valley. At the foot of the mountain the rebel

pickets were discovered; they were fired upon and one
man wounded, another being captured by the advance
guard. From this prisoner much valuable information
was obtained as to the strength, location and condition of
the rebel camp. The pickets and scouts who had escaped
had seen but a few of our advance guard, and they concluded, as we afterwards learned, that as we did not press
them closely we were only a squad of Union home guards
located somewhere near Summerville. Soon after, the advance discovered the scouts in the distance moving leisurely along toward their camp, with its smoke now plainly
visible. The advance halted until the scouts passed out of
view around a point, and then pushed rapidly forward to
where they had disappeared. Here the last halt was
made to further and more closely examine the situation;
for from this position a fair view of the rebel camp was
obtained.

The advance was ordered to charge through the camp,
as it was now evident that they were unprepared to receive us, and that there would be no engagement.
Promptly the advance charged as directed, the main column coming in on the run. The enemy scattered in all
directions, but owing to the nature of the country pursuit
was difficult.

They were taken completely by surprise, as nearly all
the guns captured were not loaded. Prisoners were
picked up in all directions, some as far as two miles from
the camp.

Owing to the severity of the weather and the scarcity
of rations in their camp, nearly all the officers and quite a
number of men were absent, intending to spend the night
at the houses through the country.

The captures were 1 captain, 1 lieutenant, 112 enlisted
men, 90 horses, 3 (rebel ?) mules, about 200 stands of arms
a few wagons, and various camp equipage. The arms,
wagons, etc. were burned and the camp destroyed. Some
of the prisoners were mounted on the captured horses, the
others being compelled to walk.

The return march commenced at 4 o'clock p. m. As the infantry had returned, and owing to the severity of the weather and the fact that we were so heavily encumbered with prisoners, it was impossible to continue the expedition further as originally contemplated by General Crook. Had the surroundings been favorable and the infantry able to co-operate, the cavalry was to push on to Covington and release Dr. Rucker, a union citizen prisoner who was on trial for his life at that place.

Among the articles captured was a fine silk Confederate flag, made for the command and but recently presented to it by their lady friends in Staunton, Virginia. At the earnest solicitation of the rebel officers the flag was subsequently returned to the donors.

From the nearly continuous march of seventy hours, the deep snow, insufficient rest and food and loss of sleep, officers, troops and horses were nearly exhausted. They fell asleep along the road, causing frequent gaps in the column, and necessitating the greatest vigilance on the part of the officers to keep it closed up in the rear of the prisoners guard.

At daybreak on the 27th the bugle sounded a halt, in response to which men cheered and horses neighed. Roll call showed all the prisoners present.

While horses are being fed, and breakfast made ready, let us attempt to draw a pen picture of our surroundings. Imagine a wild and sparsely settled region, where it was more than five miles between houses, and snow over a foot deep everywhere. All along the road the bushes added to our discomfort, by depositing great piles of snow in our faces, in our laps, and sometimes down our backs. At breakfast time with nearly frozen feet and limbs, we dismount in the snow to cook our humble meal. Are the men disheartened in the midst of all these gloomy surroundings? Not at all, but with cheerful hearts all hands join in, and soon hundreds of fires are burning; and within a few minutes the fragrant odor of coffee and bacon is borne upon the frosty air. Even the prisoners joined in to make the best of it, and were as cheerful as any.

The horses were fed by cleaning away the snow and placing the grain on the ground; or it was put in canvass bags, these strapped to the animal's head, the bag coming up just below the eyes. It was very amusing to watch the horses use this contrivance when it was first put on them, but they would soon grow accustomed to it and manage it very well.

About eight o'clock the column was again in motion, and reached Summerville shortly after noon. Quite a number of the men had their feet frozen badly, and were left at this point until they should be sufficiently recovered to resume the march to Camp Piatt.

On the 28th we marched to Gauley Bridge, where the prisoners, captured horses, etc. were turned over to General E. P. Scammon's Provost Marshall. The regiment then proceeded to the Huddleson farm, a few miles below Kanawha Falls, and camped for the night.

During the night of the 25th while the command was camped at the Hinkle farm, the men had prepared the best places they could to sleep on the bare ground, the officers faring as badly. Colonel Paxton would not go into a house to sleep while his boys were thus exposed to the weather, but shared the exposure with them. For this sacrifice the colonel was held in the highest esteem by the men; and as an evidence that this devotion was not unappreciated, some one stole the blanket off the colonel while he slept, and he woke up nearly frozen. The language used by him on this occasion was such as might have emanated from the humblest private in the ranks. But the colonel did not get his blanket.

Report of Colonel John C. Paxton, headquarters Second West Virginia Cavalry:

Camp Piatt, Dec. 2, 1862.

SIR:—In obedience to your order, I marched my command, consisting of companies G, I, F, A, K, D, E and H, Second West Virginia Volunteer Cavalry, in all 475 men, rank and file, in good order, on the morning of November 24th for Summerville, arriving there at 10 p. m. the same day, a distance of fifty-three miles. Left Summerville next morning at seven o'clock and arrived at the Hinkle farm at 4 p. m.—thirty-five miles—and, being able to obtain some hay there, remained until 4 a. m. of the 26th, when we took up the line of march, in a blinding snow-storm, for Greenbrier, via Cold Knob Mountain, where we arrived at 10 a. m. the same day; distance, twenty miles. Met Colonel Lane, Eleventh Ohio Volunteer Infantry, who was to assist me in breaking up a rebel camp at the foot of the mountain, but, on account of the severity of the weather and hard marching, he wished to return to his camp at Summerville. I asked him to take the advance until we met the enemy's pickets, which he did, and, in about one mile exchanged shots with six of the enemy, wounding one. Colonel Lane at once opened his ranks and gave us the road. We pushed rapidly into the enemy's camp, a distance of five miles, effecting a complete surprise at 12 m., the enemy scattering in all directions. We killed two, wounded two, paroled one and captured two commissioned officers (one captain and one second lieutenant) one hundred and eleven non-commissioned officers and privates, one hundred and six horses and five mules; burned and destroyed about two hundred Enfield and Mississippi rifles and fifty sabres, with other accoutrements, stores and supplies, and their camp tents, etc. I had two horses killed in the enemy's camp, and lost ten on the march from fatigue and exhaustion. The enemy was found three miles from the foot of Cold Knob Mountain, on Sinking Creek, Greenbrier county, West Virginia, at Lewis' Mill, and consisted of a part of five companies of cavalry, viz: Rockbridge Cavalry, Braxton Dragoons, Churchville Cavalry, Valley Cavalry, and Nighthawk Rangers. They were men who had been in the service fifteen months and were located at this point to guard the mountain pass, and to organize a part of A. G. Jenkin's brigade. Our success was complete. We never lost a drop of blood. After securing the prisoners and horses, and destroying the camp, etc., we marched at 4 p. m. (on the 26th) for Summerville, where we arrived on the 27th at noon, making one hundred and twenty miles for men and horses, without food or rest, except one feed of hay for horses, over the most rugged and mountainous part of West Virginia. Remained in Summerville until the 29th. Left for Camp Piatt, and arrived in camp on

the 30th at noon.   My men suffered severely from frost.
I left two men in the hospital at Summerville, whose boots
we cut from their feet.   Others were more or less frozen.
My horses were very much cut down.   I cannot close this
report without deservedly complimenting the officers and
men, but, where all behaved so gallantly, it is impossible
to particularize.   But all honor is due Major Powell, who
led the charge, and Company G, Captain McMahon who
led the column.   I have the honor to be your obedient
servant,   J. C. PAXTON,
    Col. Commanding Second West Virginia Cavalry.
    CAPT. R. P. KENNEDY, A. A. G.

CHAPTER V.

PETERS' MOUNTAIN RAID.

Following the Sinking Creek raid the regiment remained in winter quarters until January 15th, 1863, when it was ordered on an expedition commonly known among the men as the Peters' Mountain raid. The object to be obtained was supposed to be the destruction of the New River bridge. I have been at considerable trouble to discover some official report of this expedition, but have failed to do so.

The destruction of this bridge seemed to be a hobby with General Scammon, and several attempts to destroy it with a small force ended disastrously to the raiders, owing mainly to the distance to be traveled and the nature of the country to be traversed.

The command marched via Gauley Bridge, Big Sewell mountain, Meadow Bluff, Alderson's Ferry, Wolf Creek and Centerville. At the southern base of Sewell mountain the command haulted for the purpose of feeding and resting. Here a division of the force was arranged for, Colonel Paxton with one hundred picked men and horses to command the expedition in person. The regiment then moved forward to Meadow Bluff, where the command was to separate, Colonel Paxton to take his one hundred men and march in the direction of Blue Sulphur Springs, thence via Centerville. A force of rebel cavalry and infantry was known to be stationed at that point; and as Colonel Paxton had no idea of attempting to whip that body, it was necessary that strategy be employed.

Lieutenant Colonel Powell, with the remainder of the regiment, marched in the direction of Lewisburg (at a certain time, as prearranged.) He went as far as the Handley and Feamster farms, making a feint on Lewisburg. The lieutenant colonel had positive orders to burn the Handley house and the Feamster barn, and if possible induce some of the rebel commands that were in Colonel Paxton's way to march to the protection of Lewisburg.

The buildings referred to were on high ground, and when burning at night could be seen for a long distance. This act of vandalism was regarded as a necessity of war, and was carried into effect by Lieutenant Colonel Powell and his command, who then in due course of time returned safely to Camp Piatt.

Before starting from Meadow Bluff, Colonel Paxton informed his intrepid band that they were to impersonate the rebel command of Colonel Clarkson, he himself posing as the confederate colonel. Overcoats were strapped on the saddles, the men wearing blankets instead. The little column encountered the rebel pickets near Centerville, and were allowed to pass without question. The pickets informed our men that there was a force of infantry in the town, but nothing daunted, they marched boldly into Centerville, and halted. To throw the enemy entirely off their guard, the colonel ordered the men to remain in column in the street and feed their horses; this was done, the men bearing themselves in an easy, careless manner, but remaining near the horses ready to mount.

The colonel informed a rebel officer, who seemed to have some authority, that he was Colonel Clarkson, and that he had been doing duty on the Big Sandy river, and had been ordered to report in Richmond with one hundred cavalry. Soon the command was beyond Centerville, en route for Peters' mountain.

The column reached Peters' Mountain in safety, but a violent and blinding storm then raging so confused the guide that he became bewildered and lost his way, leading the detachment many miles in the wrong direction. This

pleased the little band in the neighborhood of John Mc-
Causeland's rebel cavalry regiment, and in view of all the
circumstances Col. Paxton wisely concluded to return.
This he did, via Flat Top Mountain and Raleigh, C. H.,
thus eluding all the confederate commands that were now
endeavoring to capture this pretended Colonel Clarkson.

This expedition commanded by Colonel Paxton was
not only extremely hazardous, but one of great exposure
and intence suffering from deep snows and cold weather.
These incursions (and I state it emphatically) so far into
the enemy's country with a small force, were very dangerous, and usually resulted in little loss or damage to the
foe, while imposing upon the men who made them the
greatest hardship.

This expedition closed the operations of the regiment for the winter, except the scout of Major McMahon,
with seventy men, February 5th to 8th, in Wyoming
county. The Major found nothing but snow and mountains and frozen streams.

In the latter part of February, 1863, General Crook
ordered Lieutenant Colonel Powell to proceed to Wheeling on official business, pertaining to a more efficient arming of the 2nd Virginia Cavalry. Only a small portion
of the regiment was armed with carbines, the others still
retaining the ancient horse pistols, which, as remarked before, were more dangerous to ourselves and our horses than
to the enemy.

The Cavalry had been shamefully neglected in this matter of arming; and, in view of more active service, it was
being looked into.

On the return of Lieutenant Colonel Powell to Camp
Piatt, he was taken ill with a severe attack of bilious fever,
but in six weeks so far recovered as to be able to be taken
to his home in Ironton, Ohio. His restoration to health
was so slow that he finally decided to quit the service, and
tendered his resignation as Lieutenant Colonel. Before it
was accepted or acted upon, Brigadier General E. P.
Scammon succeeded to the command of the Kanawha Di-

vision, thus relieving General Crook, who was transferred
to the army of the Cumberland.

During this time the regiment was actively engaged in
scouting over the country surrounding Camp Piatt. The
official report, as follows, of one of these scouts will suffice
for all:

Report of Captain David Dove, 2nd West Virginia
Cavalry.

CAMP PIATT, W. VA., April 7, 1863.

SIR:—I have the honor to make the following report of
the result of my late expedition through the counties of
Logan and Cabell. In obedience to your orders I marched
on the 3rd inst, with detachments of companies A, D, E,
F, G, H, I and K, in all six commissioned officers and 135
enlisted men. Marched from Camp Piatt to Red House
on Coal River, where I arrived at 12 o'clock and encamped
for the remainder of the night, resuming the march at 4
o'clock on the morning of the 4th, and arrived at Chapmansville, on Guyandotte river, at 11 o'clock a. m. Here
we captured one captain and two privates, stragglers from
Jenkin's command. After resting for two hours I started
down the river with the expectation of meeting Jenkins,
learning that he had not passed up, picking up one or two
men every few miles, but could ascertain nothing definite
as to his whereabouts until arriving at the mouth of Hart
Creek, 12 miles below Chapmansville. I learned that
Jenkins had left the river at this point, and marched
toward Big Sandy river, and, as he had some fifteen hours
the start of me, and the river was not fordable at any point
near, I thought it unadvisable to pursue him, but continued down the river until 6 o'clock, when I halted at the
mouth of Ugly creek, remaining there until 2 o'clock on
the morning of the 5th, and again started down the river.
On arriving at the falls I learned that a part of Sweeney's
Battalion, commanded by Captain Carpenter, had encamped the night before four miles below. I immediately started in pursuit of him, and upon arriving
where he had encamped I learned that he had marched
in the direction of Mud river, leaving the Guyandotte
road. Not having a guide, I had to follow his trail
through one of the wildest sections of country in western
Virginia. About two o'clock I struck the Mud river and
traveled up it one mile, to where the trail again left the

road, crossed the river and ascended a very steep and rough hill, covered by a thick wood. When the advance was about half way down the hill on the opposite side, it came upon the enemy in a very deep ravine, into which it was almost impossible to force the horses. After a sharp skirmish we drove them from their position; when a very hazardous and exciting chase ensued, the enemy scattering in every direction. During the skirmish the enemy had one man killed and we captured fifteen prisoners, fifteen horses and fifty stands of arms, which latter were destroyed. After resting an hour I started for Hurricane Bridge, arriving there at 8 o'clock, and camped there that night. From thence, marched on the 6th to Camp Piatt, leaving the prisoners at Charleston, for whom you will herein find a receipt. The result of the expedition was, killed 1, captured 34 men and 30 horses, and destroyed between 75 and 100 stands of arms. No one was hurt on our side. Very respectfully your obedient servant,

D. Dove.

Capt. 2nd. W. Va. Cav. com'g exp.

J. C. Paxton, Comd'g Reg't.

CHAPTER VI.

EXPEDITION TO LEWISBURG.

On or about the first day of May, 1863, General Scammon ordered Colonel Paxton, with the regiment, on a reconnaisance to Lewisburg. As this expedition proved so disastrous in its results, and the acts of the commander have been so severely criticised, he suffering the loss of his official position in consequence, I will endeavor to give a detailed account of it, as well as the official Confederate account.

From Camp Piatt to Lewisburg the distance is about one hundred miles. The road leads up the Kanawha river to the mouth of Gauley and New Rivers, the junctions of these two rivers forming the Kanawha. Crossing Gauley, the road leads up the east side of New river via the Tompkins farm and Hawk's Nest, over Little and Big Sewell Mountains to Meadow Bluff, thence to Lewisburg. Some lively little bouts were had with bushwhackers on the way, but no one on our side was killed.

Colonel Paxton was apprised on the road that Edgar's battalion (rebel) was in the vicinity of Lewisburg. The colonel hoped to surprise this body of the enemy and rout them, as had been done on a former occasion; hence he so arranged his march that dark found him about twenty-five miles from Lewisburg. Captain David Dove, with a detail from Company H, was placed in the advance. In going down Brushy Mountain, the advance ran into a scouting party of about thirty rebels, who succeeded in making their escape in the darkness. Captain Dove now very naturally abandoned the idea of a surprise, and informed the Colonel of his encounter with the scouts, and the fallacy of hoping for a surprise. The Colonel ordered him to push on. This intrepid and daring officer sent his orderly sergeant to the officer in command of the column, advising him to hold the column back, adding, "We are going to get into trouble, and it will be better for the advance guard to suffer alone, than for the regiment to be drawn into a trap."

At 1 o'clock a. m. on the morning of May 2, 1863, while the advance was ascending a winding road dug through a wood on the Tuckwiller farm, they were surprised by an ambuscade of the enemy, whose guns flashed right in their faces. The regiment came rapidly up to the advance, which had encountered a blockade in the road. James Smith, of the advance, was killed near the blockade, and Lieutenant George Shoemaker mortally wounded.

The regiment endeavored to fight the best it could in the darkness, and did succeed in forcing back the rebel right. Captain Dove received a wound in the foot which eventually caused his death. Geo. W. Hale was killed when the enemy's right was being turned. Alberto Harvey, of Co. G, was also killed.

After the rebel right had been turned, Colonel Paxton had the recall sounded, and in obedience to this order the regiment fell back a short distance, and remained there until 11 o'clock a. m.

The following is the report of the Confederate Lieutenant Colonel, George M. Edgar, of this affair:

CAPTAIN :—It becomes my duty to summit through you a report of the engagement which took place west of Lewisburg on the morning of the 2nd instant, between the 26th Virginia Battalion and a regiment of U. S. Cavalry commanded by Colonel J. C. Paxton. A report reached me about 2 p. m. the 1st inst. that U. S. Cavalry had been on Big Sewell Mountain the night before, and had avowed their intention of capturing Lewisburg. I immediately sent out a strong cavalry scout to ascertain the truth of the rumor, and watch the enemy, if any could be seen, and report as to his probable strength and intentions. About 11 p. m. one of the scouting party returned and reported that a large cavalry force of the enemy was advancing upon the town, and was already within nine miles of it. After ordering stores, prisoners and sick to the rear, I formed the battalion and marched it to Handley's Mills, two miles west of Lewisburg, the position selected for defense. The dispositions for battle were as follows: Company A, Captain Swann, in a skirt of woods on the Blue Sulphur turnpike, to prevent the enemy from turning our right flank; Company B, Lieutenant Hines, and Company F, Lieutenant Dunlap, along an important bend in the road on the west side of the hill with instructions to refrain from firing until the head of the enemy's column had passed the left company; Company E, Capt. Scott, and Company G, Capt. Morris, behind the barricades across the road, and the fence to the right and left of it; Company C, Lieut. Peck, and Company D, Capt. Burdett, about one hundred yards on the right of the reserve, with instructions to that officer to watch the enemy and report if he should attempt to turn our right flank. With these dispositions we awaited the approach of the enemy. We had scarcely finished our preparations when the head of the enemy's column appeared (about one a. m.) and began to file up the hill by fours, the men talking and laughing, apparently unconscious of our close proximity. Unfortunately, before the head of the column had reached the center of the line of riflemen, one of the men fired his gun. This of course obliged the whole advance to fire, the enemy retiring behind the bend in the road in great confusion. The firing then became general between the enemy's advance and ours, and lasted several minutes. In less than a minute after the firing ceased in front, I was warned by a quick volley on the right that the enemy was endeavoring to turn our position. I immediately ordered the two reserve companies to Lieut. Folk's support, and hastened in the direction of the firing. I had scarcely gone 150 yards when I met the enemy charging in line through the woods. I immediately caused Company D to file into the woods and commence firing, and afterwards hurried forward Company C (the other reserve company) to its support. The firing between these two companies and the enemy was heavy, and, realizing that our safety depended upon the enemy at this point, I ordered the two

rifle companies from the front, and formed them in supporting distance of the two companies engaged. Just as this took place, the enemy's right charged up the road in front of the barricade, but was handsomely repulsed by a volley from companies E and G. This was the last volley fired, the enemy withdrawing from both our front and right. As he withdrew I sent out squads of both cavalry and infantry to watch his movements, and very soon received information that he had formed in line in the open field in rear of our right, apparently for the purpose of charging our line from that direction. At the same time, from the noise I heard in the front of the left of our position, I conceived the idea that a portion of the enemy's force had been dismounted and would probably attack us from that direction also. I immediately withdrew my whole force within the inclosure on the left hand side of the road, and disposed it to meet the enemy in both directions, placing the rifle companies along the fences to the front, and the remaining force along the fences in the direction of which I supposed the charge would be made. With the force disposed as I have indicated, we awaited the approach of the enemy, feeling assured the attack would be renewed at daylight, if not before. At early dawn it could be plainly seen that the enemy's force, with the exception of a picket, had been withdrawn beyond the hill in our front, and about 6 o'clock a correspondence between Colonel Paxton and myself, which resulted in a truce until 11 a. m.; the enemy asking the privilege of burying his dead and taking care of his wounded. He left a surgeon and a sergeant to take care of his four wounded men, one of whom was a lieutenant. I have every reason to believe, however, that his loss was much heavier, for his ambulances were running busily for three hours, and citizens assured me that they were filled with dead when he retreated, and from the number of carriages and buggies he seized on his retreat, for the accommodation of his wounded, it is reasonable to suppose that the number was larger than acknowledged. It is gratifying to be able to report that there were no casualities on our side. The enemy returned our fire with spirit, but with no effect. They took, however, four prisoners—three infantrymen and one cavalryman. I am, Captain, etc,   GEO. M. EDGAR,
Lieutenant Colonel Commanding.

The correspondence between the Union and Confederate Colonels was as follows:

To the officer commanding at Lewisburg:—Mr. Tuckwiller consents to allow two men seriously wounded to remain at his house as they cannot be moved. They, together with the sergeant who remains to nurse, will be your prisoners of course, and I ask that you use the humanity that you would have the right to expect from us. I have the honor to subscribe myself, your obedient servant,   O. NELLIS,

First Ass't. Surgeon, 2nd (West) Va. Cavalry.

P. S.—If you will do me the favor to supply a surgeon to assist in amputating a leg, it will be received as a kindness.

[Answer.]

O. Nellis, First Assistant Surgeon, 2nd [West] Virginia Cavalry :—Your favor has been received. Any communication from your commanding officer will be received.

GEO. M. EDGAR,

Lieutenant Colonel Commanding Outposts.

ON THE FIELD, May 2, 1863.

Commanding Officer, Confederate forces before Lewisburg:—Your note received. I did not know my surgeon had gone to the front with a flag. His and my wish is to take care of our dead and wounded. I ask for nothing except what the laws of war and humanity ask for.

J. C. PAXTON,

Colonel Commanding Force.

(Answer)

On the Field, May 2d, 1863.

Col. J. C. Paxton, Comd'g U. S. Forces:—Your favor has just been received. Your dead will be conveyed to you for interment. Two of my surgeons shall assist yours in attending to your wounded. Of course the truce shall exist until formally concluded by yourself. By order of Gen. Echols.   GEO. M. EDGAR,

Lt. Col. Comd'g Advance.

On the Field, May 2d, 1863.

Major Edgar, Comd'g Confed. Forces near Lewisburg: I wish to bury my dead and take some care of my wounded. It will take until 11 a. m. this day. I leave my surgeon. Any courtesy you extend to him will be returned if occasion offers.   J. C. PAXTON,

Col. Comd'g 2nd W. Va. Cavalry.

CAPT. E. E. WILSON.

LT. COLONEL DAVID DOVE.

See page 81.

Colonel Dove was an ideal American volunteer. When the war broke out he was twenty-one years old. He promptly enlisted in the three months service and was elected a Lieutenant in the first company raised in Jackson County, Ohio At the expiration of this term he assisted in raising Co. H., Second W. Va. Cavalry, and was elected Captain of the same. Captain Dove was often entrusted with perilous missions, and in every case he ved equal to the occasion. He was severely wounded May 2d, 1863, (see page 77) after being wounded he was brought back to the house of Mr. B. S. Smythers (at his own request) where he was cared for by members of his own company and Mr Smyther's family. In July he so far recovered as to be able to return to his own home, near Jackson, Ohio. December 17th, 1863, he married Julia E. Smythers, a most estimable and accomplished young lady, of Kanawha County, West Virginia. Captain Dove was promoted to Lieutenant Colonel of the Regiment, May 18th, 1863. In October he returned to camp and assumed the command of the regiment, until Colonel Powell's return in March, 1864. His wound compelled his resignation July 5th, 1864. He died January 12th, 1868, loved, honored and respected by all.

(Answer)

On the Field, May 2nd, 1863.

Col. Paxton, Com'd U. S. Forces:---The truce you ask will be willingly granted. Everything we can do for your wounded will be done. Your surgeon will receive the attention and protection you ask.

By order of General Echols,

GEO. M. EDGAR,

Lieutenant Colonel Commanding Advance.

Our loss was four killed, eight wounded, four missing, and twenty-eight horses killed.

This was the first defeat the regiment had suffered, and, that some one was to blame for allowing the command to be drawn into an ambuscade, the humblest private in the regiment knew. Some of the best officers and men in the command had been needlessly sacrificed. First Lieutenant George Shoemaker, and Privates George W. Hale and James Smith, were fine specimens of the American volunteer. Captain David Dove was a most brave and promising officer, and the wound he received on this occasion rendered him almost incapable of further service during the war.

While the command severely criticised, and did not excuse the conduct of Colonel Paxton in permitting the surprise and making the sacrifice possible, yet, the very high esteem in which both officers and men regarded him for his many admirable qualities as a gentleman, his kindly interest in and attention to the wants of his command, his genuine and undoubted loyalty to the flag, and devotion to the union, made all deeply sympathize with Colonel Paxton. He truly and sincerely loved his "boys" (as he called them) and was frequently the central figure of a group, pleasantly taking part in such conversation as might be general about the camp.

In July, 1865, after being discharged at Wheeling, W. Va. on our way home, quite a number of us had occasion to stop off at Marietta, Ohio, Colonel Paxton's home. While on our way to the railroad depot we met the colonel and of course, all greeted him warmly. Said he : "Boys of the Second West Virginia Cavalry, God bless you," and the old warrior was so overcome with emotion that he wept like a child. The colonel has long since been "gathered to his fathers," and when we shall assemble at the great roll call above, we will want no warmer welcome from friends than that of the old commander, "Boys of the Second West Virginia Cavalry, God bless you!" On May 7th, 1863, Colonel John C. Paxton left the service. To fill the vacancy thus created a universal demand went up for the appointment of Lieut. Colonel Powell as Colonel of the regiment. The entire command knew Lieutenant Colonel Powell to be a brave, fearless and efficient officer, and all seemed fully to realize that he was the proper man to lead them. Therefore Governor Pierrepont urged the Lieutenant Colonel to reconsider his purpose of leaving the service, and to accept the command of the regiment. This proffer, endorsed as it was, induced Colonel Powell to recall his resignation and accept the command; and thereupon Lieut. Colonel Wm. H. Powell was commissioned as Colonel of the 2d W. Va. Cavalry, May 18, 1863.

CHAPTER VII.

THE JOHNNIES AFTER THE LOUP CREEK WHARFBOAT.

The time immediately following was occupied in drill‧ing and scouting. The most important event that transpired was about June 27th, when the officer learned that the rebels had formed a plan to burn the Loup Creek Wharfboat. Preparations were made to capture the raiders, as it was known they would be in small force. Captain Chas. E. Hambleton was sent to Loup Creek with two companies, and other forces were distributed in such a manner as the exigencies of the case seemed to require. The wharfboat was moved across the river out of danger, and the coming of the enemy awaited.

The enemy came, but with all the precautions taken, made good their escape. As they came in on the road guarded by Captain Hambleton's force, I will give that officer's version of the affair, without further comment.

Camp Piatt, Va., June 28, 1863.

Sir:----In obedience to your order I started with Companies B and I, 75 men, June 26th, at 7 p. m. Crossed the river at this place and proceeded to Loup Creek Landing, where I arrived at 3:30 a. m. June 27th. I immediately sent out a picket of twelve men to stand on the road below Loup Creek bridge, about three-quarters of a mile above the landing. I then ordered my command to unsaddle and cool their horses, and then saddle and feed. They had unsaddled and were lying down, when my picket, having gone to the place designated, found a picket guard of Company F already stationed there, when they returned. But I was not aware they had returned until afterward. They had been back fifteen or twenty minutes

and my men were just saddling, when the rebels came
dashing in, yelling and shooting, which was the first
notice I had of their approach. The picket had retreated
up the road instead of towards us. My men sprang to
their arms and fired into the advancing column, but on
they came. The first squadron dashed right through us,
so we were between them. I ordered the men that were
near me to get under the river bank some twenty feet from
the road. Some few got into the woods above, and some
were taken prisoners. Some eight or ten infantry on the
opposite side of the river fired into them, while my command who were near the river bank also fired on them,
which was the means of starting them down the road.
While they were passing us Lieut. Carlisle called to those
who were prisoners to rally under the river bank, and some
ten or twelve saved themselves by running and jumping as
directed, the rebels not daring to follow. They----the
rebels----started to return, but again fell back and went up
Armstrong Creek on the gallop, while about thirty, supposed to be the rear guard, did not get past us at all, but
retreated up Loup Creek. Their force has been variously
estimated, but from what I could see, and from the best
information obtained, I judged them to be about 225
strong, under command of Major Bailey. The whole affair did not last over fifteen or twenty minutes. That we
did not allow the rebels to do this without resistance is
evidenced by the fact that they left one dead, three badly
wounded, five horses killed and three wounded. I am,
Your Obedient Servant,
CHAS. E. HAMBLETON,
Captain Comd'g.

Col. W. H. Powell.

In the interim between the 18th of May, 1863, the
operations of the regiment were of minor importance.
During this time Col. Powell's health had been restored,
and the regiment reorganized and fitted for active service.

The camp life at this time was of the highest type of
enjoyment. The quarters were in the shape of a square,
and consisted of good log houses, with kitchens for the
different messes. The houses on the east side of the
square were occupied by the company officers, the regimental headquarters being in a house near the Kanawha
river on the west. The stables were a short distance north

of the camp. To the rear of the officers quarters there was a mountain of considerable height, its sides steep and almost inaccessible. In front of the camp, flowed the Kanawha river, with Brownstown on its opposite bank. It was four miles down the river to Malden, and ten miles to Charleston. During the month of June the regimental surgeon recommended that the men be supplied with ale, as it would be conducive to their health. When this became known, the file of the regiment readily expressed their willingness to take the perscribed medicine, and were ready to bless the name of Dr. McKeown. Word was sent to some Jewish merchants in Charleston that they might sell a few dozen bottles of ale to the regiment daily. Two or three of those enterprising dealers soon appeared in camp, and disposed of their merchandise at a good profit. This was a bonanza for the vendors, for ordinarily they were not allowed to sell to soldiers. There was no indication that the men would abuse the privilege, and the merchants obtained leave to make another visit within a few days. On the next trip they brought a considerable quantity of the stimulant, and with the large demand and their former success, determined to make a larger profit. The soldier has his own ideas of right and wrong, and will quickly resent a wrong, especially when his finances are involved. No sooner had they learned that ale was suddenly advanced in price, than they reached the conclusion that ale was a contraband of war, and so confiscated the entire lot. This ended the administration of ale as medicine in the regiment; but by this time it was unnecessary, as the men were in splendid health, the result, no doubt, of the ale.

The following order will explain itself:

Charleston, W. Va., July 8, 1863.

General Order
No. 9.

The thirty-fourth mounted Ohio volunteer infantry, second (West) Virginia Cavalry and two companies, First (West) Virginia Cavalry, under Captains Gilmore and

Delaney, will constitute a brigade under the command of Colonel John T. Toland, and, until further orders, be designated as the Third Brigade, Third Division Eighth Army Corps. By command of

BRIG. GEN. E. P. SCAMMON.

JAS. L. BOTSFORD, A. A. G.

The following incident is only illustrative of the many perilous times experienced by small detachments of cavalry making night marches over mountainous roads. Comrade Richard Barron, of Company G, and who was so severely wounded on the occasion as to have been, for awhile at least, left for dead, has furnished me these particulars. During the summer of 1863 Companies G and K were attached to Colonel White's brigade, which force occupied Fayetteville. The cavalry were kept busy scouting and doing patrol duty. A force of confederates under General McCausland was camped at Piney Creek, three miles beyond Raleigh C. H. and about thirty miles from Fayetteville. Twice a week, in addition to the day scouts, the cavalry made night marches, attacked and drove in the rebel pickets, thus alarming their camp. General McCausland learning that these little incursions on his outposts and camp were only by a small force of cavalry rarely exceeding fifty men, devised a plan to punish them. Their plan was eminently successful, as this narrative will show. Early on the night of July 3rd the enemy posted four companies of infantry about eight miles from Raleigh on the steep sides of a mountain, where they lay concealed until the little band of cavalry passed their position.. They then came into the road, where it had been dug and hewn along the side of the mountain. For some distance along the lower side of the road was a sloping precipitous bank about sixty feet high which led down to a small stream of water. The side of this bank was covered with jagged rocks, most of them having been torn from the roadway in its construction. At sun down on July 3rd, fifty-one men of companies G and K, under command of Captain Joseph Aukrom, started out the Raleigh road with orders to ascertain if the enemy's pickets were still posted as usual. After the little band passed the point where the enemy lay concealed, the latter came into the road, felled a tree across it, and by sharpened limbs, and other material hastily gathered formed an impassible barrier for cavalry. They then posted themselves in advantageous positions and awaited the return of the scouts. The latter proceeded to near Raleigh C. H., where they encountered and drove in the rebel pickets, and soon after started on their return. About 3:30 a. m. on the morning of July 4th, when the advance of the scouts encountered the blockade, and while many of the men in the column were sleeping on their horses, they were suddenly surprised by a volley being fired into their ranks from front and flank. The rear men dashed forward to the relief of their comrades, and thus adding to the confusion, which was intensified by the yelling and firing of the enemy. Dead horses were piled on top of each other, and the only escape for the men was over the rugged rocks referred to. Every man in the command was either wounded with ball or cut and bruised by the rocks in making their escape. Of the fifty-one horses only one came out uninjured. Only three men were killed outright, (see death roll) as the fire of the enemy was low. Eighteen prisoners were taken away, the wounded were carried to a house some distance to the rear, the enemy remaining until after sunrise and caring for the injured as best they could. The rebel captain in command (Mr. Phil. Thurman) recognized in Mr. Barron an old acquaintance, and it was by his orders that the wounded were carried to the house and cared for.

The narrator says that when the prisoners, by their own request, were brought to the house, that they might see their wounded companions, they looked like they had gone through a threshing machine they were so cut and bruised and their clothing so torn. The same day a portion of the 91st O. V. I. came out and removed the wounded to Fayetteville.

CHAPTER VIII.

THE WYTHEVILLE RAID.

On the 13th day of July, 1863, the expedition to Wytheville was organized, the object being to destroy the East Virginia and Tennessee railroad. Much care has been taken to obtain all the information possible in this connection, and this is submitted as being correct almost in detail.

The raiding party consisted of the 34th O. V. I. mounted infantry, numbering 505, officers and men, under Lieut. Colonel F. E. Franklin; seven companies of the 2nd West Virginia Cavalry, viz. companies B, C, D, E, F, H and I,365 officers and men, under the command of Colonel Wm. H. Powell. The expedition left Camp Piatt, West Virginia, on the 13th day of July, 1863, at 4 o'clock p. m. The movement was made through Fayette, Raleigh, Wyoming, Mercer, Tazewell, Bland and Wythe counties. The route was mostly over a rough, rugged, mountainous country, this being the first time that much of it had been traversed by union troops, as owing to the topography of the region, the execution of rapid movements so essential in making a raid, was very difficult. The entire route, after leaving Fayette, was sufficiently occupied by detachments of the enemy's cavalry, or by bushwhackers and local organizations, as to cause delays, and thus retard our progress. The command reached Piney Creek, near Raleigh C. H. on the night of the 14th, when the head of the column was fired upon from an ambuscade, by which the 34th O. V. I. lost three men killed and four wounded.

LT. JOHN M. CORNS,

Now honorably serving his twenty-third consecutive year as Mayor of Ironton, Ohio.

Yours Truly,
W. H. Powell
Late Bng. & Bn. Maj. Genl. U. S. Vol's.

This was understood to have been caused by a blunder of the commander in not providing a sufficient advance guard thus allowing the column to be drawn into a trap.

While going into camp here a communication was received from General Scammon referring to order sent by Captain Gilmore, and directing Colonel Toland to return to the forks of Coal River roads and move immediately upon the Virginia and Tennessee railroad at Wytheville, Virginia. Owing to the darkness of the night and the confusion caused by the ambuscade, only a portion of the command received or understood the order, and in consequence the column became broken and separated. One part of the command proceeded under command of Lieutenant Colonel Franklin to the town of Raleigh C. H., and a portion with Colonel Toland struck the Wyoming pike five miles from Raleigh C. H. This occupied nearly the whole of the night. The horses had now been under saddle for thirty-six hours and had marched a distance of sixty-five miles, according to information received from the guides. Lieutenant Colonel Franklin was immediately ordered to that point, and at ten o'clock a. m. the whole command was united at the Harper farm, six miles west of Raleigh on the Wyoming pike. Here Captain Gilmore, of the 1st West Virginia Cavalry, with two companies of that regiment, joined the column with the train containing supplies. From this point the commanding officers were ordered to send back to Raleigh all unserviceable horses and all men who were unfit to continue the march.

At 1 o'clock p. m. Colonel Toland moved forward, having in his command a total force of 818, exclusive of one company of the 2nd West Virginia Cavalry, which was to escort the train back. The forces were as follows: Thirty-fourth O. V. I., (mounted) 441 officers and men; 2nd West Virginia Cavalry, 298 officers and men; First West Virginia Cavalry, 79 officers and men.

At the marshes of coal river the command was halted and supplied with four days rations for the men and three days forage for the horses. From this point the train was sent back, and the force camped for the night on the Jones farm. The Marsh fork of Coal river being impassable for horses without swimming, a bridge was constructed, and on the morning of the 16th the column crossed the river, pursuing a course that led over Little Guyandotte mountains, and by way of Wyoming Court House. The command camped here on the night of the 16th, having marched a distance of about forty miles.

On the 17th the route was pursued in the direction of Abbs Valley, via Tug mountains. While on the mountain it was ascertained that a small force of the enemy was stationed at the head of the valley, picketing the gap or road through which our route lay. Colonel Toland ordered Colonel Powell to go forward with three companies of the 2nd West Virginia Cavalry, and endeavor to surprise and capture the pickets.

On the road the advance captured an old man with a squirrel rifle on his shoulder, the report of which had just died away. But on account of his age he was not summarily punished. The Colonel questioned him closely as to the location of the enemy's picket, and the location and strength of the force camped in the valley. The old man gave the required information in a straightforward and correct manner. The force in the valley consisted of J. E. Stollings' company of rebel infantry, about sixty strong. Lieutenant Davidson, who was ever anxious for such duty and very efficient in performing it, was sent forward to capture the pickets, without firing a gun, if possible. It was raining, and the outpost of six men were all inside a tent, which was revealed to the advance by the barking of a dog. They rode up quickly and captured the entire picket before one of them had time to get outside the tent. This made the capture of the company an easy matter. Approaching to within a short distance of the house where the company was quartered, a charge was made, the house surrounded and all the inmates captured while they were enjoying an old Virginia hoe-down.

The captures consisted of forty-five prisoners, twenty

horses and five hundred stands of arms, the arms being intended for recruits. The prisoners were taken along, the arms, quarters, etc. destroyed.

Pushing on that day over very rough roads, the column camped that night on the Taylor farm, six miles from Jeffersonville and forty-five miles from Wytheville, having marched forty-five miles on the 17th. We had been driving a small force all the previous afternoon, but they kept out of our way and did not retard our progress materially. This force was in our rear on the 18th, they having taken the road to Jeffersonville, supposing that we were going in the direction of the salt works. On the 18th the command marched rapidly in the direction of Wytheville, the rear constantly skirmishing with the enemy. During the day the Abbs Valley prisoners, proving to be an incumbrance, were paroled.

The pickets of the enemy were encountered about one mile from Wytheville. They fell back at our approach, and a skirmish line of the enemy was discovered along a low ridge that covered our view of the town and concealed the position and strength of the enemy.

The First and Second West Virginia Cavalry companies were in the rear at this time, and Colonel Powell was ordered to the front with the cavalry to charge the skirmishers. Colonel Powell, seeing the position on the ridge and not knowing the position of the enemy beyond, requested Colonel Toland to dismount a portion of the infantry and drive the skirmishers in. This suggestion was characteristically disregarded, and the order to charge vigorously renewed in unnecessary language. The order was promptly obeyed, and the charge in column of fours down the road began. The little line of Confederate skirmishers fled, and, when the point was reached where they had been stationed, it was seen that we were within a short distance of the town, hemmed in by a high stake and rider fence, and the enemy posted in houses along both sides of the street. Into this avenue of death the column dashed, and, although it received a volley from the command stationed in the street and from the houses, it rode through, capturing the command in front. The column was now checked, owing to the dead horses and to the fact that Colonel Powell had been wounded and Major Hoffman's horse killed, stunning the major in the fall. Colonel Toland hurried forward, evidently seeing the mistake he had made by charging in column, when there was plenty of open ground on each side of the road. A company of the Thirty-fourth was dismounted and deployed as skirmishers on the right of the road, while some of the Second West Virginia pulled down the fence to the left and deployed also. This soon cleared the town of the enemy, but not without fearful loss. Colonel John T. Toland was killed under the following circumstances: After Colonel Powell was wounded, Colonel Toland came to the front to direct the movements of the dismounted men. He was sitting on his horse near a pond of water. The rebels were firing from the upper windows of a two-story brick house, and by the bullets striking in the water, it was evident that the Colonel was the object of their aim. His attention was called to this fact, but he replied in inelegant language that the bullet to kill him had not yet been moulded About this time he was shot through the heart and killed instantly. I was near him, and distinctly heard the fatal ball strike his body. Captain Dennis Delaney of the First Virginia Cavalry was killed, and First Lieutenant William E. Guseman of the same regiment was mortally wounded. Our loss was fourteen killed, thirty-two wounded, seventeen prisoners and twenty-six missing. This loss includes the entire trip, but nearly all the casualties were at Wytheville. We captured about one hundred prisoners in the town, two pieces of artillery, and about five hundred stands of arms. The damage done the railroad was only a small matter, but the reason of this was undoubtedly the loss of our commanders, namely, Colonel Toland killed, and Colonel Powell severely wounded. The rebel General Sam Jones, at Dublin Depot, in his official report says that this was

all that saved the destruction of the railroad, as there
were not enough rebel troops at hand to prevent the raiders destroying considerable property, as they supposed
our object was Saltville, and their energies were spent in
preparing to defend that place. Our men became so in-
censed from having been fired on so fatally from the shelter
of houses, that they set fire to that portion of the town,
and quite a number of houses were burned. Most of this
shooting from houses was done by armed citizens, and
hence the destruction of this part of the town was certainly
justifiable according to the rules of war. Many of the
Second West Virginia assisted families to places of safety
and no wanton acts were committed. The fight commenced obout sun-down, and did not last over twenty minutes, when we had entire possession. All our wounded,
together with the assistant surgeon, Ozias Nellis, of the
Second Virginia Cavalry, Sergeant E. A. Thomas, John
N. Stewart and a few others who had been detailed to care
for the wounded, fell into the hands of the enemy as prisoners of war, and were subsequently taken to Richmond.
About ten o'clock at night, Lieut. Colonel Franklin, of
the 34th O. V. I., who now was in command of the brigade, reported to Colonel Powell, through his adjutant,
Lieut. Clark, for instructions. Colonel Powell replied, "say to Colonel Franklin to be governed by
existing circumstances, and to exercise his best
judgment in getting the command back to the
Kanawha Valley. And that in his opinion it was impracticable to attempt to continue the raid as originally intended, as the force was too small to cope with the enemy,
now gathering from all directions. It was near midnight
when the force left the place on the eventful return march.
About twelve miles from Wytheville all the prisoners
were paroled, and the two pieces of artillery destroyed.
About twenty miles on the Tazewell road the command
left the main road, and took a mountain route to the right,
crossing Queen's Knob, Walker's Mountain, Brush Mountain and thus through Hunting Camp, leaving Rock Gap

on our right. (See John McCauseland's report, rebel,)
thence northwest over Wolf Creek and East River Mountains, crossing the Tazewell and Mechanicsburg, the Tazewell and Parisburg and the Tazewell and East River main
roads or pikes, thence across the Stone Ridge into the
north of Abb's Valley on the Laurel fork of Bluestone.
Here we camped on the night of the 19th, having marched
forty-five miles from Wytheville. On Sunday evening
the 19th the first attack was made on the rear guard,
which was in charge of Lieut. Davidson, but though the
little force of rebel cavalry in pursuit made repeated attempts to cut the guard off from the main column, yet
they did not materially interfere with the march.

Monday morning, July 20th, at 3 o'clock a. m., the
march was resumed, and a continued attack was kept up
on the rear by an increasing force of the enemy commanded by Major May. At one time they charged into
our rear guard with saber, a rebel officer cutting Lieut.
Davidson severely on his wrist, the lieutenant replying
with a pistol shot which unhorsed the daring confederate.
Soon after this occurrence some of our command dismounted and formed an ambuscade into which the pursuers were drawn, and so badly used up that they did not
again attack the rear. The march was by mountain paths
across the west of Great Flat Top Mountain, over Indian
Ridge, Pinnacle Ridge, and down Pinnacle Creek, and
thence across Casey's and Barker's Ridges, and along
Pond Mountain, finally crossing Guyandotte and Pond
Mountains to to the marshes of Coal river, where we
struck Maple Meadow road, at a distance of nine miles
from Raleigh C. H., from which point we marched
through the town of Raleigh, and rested at Francis'
farm on the Raleigh and Fayetteville road at 5 o'clock p.
m. of July 22nd. I do not know where we camped the
nights of the 20th and 21st. Our rations had long since
given out, and the command was nearly in a state of starvation, as the country traversed produced nothing but
timber and rocks. On the evening of the 21st a portion

of the command obtaind four small steers, and a small quantity of corn meal. The paths along which we passed presented obstacles almost impassable, being filled with fallen timber and winding over rocky steeps which are beyond description; and now, at this late day, it seems almost incredible to think of a mounted command pursuing such a route. Owing to the lack of forage and the severe labor undergone, many horses gave out from exhaustion and were left on the road. The number has been roughly estimated at three hundred. Quite a number of horses were captured in Tazewell and Wythe counties, so that probably not more than one hundred men were marched into camp dismounted. On the night of the 22nd two messengers on fresh horses were dispatched to Fayetteville for supplies for the famishing horses and men. The next morning a train of supplies and forage reached us from Fayetteville under escort of a company of cavalry and two pieces of artillery. As the train came rumbling into camp, arousing the men from a sleep of exhaustion, they greeted the deliverers with cheers. As it would take some time to issue the rations in regular form, to appease the hunger of four days, crackers or hard tack were scattered about the camp, which were eagerly seized and eaten. By eight o'clock all had partaken of a substantial breakfast of genuine "Lincoln" coffee, bacon and hard tack. The poor, jaded horses also enjoyed a good feed of oats and hay. The column, in high spirits, headed for Fayetteville about 10 o'clock. Boxes of crackers were placed by the roadside every few miles, and it is safe to say that most of us ate hard tack all day. On the evening of the 23d we were safely within our lines at Fayetteville, where we camped for the night.

A very amusing incident took place soon after our arrival at Fayetteville. The personal appearance of troopers after a long march such as this had been, is generally not very prepossessing. The use of soap and water had been shamefully neglected, our hair was unkempt, our clothes dirty and ragged, and altogether we were a very hard looking set of boys. A lieutenant of Company I, who was no exception to the rule as regarded personal appearance, went at once to a sutler of the post at this place, bought a paper collar, put it on, and came over to the camp. The marked contrast between the clean white band about his neck and the other parts of his apparel was so ludicrous that he was greeted on all sides with laughter and with shouts of the then familiar salutation, "here, ring," "here, ring."

On the 24th we marched only as far as Loup Creek, and about noon on the 25th reached Camp Piatt, our old quarters. The whole march occupied twelve days, and covered about four hundred miles.

About the 21st Captain West, of the 34th O. V. I., left the column for the purpose of finding a house in the hopes of being able to procure something to eat. When he came in sight of a little farm house, some distance from the road, he met one of his own regiment coming away. He inquired of the man if there was anything there that would appease hunger? The man replied: "Nothing but some buttermilk." The officer was very fond of that delicacy, and went on his way. On arriving at the house the gallant captain was met by the lady, who, at sight of him, threw up her hands in holy horror, and, in a despairing tone of voice, exclaimed: "Take anything I have in the world, but save my honor." When the officer had somewhat recovered from the shock this gave him, he replied: "Hang your honor, madame,—I want some buttermilk."

Report of Major T. M. Boyer, C. S. Artillery, Chief of Ordinance, etc.

Dublin, July 26, 1863.

GENERAL :—In obedience to your orders of July 18th, directing me to take command of the two companies at this post, and such of the employes and citizens as could be hastily collected together, and to proceed to Wytheville for the purpose of meeting a raiding party of the enemy reported approaching that place, I have the honor to report: The mail train was stopped, the passengers notified to leaves the cars, and my command, numbering about 130 men and two pieces of artillery, placed upon them. Not-

LT. COL. J. J. HOFFMAN.

withstanding the delay consequent upon getting citizens
hastily together, organizing, arming and equipping them,
we were enabled to leave this place for Wytheville at 3 p.
m., one hour and a half from the time your order was first
placed in my hands. The train was subject to further delay, owing to the fact that we were running out of time,
and a freight was upon the track meeting us. The train
arrived at Wytheville depot (three fourths of a mile from
the town) at 5:10 p. m. My artillery was disembarked at
once, but as there was neither horses nor harness ready at
hand, it became necessary to procure them, which in the
great state of alarm and confusion in which everything in
the place was found, rendered a considerable delay unavoidable. As no reliable information could be obtained either
of the force or whereabouts of the enemy, Lieut. C. L. C.
Minor was ordered to procure horses enough to mount himself and half a dozen men, move as rapidly as possible in
the direction in which they were reported to be approaching, and furnish me with reliable information, if possible.
After about half an hour's delay in making arrangements
for organizing the citizens of Wytheville, and distributing
the small arms to them, which I had carried with me for
that purpose, (in which I was promptly and efficiently aided
by Lieut. Colonel Umbarger, of the militia and Maj. Joseph
F. Kent, a resident of the place.) I received information
from Lieutenant Minor that the advance guard of the
enemy, numbering about forty men, was within one mile
of the town. I could then wait no longer for my artillery,
but put my small command in motion in the direction of
the town, and ordered Captain Oliver to follow me as rapidly as possible when he should have procured the means
for moving his guns. Before reaching the town I again
received information from my scouts that the main body of
the enemy, numbering about 1,000 men, was within half a
mile of the town, moving steadily and rapidly forward. I
pressed on as rapidly as was practicable with an undisci-
plined command, and succeeded in reaching the town just
as the enemy made their appearance in sight of Main street,
some 1,200 yards distant. Not being familiar with the
streets or topography of the town, I was forced to be
guided by circumstances, and first moved my command in
the direction in which the enemy were approaching, but,
after advancing a short distance in that direction, I found
it impossible to procure a position which would be tenable
for so small a force against so large a one. I therefore

ordered Lieutenants Bozang and Alexander to move their company forward to check the advance, while the remainder of the command could be brought back to Main street where resistance might be more successfully made. This order was obeyed promptly, and the officers and men behaved most gallantly. Lieutenant Bozang's conduct on the occasion was conspicuously brave, and his services most valuable. Although a deadly volley of buck and ball was fired into the head of the advancing column at a distance of not more than thirty yards, yet the impetuosity of the charge was so determined as to be irresistible, and Bozang and his gallant little command were forced from their position in a narrow street, and compelled to surrender to overpowering numbers. By this time the remainder of my force had been removed from Tazewell street (the one by which the enemy were approaching) and posted in such of the houses on Main street as could be entered, many of the doors being closed and securely fastened. This position was held for about three-quarters of an hour, when we were forced to abandon it by overpowering numbers of the enemy, deployed as skirmishers on foot through the town. I ordered a retreat, and the town was left to the mercy of the foe. Had I remained longer the result could not have been different, excepting that all the brave men under my command must certainly have been killed or captured. Owing to the severity of the enemy's fire and the unorganized condition of my command, they could not be withdrawn in order, and were therefore directed by me to quit the town as best they could, and to rally at the water tank, a point on the railroad a mile below the depot, whither I had ordered the train to be removed for greater safety. This they did, but before that point could be reached, the conductor, for some reason which has never been explained to me, moved off with his train, thereby compelling the command to make their way back to Dublin on foot. About twenty-five of the men who accompanied me were captured; Captain Oliver and two men were killed; Lieut. Bozang and three or four wounded; and I have been informed that two of the citizens of Wytheville were also killed, and some fifty or sixty captured. They, however, with the other prisoners, were subsequently released upon their parole. Owing to the great advantage we secured in fighting from houses and other shelter against mounted men in the streets, we were enabled to inflict far greater loss upon the enemy than we sustained, notwithstanding the disparity of numbers. The colonel commanding (Toland) was killed, the second in command [Colonel Powell] was wounded and afterwards left in our hands. Captain Delaney was killed; Lieutenants Livingston, Guseman and——————were wounded and also left in our hands. Nine others were left dead in the streets, and a number, which I have not been able to ascertain, were left wounded in and around the town. It was owing to these losses, doubtless,—especially the loss of the two colonels, that after burning eight or ten houses and inflicting an in-injury upon the railroad which was repaired in an hour's time, they abandoned their undertaking, and retreated at ten o'clock that night toward Tazewell C. H., carrying off one of our six pounders, which had not been brought into action, and which they abandoned before they had gone twenty miles. I am, General, very respectfully, your obedient servant,

T. M. BOWYER,
Maj. Com'dg Expedition.

To Major Genl. Saml. Jones, Commanding Department of Western Virginia.

Dublin, Va., July 18.

Mayor of Lynchburg, Va.—Thirteen hundred of the enemy's cavalry were reported this morning between Tazewell C. H and Wytheville. They are on a large raid on this road. I have sent all the troops I had on the road to General Lee. If there are any available volunteer companies in Lynchburg, please send them at once. By so doing we may not only save this line of road but intercept and capture the raiders. The citizens about here are turning out well. If any of your people can come here, Mr. Thomas Dodamead will soon be sending a train. They can come on that. If Captain, or Major, or Doctor H. Grey Latham is about Lynchburg, present my regards to him, and ask if he has any men at his disposal, to bring them on here at once.   SAM JONES.

Report of Colonel John McCausland, Thirty-Sixth Virginia Infantry, commanding Fourth Brigade.

Headquarters Fourth Brigade, }
Mercer Court House, Va., July 30, 1863. }

SIR:—In accordance with your letter of the 29th calling for a report of the movements of my troops and the part taken by them in connection with the recent raid on Wytheville, I will submit the following brief report:

Having been forced from my position at Piney, near Raleigh C. H., Va., by a superior force of the enemy under General A. P. Scammon, I retired to the top of Flat Mountain, and, finding that the enemy did not follow me with his main body, and was endeavoring to pass in my rear with a large cavalry force, I continued the retreat to this place, where I learned that the enemy had passed through Abb's Valley in Tazewell county. I at once sent some cavalry to intercept them and some infantry to obstruct the roads. When they arrived in Tazewell the enemy had gone in the direction of Wytheville. The cavalry pursued them until they met with Colonel (A. J.) May, of Brigadier General William's command, who presumed to give them orders, etc., so that they accomplished but little, owing to the interference of those named above. On the morning of the 19th I moved with a part of my infantry and cavalry and artillery through Rock Gap, in the direction of Wytheville. I halted the infantry and artillery at the Gap, and went on with the cavalry, but on reaching Bland C. H., I found that the enemy had retired, and had gone back toward Tazewell county, coming at no time in my direction, or passing the mountains at any of the crossings guarded by my forces. They passed beyond me, and as soon as I found I could not come up with them, I stopped at Rock Gap and remained there. On the morning of the 19th I also sent a sufficient garrison to the narrows. I am sure that some one is to blame for the escape of the enemy. I am also of the opinion that the cavalry force that was in Tazewell, under General Williams and Colonel May, was sufficient to have captured the enemy if it had been properly managed. Your attention is called to the report of Captain Bowen, of the Eighth Virginia cavalry, herewith submitted, from which it appears that if the Gap at Crabtree's had been occupied by Col. May, or had he permitted Captain Bowen to have occupied it (which he would have done) the enemy would have been driven upon me at Rock Gap, and they could not have escaped. Again, if General Williams had moved with the celerity that the occasion required, and attacked the enemy in force, instead of skirmishing with his rear, he would have defeated them, and taken or scattered the most of them. I never could come up with them with my infantry, and those commanding the cavalry failed because they did not charge the enemy with their whole force when they did overtake them. I have the honor to remain, your obedient servant,

JOHN McCAUSLAND, Col. etc.

MAJ. C. S. STRINGFELLOW, A. A. G.,

To MAJOR GENL. SAM JONES, Dublin, Va.

CHAPTER IX.

COLONEL POWELL IN PRISON.

In connection with the Wytheville raid I will here relate some of the prison experience of Colonel Powell, which he has furnished me at my request. It was well known in the regiment that the confederate authorities had placed Colonel Powell in a dungeon for some imaginary wrong which he was accused of committing. I read an article in the Richmond Dispatch, in July, 1863, which contained the most virulent abuse of that officer. In January, Colonel Powell had, under orders, burned the Austin Handley house and the James A. Feamster barn, near Lewisburg. This was the principal cause of the abuse. Colonel Powell says:

"I find in my Prison Dungeon Diary, the following record: Saturday, August 29th, 1863. I wrote a letter this morning by permission of the rebel department at Richmond, Va., to the rebel general, Sam Jones, Dublin, Virginia, in reference to the charges made against my conduct as an officer, and asked him to arrange for an early examination of my case, and advised him of my condition of health, and of my close confinement in a dungeon, subsisting on bread and water. Also, under date of September 9, 1863, the following record: Lieutenant and Adjutant Latouch, of Libby prison, visited me and placed in my hands to read an answer to my letter of August 29th, as follows: General Sam Jones states that Colonel W. H. Powell, 2nd Regiment West Virginia Cavalry, had not been placed in close confinement by his order, and that there had been no charges preferred against Colonel Powell that he knew of, and that he should be released from close confinement and returned to the officers' general prison. "At ten o'clock, September 9th," adds General Powell, "I was taken from the dungeon to Colonel Straight's room in Libby prison, where I remained in company with my fellow officers until January 29th, 1864, at which time I was paroled for thirty days, to go to Washington to effect the exchange of Richard H. Lee."

This concludes the statement furnished me by General Powell. In the records of the War Department I find the following:

Headquarters Department of Western Virginia, }
              Dublin, July 23, 1863. }

Hon. James A. Seddon, Secretary of War.

Sir:—Colonel W. H. Powell, who was wounded and taken prisoner at Wytheville on the 18th inst., is believed to be the same officer who, on the evening of the 10th of January last, caused the houses and barns of Mr. Austin Handley and Mr. James A. Feamster, near Lewisburg, Greenbriar county, to be burned, under circumstances set forth in the accompanying affidavits. I entered into a correspondence with Brigadier General Scammon, U. S. army, commanding in my front, on the subject. He disclaimed any knowledge of the outrage, and condemned it in the strongest terms, and assured me that it should be investigated. It seems, however, that Lieut. Colonel Powell was retained in the service, and I have been informed that he has since been promoted. Colonel Powell is not so severely wounded as was supposed, and I bring his case to your notice, and forward the accompanying affidavits, and ask that he be not exchanged until it is ascertained from the government of the United States if he burned the property I have mentioned under orders from superior authority. His conduct as I understand it, was in violation alike of the laws of this state and the rules and usages of civilized warfare. If his government avows the act, and declares that he acted under orders, or if he can show that it was done under the pressure of military necessity, he may be excused. Otherwise, I submit that he should be held to answer for his crime. He is a bold, daring man, and one of the most dangerous officers we have had to contend with in the northwest of this state, and I am particularly anxious that he should not be allowed to return to the Kanawha Valley if it can be avoided.

SAM JONES, Major General.

P. S.—The prisoners captured at Wytheville declare, as I am informed, that this Lieut. Colonel Powell had given orders to burn Wytheville, and he himself admitted to an officer that he had given the same order in regard to Lewisburg.

Following the Wytheville raid, the regiment was not actively engaged in campaigning for some time. About the middle of August Brigadier General Alfred N. Duffie was assigned to the command of the cavalry in the Kanawha Valley. General Duffie was a Frenchman, had been engaged in wars in Europe, and was one of the best drill masters we had during the war. As soon as he was fully installed in his new command, he detailed Company H as a body guard. The company reported at once at Charleston, and took up quarters in the Clarkson House. Some time after this the general and his staff occupied this house as headquarters, and the body guard built comfortable quarters near by. The brigade was also moved to Charleston, and comfortable quarters were built for all.

General Duffie at once began drilling the cavalry and fitting them for active service. A large number of blank cartridges were used in skirmish drill, and the regiment was instructed thoroughly in this and all movements pertaining to cavalry in action. How well this efficient school of preparation served the command will be seen when some of the engagements in which they subsequently participated shall be described. Especial care was taken to put the 2d West Virginia Cavalry in good condition for more active service than they had yer experienced. Frequent scouts were made through adjoining counties, some of them occupying several days. The body guard was not allowed to remain idle, but did its share of scouting, picketing, etc. On one occasion they were sent on a little forced march of about three-quarters of a day, all equipped for light marching. Their object being accomplished, the company arrived in camp late in the even-

ing, drenched to the skin, having been caught
in a shower of rain. To overcome any ill af-
fects that might follow the drenching, the general who
was ever mindful of the comfort of his boys, ordered a
large ration of commissary whiskey to be issued to them.
In order that the commodity might be more easily and
equitably distributed, the company was formed in line at
the head of the company street, each man with tin cup in
hand, ready to take his ration from the bucket as Sergeant
Kramer passed down the line. It was nearly dark, and
the Sergeant being in a hurry, did not notice that the
line did not diminish, for as soon as the men at the head
of the line were served, they immediately fell in at the
foot, in order to get another ration. The general came out
to the company quarters several times during the evening
and was forced to go back smiling; and though he was
greeted in a very warm and familiar manner, he seemed to
take peculiar pleasure in being introduced to one
of the privates represnting General Grant. Although
more than twenty-seven years have passed, and many
changes have occurred with the passing of time, I am yet
forced to smile at the recollection of that evening in camp
on the banks of the Kanawha.

General Duffie and his staff took their meals at the
house of Mr. Jeffries, a very dignified gentleman of French
decent. The sympathies of Mr. Jeffries and his family
were with the South, yet they at all times treated the
officers and soldiers of the union with that respect and consideration so characteristic of refined people. Whenever it
was necessary, as it frequently was, to have a guard placed
at the house, one of the young ladies usually brought him
some delicacy, in the shape of fruit or confections.

The fall of 1863 was the most pleasant time we experienced during the war. The soldiers seemed determined to get all the enjoyment that was possible out of
this kind of life, and to that end they were constantly on
the lookout for fun. The little scouting expeditions that
were sent out afforded diversion to the troopers, and often

furnished incidents bordering on the romantic or tragic.
I will relate a case in point to illustrate the latter.

Once, a scouting party of twenty men of Company H
had been sent up Elk river some twelve or fifteen miles.
In the party was a young man who had enlisted from
Kanawha county as a recruit. He was an easy, steady-go-
ing, all-around good young fellow, and did not impress
one as having any distinguishing characteristics, other
than that he appeared to have been born lazy. He was a
confirmed book worm, and was engaged in reading most of
the time when it was possible for him to do so. When
engaged in this favorite pastime, he usually reclined in a
position of such perfect abandon that he looked the em-
bodiment of laziness. Physically, he was a magnificent
specimen of the camp soldier. While we were returning
from this little expedition, our lazy man, as was his custom, kept in the rear, with one leg thrown carelessly over
his saddle, deeply absorbed in reading a novel, oblivious
to his surroundings. One of the men conceived the idea
of giving him a scare, such as might afford rich amusement for all. The plan proposed by the fun-maker was
that he should dismount, let the command proceed on the
road with his horse, while he would go a little ways
up the hill-side, conceal himself behind a tree, and bush-
whack the straggler, while we should enjoy seeing the
trooper gallop up to the command in a demoralized condition. The first part of the program was carried out to the
letter. But the funny part didn't work. As soon as the
shot was fired, and the bullet went whistling over the
rider's head, he quickly stopped his horse, looked in the
direction from which the shot came, and seeing the smoke
near the tree, he called out in a loud voice, "Oh, you are
there, are you, bush-whacker? I'll soon bring you out of
that." He seized his pistol, and was soon at the tree.
The pretended bush-whacker laughed, but the other was
so enraged that he came near shooting his comrade. It is
needless to add that when the dismounted man came up
with the column he did not look more demoralized than

he had proposed the literary young man should had his plan worked more to his liking.

On another occasion while on a scout on Guyan river, in April, the command halted for dinner; the advance, consisting of twelve men, went on about half a mile as a picket, with orders to feed and get dinner. It was a beautiful day, and as they came to a farm house, the noise of poultry suggested the idea of having eggs for dinner. One of the party was sent into the house to see what amicable arrangement could be made to that end. After the mother and her two daughters were satisfied that their lives were to be spared, it was arranged for a dinner to be cooked by them, we to furnish the coffee, bread and pork, they to furnish three dozen eggs. For their trouble we were to give them some Lincoln coffee. We had a royal dinner and a grand, good time, for just after dinner two more Guyan girls came to the house, and as the command did not march until late in the afternoon, we became very well acquainted. One of our number, who evinced a strong disposition to remain in that country or to return after the war, got information from one of the girls that there was to be a wedding there that night, and in accordance with the custom, a dance.

Soon the main column came in sight, and we again took the advance. Two or three miles from the house we met a young lady, and a Confederate soldier with a violin. We took the Johnny in charge, gave the violin to the lady, and sent our regards to the dancers, with regrets that the usages of war compelled us to deprive them of their musician.

On October 21st a scout was organized for the purpose of marching in the direction of Boone C. H. The force consisted of a part of the 2nd West Virginia Cavalry and the 34th O. V. I., mounted, in all about 300 men. The expedition left Charleston at 7 p. m., the Second West Virginia marching to Camp Piatt, where they arrived at 10 p. m. Here the command crossed the ferry and left

Brownstown at 2 a. m. on the 22nd. The force was divided into three columns, all taking different roads for Boone C. H., where it was reported a rebel force was camped.

The expedition, under command of General Duffie, was well handled, and the three columns all reached Boone C. H. some time before daylight, nearly together. The columns swooped down on the rebel camp and made a "water haul," capturing two or three stragglers and one man who was supposed to be a deserter. The information upon which this movement was made had no foundation in fact, as at no recent time had there been over fifteen or twenty rebels at Boone C. H., nor more than one hundred and fifty in the county. On the 22nd at 5 p. m. the command reached Camp Piatt and rested for the night. Reached camp on the 23rd. The distance traveled was eighty miles; prisoners captured, 4; horses captured, 3.

CHAPTER XIX.

THIRD EXPEDITION TO LEWISBURG.

The next move was an expedition to Lewisburg. The force consisted of the 34th O. V. I., mounted, the 2nd West Virginia Cavaly, and one section of Simmond's Battery, numbering 970 in all, officers and men. On the 3rd of November the command marched thirty miles and camped for the night. On the 4th it marched to Gauley, and crossed the river by means of a small ferry boat, and went forward on the Lewisburg pike. The march was much delayed by blockades in the road. This was unexpected, and the obstacles presented themselves for a distance of eight miles, so that in some places a new road had to be dug around them. The force went into camp for the night at the Hamilton farm, eight miles from Gauley. On the 5th it marched to Tyree's a distance of twenty-two miles, being again delayed by blockades. At this place the command was joined by Col. White, with detachments of infantry. On the 6th the whole command marched to Meadow Bluff, about eighteen miles from Lewisburg. The enemy's pickets were encountered on Little Sewell mountain, and our advance succeeded in capturing two of them. On the morning of the 7th the force started for Lewisburg, the object being to intercept the rebel forces that had fought General Averill at Droop mountain. On the 7th of November, at 9 a. m. the cavalry occupied Lewisburg, and learned that General Averill had badly defeated the enemy at Droop mountain, and that they had passed through in the direction of union. We gave pursuit, but they could not be brought to bay, although the 2nd West Virginia captured 110 head of cattle, 2 caissons and a few prisoners.

At Lewisburg we captured the rebel camps anp a considerable quantity of stores, which we destroyed; also the knapsacks of the 22nd Virginia infantry and the regimental tents.

On the return march the command found five inches of snow on Sewell mountain, which made it very difficult to move artillery and trains. However, at 10 a. m. on the 13th the command reached Charleston, having been absent eleven days and marched 250 miles.

The result of this expedition, summed up, is as follows:—Prisoners captured, 34; horses captured, 50; cattle captured, 110; small arms, 102. The above were brought away. Besides this 350 small arms, a large quantity of ammunition, tents for a regiment, knapsacks for a regiment, with the clothing in them, 2 artillery caissons, 10 wagons, and some quartermaster's stores were destroyed.

General Duffie has stated in his report that if General Averell had not whipped the enemy so hard at Droop mountain, he would have gotten in their rear, and the whole force could have been captured.

About the 20th of November the enlistment of the regiment began. The inducement offered by the government was $400 bounty and a furlough for thirty days. Under this arrangement the following number of men in the regiment re-enlisted for three years or during the war, the latter applying if the war should end before three years:—

Company A, 43 men; Company B, 28 men; Company C, 38 men; Company D, 49 men; Company E, 23 men, Company F, 51 men; Company G. 35 men; Company H, 42 men; Company L, 23 men; Company K. 32 men; making a total of 364 men, exclusive of those whose death occurred between the 20th day of November, 1863, and the date of first muster out, November 28, 1864. Probably 400 officers and men re-enlisted at this time.

On November 24th, 1863, the first installment of furloughed men left Charleston for Gallipolis, Ohio, on the steamer Victress. What a happy crowd that was. The boat landed in Gallipolis at about 5 p. m. the same day. Thousands of people gathered on the river front, being attracted there by the cheers of the men when they caught sight of God's country, as they called Ohio.

It would be impossible to describe the pleasures of these veterans during their visit to home and family, and I shall not attempt it.

By the 24th and 25th days of December all had returned to once more take up soldier life, with its sorrows and its joys, the softening influences of the home associations making them more willing to bear whatever hardships might befall them.

About the 12th of December another expedition was sent to Lewisburg in which the regiment bore a conspicuous part. The raid was under command of General Scammon, and was principally for the purpose of co-operating with General Averell, who was making a raid on the Virginia and Tennessee railroad. General Kelley, in his report, says that General Scammon moved too slow to accomplish anything other than to draw some forces from interfering with the plans of General Averell. In due course of time the command returned to camp without loss.

During all the winter and spring, detachments of the regiment were scouting and engaged in skirmishes with bush-whackers or small parties of the enemy.

About the 4th of February, 1864, we learned that Colonel Powell had been released from Libby prison, and would probably return to the command of the regiment in the early spring. The conditions and particulars of his release were as follows:

On the 29th day of January, 1864, Colonel William H. Powell was released from Libby prison on executing this parole:

Richmond, Va., January 29, 1864.

I, William H. Powell, Colonel of the 2nd Virginia Cavalry, U. S. A. Volunteers, in consideration of being released from imprisonment, do hereby give my parole as a soldier, and pledge my honor as a gentleman, to effect the release of Colonel Richard H. Lee, C. S. A., now held as a

prisoner of war by the U. S. Government, and his delivery
to the Confederate States authorities at City Point, Virginia within thirty days from this date; or to return to
City Point, Virginia, and deliver myself a prisoner of war,
to the confederate states authorities, within said period of
thirty days. And further, that I will not give any aid to
the U. S. government or its authorities, or any information to any person whatever, prejudicial or injurious to the
confederate states.

Witness,   (Signed) WM. H. POWELL,
    W. H. HATCH,   Colonel 2nd West Virginia Cavalry,
    Capt. and A. A. G., C. S. A.   U. S. A. Volunteers.

After this formidable document had been signed and
witnessed, the colonel was delivered to our forces at or near
City Point, Virginia. From there he proceeded to Washington and procured the release of Colonel Richard H.
Lee, C. S. A., in accordance with the terms of the parole,
and was a free man, so far as the rebel authorities were
concerned. He was then granted a leave of absence by the
Secretary of War, and visited his home in Ironton, Ohio.
He so far recovered from the effects of the wound received
at Wytheville eight months before; that he was able to return to the regiment, and took command at Charleston on
the 20th of March, 1864. When Colonel Powell returned
to the regiment he was given a magnificent reception.
Lieutenant Colonel David Dove, who had been in command, delivered an address of welcome on behalf of the
rank and file, which was feelingly responded to by the
colonel. Cheers greeted his remarks, and the reception
given him on this occasion, certainly justified the colonel
in expecting such confidence and co-operation on the part
of the officers and men, as would render the command
effective.

CAPT. JOSEPH ANKROM.

See page 156

CHAPTER XI.

GENERAL AVERELL ARRIVES IN CHARLESTON AND ASSUMES COMMAND.

Soon after this preparations were begun for some important movement. General George Crook had been assigned to the command of the Kanawha Division, and all was now activity. Horses were supplied for the dismounted men; arms, ammunition and clothing were issued. About the last of April General Averell arrived in Charleston with about two regiments of cavalry, and assumed command of all the cavalry intended for the expedition, which was now understood to be against the Virginia and Tennessee railroad. Some additional infantry regiments also arrived, among them the 36th O. V. I. General Crook pleaded for the return of his old regiment, and it was sent him by order of General Grant.

On April 30th, 1864, the expedition left Charleston, the infantry and artillery in the direction of Fayetteville, and the cavalry in the direction of Logan C. H. The cavalry numbered 2,079 officers and men. The command took only four days rations and one days forage after leaving Logan C. H., owing to the condition of the wagons and teams. The latter were sent back from Logan C. H. on the 5th. The division then found its way over mountains and streams to Abbs Valley, where we had been almost a year before. On the 7th a rebel picket was captured in much the same way as we had captured J. C. Stolling's rebel company on our first trip. A small force of rebel cavalry met us in the valley. They made a show of trying to stop us, but we pursued our way until the 8th, when the advance had an engagement about fifteen miles from Tazewell C. H., in which the enemy suffered a loss of four killed and five wounded.

The original intention was for the expedition to strike the railroad at Saltville, and then proceed toward Dublin, Va. Near Jeffersonville it was learned that Saltville was defended by a large force of infantry and artillery. Captured mail and information received from deserters showed that the enemy were fully informed as to our strength and intentions. Here General Averell decided to march to Wytheville, in order to prevent the enemy from concentrating against General Crook. On the way a train of wagons was captured. Near noon on the 10th the enemy was met in force at Cove Gap, or Grassy Lick. From all sources of information, including Confederate newspapers, it is estimated that their force was about 4,000, under command of General J. H. Morgan. On the 2d day of May, 1864, the following order had been issued:

Richmond, Va., May 2, 1864.

Special Order,
　　No. 102.
Brigadier General John H. Morgan, with his brigade, is relieved from duty in the department of East Tennessee, and will report to General J. C. Breckenridge, commanding department of Southern Virginia. By command of Secretary of War.   JOHN WITHERS, A. A. G.

To show that the enemy was fully informed as to our intentions, the following is inserted:

MAY 3, 1864, 11 A. M.

Major General Breckenridge, Dublin:----My two best scouts are just in directly from Averell's camp on Kanawha. They left there last Wednesday. Averell is certainly there. There were eight mounted regiments and eleven regiments of infantry, and others expected from Parkersburg. This force is called, on the Kanawha river, the right wing of Grant's army. Their intention, as expressed there, is to strike the Salt Works and New river bridge. There is no mistake about this information. They were expected to move very soon.

JOHN ECHOLS,
Brig. Genl.

The enemy in force were found to have taken possession of the gap, which was a strong natural position, and defended by artillery. It was at first intended to carry that gap by a charging column, and for this purpose the 2nd West Virginia cavalry was ordered forward, and stood near the gap with drawn sabers, awaiting the order to charge. While thus waiting, a member of Company H (which was General Duffie's body guard) dismounted and crept up into the timber, and plainly saw the rebel position, and heavy reinforcements being hurried forward. This information was at once communicated to General Duffie, who went with the informant and viewed the strong position of the enemy. The charge was abandoned, which from the first had been regarded by Colonel Powell as suicidal. We afterwards learned that the rebels were eagerly watching our movements, and, seeing the regiment with drawn sabers, had placed a battery in the road, shotted with grape and canister, and masked by brush in front of it, while a force of infantry was on either side of the Gap. Our command fell back a short distance and formed in line of battle, the Second West Virginia Cavalry occupying the left of the line. This drew the Confederates out of the Gap, and the fight commenced. The rebel right overlapped the Union left, and the enemy could be plainly seen and heard moving down the mountain side. But our position or alignment was not seriously disturbed. The battle raged for four hours, and was stubbornly contested by our little command. General Averell was slightly wounded early in the engagement by a ball cutting the skin across his forehead, causing some inconvenience from the freedom with which it bled. While under a heavy fire, Colonel Powell divided the regiment into platoons, and when it became necessary to fall back, the voice of the commander would ring out above the battle's noise, "Platoons, right about, march," and the order would be executed with the same precision as if on parade; then the same order would again face the regiment toward the enemy. The left was the key to the position, and the bold stand taken there added to the discomfiture of the enemy, and prevented him from breaking the union lines, notwithstanding his superior numbers.

This was one of the best conducted engagements we ever witnessed. During the four hours it lasted, there was but one break in our line, and that was made by the 14th Pa. Cavalry. The 34th O. V. I. was thrown into the breach, the 14th Pa. was reformed and resumed their places. Darkness put an end to the conflict, the enemy retiring to their position at the Gap. General Averell moved his command across the mountain to Crab Orchard, on the right flank of the enemy. This so fatigued men and horses that it was necessary to rest for half a day. By this engagement at Cove Gap, of Grassy Lick, with the forces of Gen. John H. Morgan and Gen. Wm. E. Jones on May 10, 1864, the concentration of the enemy's force against General Crook was prevented. Our loss was 114 killed and wounded, that of the enemy not known.

From Crab Orchard the command moved to Dublin, intending to join General Crook. When New river was reached, it was rising rapidly, and would soon be unfordable, from recent heavy rains. The stream at this point was about one-third of a mile wide, with a small island near the center. The current was rapid, and as it ran over a rocky bed, crossing was extremely perilous. I do not recollect having witnessed a more thrilling scene than when I reached the bank, and saw men and horses struggling in the surging water. Many of the horses had fallen, and being carried into deep water, were drowned, while the riders engaged in a desperate fight for life, battling with the beating waves, until rescued by some bold rider who took them by the hand and helped them to land and life. Several men were drowned. One I saw carried below the ford into deep water, divested himself of all his arms and attempted to swim ashore. But he could not, and drowned before our eyes, with no hand able to save or even render him help.

After crossing, the command moved to Christianburg,

distant two or three miles from the ford. From here the 2nd West Virginia was sent back to the ford, and witnessed the forces of Morgan and Jones baffled and unable to stem the torrent, which had now risen so as to be impassable.

At Christianburg General Averell communicated with General Crook at Blacksburg, and was directed to destroy the railroad east of the town. This was done for a distance of four miles in that direction.

Our ammunition being exhausted or rendered useless by the incessant rains, the general commanding dscided to start on the return march, which was in the direction of Blacksburg.

The Confederate General, John McCausland, in his official report under date of May 15th, says that he tried to intercept General Averell at Blacksburg, but, on reaching that point, found that he (Averell) had passed on. He also says that French and Jackson (Mudwall Jackson) occupied a position at Gap Mountain, intercepting our command, and scattering us in all directions, etc. The truth of this matter is when our column came in sight of this position in Gap Mountain, they were fired upon by the rebel artillery. General Averell threw out two companies as skirmishers, who engaged the enemy in the Gap, while our command was crossing the mountain below the rebel position. General McCausland also says: "I reached Gap Mountain with a small cavalry force about the close of the fight, just in time to see Averell pass into the woods."

The command joined Crook at Union on May 15th, Sunday, after marching along narrow and unfrequented paths and roads and crossing swollen streams. Our rations and forage had been exhausted, and the country was so poor that only an inadequate supply could be had. Our clothing was soaked with rain and our feet so badly swollen that our boots had to be cut open to get them off. One hundred and eighty-eight men of the 2nd West Virginia alone were barefooted. About thirty miles of the journey was made by file on foot, leading the horses. The whole distance marched was about 350 miles.

From Union we proceeded leisurely to Bunger's Mills, near Lewisburg, arriving there on the 18th, and went into camp. In this splendid blue grass country the horses speedily recovered strength.

As a whole the expedition was successful; as it accomplished the destruction of the New River bridge. But such raids on our part, owing to the long distance we were compelled to travel, certainly cost us more than the harm done the enemy. New River bridge was soon rebuilt, probably before our command started on its next raid.

While in camp at Bunger's Mills, the following congratulatory orders were read to the command:

Dep't West Virginia, May 23, 1864.

General Orders
No. 5.

The Brigadier-General commanding Cavalry Division desires to express his sincere thanks to the officers and men of this division for the uncomplaining fortitude with which they have endured the terrible vicissitudes incident to the recent march, and for the unwavering courage with which they attacked and held a superior force of the enemy near Wytheville on the 10th instant, thereby enabling another column to accomplish its purpose without the opposition of overwhelming numbers. Your country will remember your heroism with gratitude and the noble sacrifices and sufferings of our fallen comrades will be forever cherished in our memories. The 14th Pa. and 1st West Virginia Cavalry first received the shock of battle, while the Second and Third West Virginia Cavalry and Thirty Fourth Ohio Mounted Infantry, established a line which the enemy had reason to respect and remember. Great credit is due to the brigade commanders, Brigadier General Duffie and Colonel Schoonmaker, for the energy and skill they displayed, while the conduct of all was admirable, and worthy the praise of the brigadier general commanding. He desires, without making an invidious distinction to express his high appreciation for the skillful and steady movements of the Second West Virginia Cavalry under Colonel Powell upon the field. It was a dress parade which continued without disorder under a heavy fire during four hours.

The purposes of the enemy were foiled by the engagement; the railroad was reached and destroyed; New river crossed, and the baffled columns of the enemy arrived in time to witness the destruction, which all the energies of their superior force, even with artillery, had failed to prevent. The division commander also wishes to thank those officers and men of the division who have treated the inhabitants of the country with that courtesy, dignity and magnanimity which is inseparable from true courage and greatness; such conduct can not fail to awaken in the hearts of the deluded people, a respect and love for the government we are determined to restore and maintain. While we bring death and destruction to rebels in arms, let our bearing toward the people and peaceful citizens become soldiers of the United States. Those few unworthy persons who have disgraced themselves and us by acts of lawless pillage, should receive the scorn and contempt of every honorable soldier in this command, and every effort should be made to bring them to the punishment they deserve.

By order of Brigadier General Averell.

WILL RUMSEY, A. A. G.

Headquarters Third Cavalry Brigade,
Camp at Bunger's Mills, W. Va.,
May 20, 1864.

General Orders, No. 18.

It is with sentiments of profound satisfaction that I give to the officers and men of this brigade my hearty thanks for their gallant and faithful behavior on the battle-field near Wytheville. Their conduct has been admired, not only by me, but by the general commanding the expedition, and by the troops called to co-operate with us in our hardships.

Officers and soldiers of the Third Brigade, you have not deceived my expectations. My hopes and desires as to your conduct have been fully realized; and for this I thank you all. My thanks to the Second Virginia Cavalry, who, under the leadership of their gallant colonel, while retreating under a galling fire from the enemy, preserved their ranks unbroken as on parade, and by their vigorous return of the enemy's fire, saved the left of the division. *
* * * But while you receive my congratulations, do not forget that there is yet much for us to do. Do not be blind to the fact that our duty is yet only partly performed. We have much yet to suffer; many labors to undergo. The

whole army of our country is actively engaged to destroy an active and determined foe. Let us see that our part is performed without disgrace, and without murmur. In a word, do as you have already done. Let every man be at his post, and discharge his duty as a patriot and a soldier.

A. N. DUFFIE,
General Com'dg Cavalry.

During the war, in the active life of the cavalryman, many, very many "narrow escapes" might be related of the men of the regiment. The following "narrow escape" of one Mark King of Company G so combines the amusing, the romantic and the tragic, that we gladly give it space in these pages:

In the early fall of 1862 Companies A and G were in camp near Raleigh C. H., West Virginia. The paymaster had just made the troops one of his welcome visits, and their hearts were so gladdened that King proposed to some half dozen of his comrades that they go out into the country and have some fun. What the latter was to be did not seem clear to them at the time, but the idea of a free stroll away from the restrictions of camp was in itself suggestive of personal enjoyment. The little party saddled their horses and were soon away from the restraints of the camp. After riding for some time with no apparent object in view, a halt was called for the purpose of ascertaining the time of day. Nearly every soldier carried some kind of a watch, and after comparing theirs, and finding such a radical difference in them, they looked at the sun and concluded it was near eleven o'clock. The brisk ride had sharpened their appetites, and the idea of a country dinner now suggested itself, which suggestion was at once acted upon. The party again started, and soon came to a typical Virginia farm house. On the front porch sat an elderly lady and three younger ones, who proved to be mother and daughters.

The little party of ladies were very much frightened at the presence of the "Yankees." One of the men dismounted, went forward to the house, and, when the "folks" learned that the men wanted dinner and were willing to

pay for it, they became reassured and invited the boys to
"come in." Chairs were placed on the porch, and while the
girls disappeared to prepare dinner the old lady acted the part
of hostess and entertained her visitors. She asked innumer-
able questions, such as where they lived, whose command
they belonged to, and if they wrote letters often to their
mothers? The lady said that she had two boys in the confederate army, and once when they had been at home they
talked just like you "alls". One of the young ladies announced dinner, and the party was conducted through the
house to where the table was spread. On the way the hostess
delighted the visitors by remarking that, "when her boys
had been at home, they amused them by telling of the
many plans the soldiers would devise to obtain whiskey.
"Boys," said she, "here is some that we had on hand
before the war, and I am going to treat you "uns." With
that, she produced a well-filled bottle and glass, and the
boys took a drink. After a hearty dinner had been eaten
they again repaired to the front of the house. Soon the
conversation—on the part of the boys at least—became
quite animated. B—— then proposed to have another
drink, and producing some money, offered to pay for it.
The lady said that she could not spare any more of the
liquor, as she would need it to make "camphor." After a
little solicitation on the part of the boys, backed by the
sight of the money offerd her, the lady produced the
bottle, and the men drank to the health of the young
ladies. By this time, King, who was the leader of the
party, observing that his companions were getting under
the influence of the "mountain dew," concluded to draw
off his force at once. Biddle Y--s suddenly jumped to his
feet, and proposed drinking to the health of their friends
in Lawrence county, Ohio.

King quietly told the lady to give them the drink
asked for, and he would induce the party to leave. The
bottle being nearly empty the old lady disappeared, and
soon returned with a fresh supply of the liquor. This
action on the part of the old lady, was closely observed

by King, and thereby hangs the sequel to the story.
Drink number three was taken as proposed, and after the
boys had shaken hands with the girls, they mounted their
horses, and waving a parting salute, galloped off
down the road.   Under the exhilarating influences of the
liquor the party rode rapidly toward camp, and when near
it, they raised a "wild yell," charged through the camp,
over everything that came in their way, playing havoc with
the out-door kitchens.   This grand entry into camp
caused no little excitement, and under the directions of the
officers, the revellers were soon in custody. Exceptions
however, should be made to King who quietly sought his
quarters, and was not included in those who were arrested.
The officer in command ordered the disturbers taken to his
quarters, and he at once questioned them as to where they
had found the liquor.   "Found a cave full," shouted Biddle Y——.   "Found a mountain distillery," yelled Al.
H——.   At this the officers exchanged significant glances,
which meant well for the boys, if they would tell where
the whisky had been obtained.   Soon after this Mike M——
came to the tent where King was, and remarked that the
officers were getting the company team ready to go after
the liquor and bring it into camp, presumably for the use
of the hospital.   Said Mike M——, "if I only knew where
it was, I would go and get it before they could get there
with the team.   King then came to the rescue telling those
present that he had been with the party who found the
liquor and that he knew where it was.   A plan was quickly devised to circumvent the officers and procure the
liquor.   Between the camp and Raleigh a small creek
crossed the road where the command usually watered their
horses.   Under pretence of going to water, King and three
companions saddled their horses and rode toward the creek.
Just outside of camp they found another one of the plot-
ting party, who gave the riders a dozen canteens.   The
latter then by a circuitous route, struck the pike above
the camp, and being well mounted and the spirit of adventure, uppermost in their minds, they soon left the camp far

behind. The sun was sinking behind the western hills when the little party galloped up to the house where they had been entertained at noon. Their minds were so intent on the object of their trip that they scarcely noticed that three men were sitting on the porch, and who at once disappeared. The ladies were badly frightened at the re-appearance of the troopers. King leaped from his horse, approached the little party of females, and said: "Madame, I am afraid your kindness to the boys to-day has brought trouble on you, for," said he, "those boys who were here got drunk on your liquor, and when they arrived in camp they shot and killed one of their comrades, and now the officers are on their way out here, and, if they find any liquor on these premises, they will burn your house and carry you and your daughters to Camp Chase as prisoners." This announcement created the wildest excitement in the household, and the girls commenced screaming: "Mother, throw it out! throw it out!" "No! no! said King, that wont do, give it to us and we will carry it away before they get here." "Come this way," said the old lady, and leading the way the party followed through the house and into a small corn field, where under a projecting rock a cave had been built. One of the girls opened the door, and entering, handed out to our delighted "plotters" a demi-john containing about three gallons of "mountain dew." With this—to them—prize, the boys left, after assuring the ladies that no harm could befall them now. When well out of sight of the house the contents of the heavy vessel was poured into the canteens, and the "vessel" thrown over into an old field. It was now nearly night, a storm was gathering, and it was six miles to camp. Approaching a low gap in the hills our party was surprised to see themselves confronted by some half dozen guerrillas who commanded them to halt. This was an unexpected dilemma, and, as Mike M—— quickly realized that it was less dangerous to run the gauntlet as it were than to go back, he exclaimed: "Boys, lets go through," and suiting the action to the word, he dashed into the enemy, cutting right and left with sabre, the rest of our party following. King was so burdened with canteens that he, being behind the others, did not escape so easily. One of the rebels seized his horse by the bridle, while another at the same time struck him on his left arm with a gun, nearly breaking that member. King used his sabre with such effect that—saving the loss of three of his canteens which the gun knocked loose—he effected a very "narrow escape."

CHAPTER XII.

THE LYNCHBURG RAID.

From the 18th of May until the 1st of June, we waited, upon half rations most of the time, for supplies of horse shoes, nails and clothing; but, owing to the miserable, inadequate transportation furnished from the Kanawha, we were obliged to set out again, almost as destitute as when we came.

While here the Eighth Ohio Cavalry arrived in camp from the Kanawha Valley. This was a new regiment, composed of the old 44th Ohio Infantry, recruited up to about 1,100 men. As they filed into camp with new men, new horses, new arms and new clothes, we felt our littleness compared to that grand body, and, with open mouths, as we stood in our half naked condition, saw them file by and go into camp.

On the 2d day of June a Mr. Creigh, a citizen of Lewisburg, was tried by a military commission and found guilty of murdering a Union soldier in November. The proceedings were subsequently approved, and Mr. Creigh was hanged at Belleview, on Friday, June 10th.

On the 2d of June the march was taken up in the direction of White Sulphur Springs. The command consisted of about 2,000 mounted, and 1,200 dismounted men, many of whom were without shoes and other articles of clothing.

The march from White Sulphur Springs to Staunton was via Morris' Mill, Warm Springs, Goshen and Middlebrook, occupying five days. The infantry under General Crook had arrived in Staunton by another route, and a junction was formed with General Hunter, who came up the Shenandoah Valley. At Staunton the much needed supplies were received.

On the 9th of June General Duffie was placed in command of the First Cavalry Division, and the Second Cavalry Division, commanded by General Averell, was reorganized as follows: First Brigade, Colonel Schoonmaker, Fourteenth Pennsylvania Cavalry, Eighth Ohio Cavalry; Second Brigade, Colonel Oley, Seventh West Virginia Cavalry, Thirty-fourth Ohio Volunteer Mounted Infantry, Fifth West Virginia Cavalry; Third Brigade, Colonel Powell, Second West Virginia Cavalry First West Virginia Cavalry. The Third West Virginia Cavalry was assigned to the division of General Crook.

Here the Lynchburg campaign was arranged and begun. On the 10th of June the command marched via Summerdean to Belleview, where Mr. Creigh was hanged. On the 11th the march was resumed via Cedar Grove. North river was crossed at or near Rockbridge Bath for the purpose of endeavoring to cut off McCausland who had burned the bridge at Lexington, and was trying to oppose the crossing of Crook. The enemy hastily fled, and Lexington was occupied by the Infantry and the cavalry at about the same time. The military institute at this place was burned, the cadets fighting for their town in a manner which would have done honor to veterans. A young man, or rather a mere boy, went to the cemetery and removed a flag from the grave of Stonewall Jackson; and although efforts were made to capture the lad, he mounted a horse, and waving his flag at the pursuers, boldly and defiantly made his escape. It is needless to add that this chivalrous act elicited the admiration of all who saw it.

At 2 a. m. on the 13th, the cavalry moved toward Buchannon, driving the rebel force under McCausland before it. The last eight miles were made at a trot, the advance endeavoring to save the bridge over James river; but as there was a convenient ford at hand, its loss did not stay the progress of the troops. In view of this fact, and of the danger to private property, the citizens protested against burning the bridge, but McCausland, with his characteristic recklessness, persisted in the needless destruction, involving eleven private dwellings in the conflagration. Further extension of this destruction was stopped by the friendly action of the union cavalry, who extin-extinguished the flames. Several batteaux loaded with ammunition and stores were captured near this place. A rebel spy was found in camp, and by order of General Averell, was shot.

Orders were here received to await the arrival of General Hunter and the main body of the army. On Tuesday, the 14th, some important iron furnaces in the vicinity of Finncastle were destroyed. On the 15th the column crossed the Blue Ridge between the peaks of Otter, to Fancy farm, where the division again awaited the arrival of the main army. Our brigade, under Colonel Powell, was sent forward to Liberty, and the country in that direction was scouted most effectually. While on one of these scouts a body of about thirty rebel cavalry were seen observing our movements, and their capture was attempted. Our main body halted, and it became evident that the little force of the enemy imagined that they had checked further advance. Company H of the 2nd West Virginia was dismounted, and sent to gain their rear. As they were making their way along the mountain side for this purpose, and had reached a point where the descent could be made, one of the men was horrified to see a huge mountain rattlesnake poise himself in a position to strike. The soldier was so excited at this demonstration of an unexpected enemy, and so far forgot his orders of secrecy, that he immediately raised his carbine, and shot the rattler dead. The echoes reverberated down the mountain side, and the Johnnies beat a hasty retreat. No one was more chagrined at this result than the man who fired the

shot. He afterwards said that it seemed to him that that
snake was eight feet high, as it prepared to strike.

To show what the confederates thought of this rapid
advance of General Averell, I insert the following dispatch:

June 13th, 1864.

The enemy drove my cavalry brigade from Lexington on the Eleventh. They now occupy the town. Scouts
report the force to be Hunter's, Crook's and Averell's.
They have destroyed the Military Institute. I have
driven their cavalry back several times. They are now
advancing on the Buchanan road.

(Signed) John McCausland,
Brigadier General.

Genl. S. Cooper,
    Richmond, Va.

On the 16th the main cavalry column marched to
Liberty, rebuilt the bridge over Little Otter river, forded
Big Otter, and attacked McCausland at New London
about dark. General Imboden had re-enforced General
McCausland with one regiment of cavalry and two pieces
of artillery. After a short engagement the enemy gave
way, losing a dozen men. The following is General Imboden's report of the affair:—

June 16th, 11 p. m.

General:—After writing you this evening the enemy
renewed his attack upon me. General McCausland, occupying the left, just after dark reported the massing of a
heavy force in his front to charge his position. A few
moments later it was discovered that a double line of infantry was formed in front of and overlapping my right.
Finding our position very critical, and involving the
almost certain loss of all our horses (the men being on
foot and the horses tied) if the enemy succeeded in driving our lines back, I quietly withdrew, and have encamped
at the first creek this side of New London, on the pike,
where we shall have a fight early to-morrow morning. * *

J. D. Imboden,
Brigadier General.

Maj. General Breckenridge,
    Comd'g Lynchburg.

At sunrise on Friday, June 17th, the division moved

MAJOR C. E. HAMBLETON.

towards Lynchburg on what was called the old road, about two miles to the right of the road on which the infantry of Crook was marching. There were frequent skirmishes during the day, and when within eight miles of the city, our advance was contested at every step. When the stone church, four miles from the city was reached, the enemy seemed determined to give battle in earnest. As near as can be learned the dispositions for battle were as follows. The ground made it very difficult to handle cavalry, being rough and broken by sharp ravines.

Schoonmaker's brigade formed a strong skirmish line mounted across the open ground, supported by squadrons at intervals in columns of fours open order ready to charge on, or dismount to fight. Oley's brigade formed on the right, and Powell's on the left, in the same order. As this attack was developed, the enemy retired with only a slight skirmish, but as we neared the crest of the hill upon which the church stood, a rapid artillery fire opened upon us, and their small arms were unmasked, Schoonmaker's and Oley's brigades dismounted and ran to the front, a section of artillery, supported by Powell's brigade, galloped up to the church, and opened fire. At this juncture Crook's infantry arrived, and forming in line, charged the rebel position, driving the enemy in great confusion. It now being dark, the whole army went into camp in line of battle.

This action has occasioned much comment, but, in the light of all subsequent events, it was the proper thing to do. A large part of Early's corps was already in the city and occupying strong works on the outside. On the night of the 17th the enemy were busy strengthening their works and re-inforcing their lines. As new forces took their positions, the men could be heard cheering. On the morning of the 18th it became evident that Lynchburg was defended by a force larger than our own. During the night Powell's brigade was sent to the right, either to attack the rebel right or endeavor to capture and burn Lynchburg. This was a perilous march, the advance constantly skirmishing with the enemy. The little command was led in the wrong direction, it was thought intentionally, by the citizen guide, whose life paid the penalty of the act. At one time the command was in a position where the church spires of the city could be plainly seen. Some time in the morning a courier arrived with the information that the army was in full retreat, and that Powell's command would have to join the main force as best it could. This was the first intimation had that a retreat was ever contemplated, and the information seemed to daze the officers. Fully realizing the dangerous position of his command, Colonel Powell commenced to withdraw, and, by keeping well to the left of the main road or pike, succeeded in joining the main force at New London, just in time to take the rear, and to receive the first fire of the enemy, who had overtaken us.

The failure to capture Lynchburg is thus explained by General Averell:

"The delay at Lexington, rendered necessary by the deviation of the First Cavalry Division (Duffie) from the course ordered for it, and the change of place made by ordering it to join the main body, instead of going around Lynchburg, had proved fatal to the successful execution of the original project."

Averell's Division composed the rear guard until Liberty was reached, where we went into camp. The enemy was pursuing us in heavy force, and our rear was constantly skirmishing, often delaying the enemy, so that the entire column was enabled to march rapidly and securely, bringing off all the trains and artillery.

The Second West Virginia was rear guard on the 19th and often dismounted and fought as infantry. At Liberty an engagement lasting two hours occurred between Averell's Division and the enemy's advance. In this little battle the cavalry held their position until their ammunition was exhausted, and then withdrew behind Crook's Division of Infantry, which was drawn up in line of battle. The cavalry suffered the loss of 122 men. At three a. m. the march was resumed in the direction of Buford's Gap. After passing the Gap, the cavalry and Crook's division were placed in a position to rest. At sundown the column was again in motion toward Salem, Powell's brigade in the rear. The Second West Virginia encountered a force at Bonsack, and held them in check for some time. A portion of the regiment and two companies of the 36th Ohio formed an ambuscade, but owing to the accidental discharge of a gun by some member of the 36th, the ambuscade failed.

About this time the extreme rear guard was composed of one squadron of the First Virginia, and one squadron of the Second West Virginia Cavalry, under command of Major Carman, of the First. The men of the rear guard were much annoyed at the demonstrations of a cavalry force of the enemy, which acted as if it were driving the whole federal force before it; so they were greatly elated when the order came, "Let's stop and whip them." The Major formed his force, and when the Confederates came up in line, expecting to crush our little band, they met with a very unexpected reception, and were completely thrashed in short order.

The march was then resumed to Salem. Just after passing that place another ambuscade was formed, but failed of its purpose, as the enemy appeared to be less impetuous and less inclined to attack the rear.

It was late in the afternoon when the march was again taken up in the direction of the mountains. All were in excellent spirits, and notwithstanding the reverses lately met, as we filed up the Catawba Creek, the usual good nature of the soldier asserted itself. The setting sun cast long shadows on the mountain slope, and the beautiful panorama, spread out before us was duly appreciated by the warriors. Little did they think that but two miles ahead of them was to be enacted one of the most distressing scenes it was their lot to witness during the war, all the more deplorable because it was occasioned by the lack of judgment and criminal carelessness of the officer commanding the rear guard.

During the march up Catawba Creek, a well known

member of the Second West Virginia cavalry was in an
unusually good humor. He was known as the wit of the
regiment, and when others, through their surroundings
became gloomy and disheartened, his good nature asserted
itself, and like a gleam of sunshine, lightened the burdens
of others. Such in brief was the character of Scott Gard,
of Company H. At the time of his enlistment in 1861,
Scott was nineteen years of age, full six feet tall, of magnificent physique, and one of the finest athletes in the
regiment. He was promoted to the position of corporal,
the officers hoping that this little official responsibility
might be the means of restraining to some extent his ex-
urberance, and of freeing them from some of his harmless
pranks. He was the ideal American volunteer. Alas!
the cruel hand of fate was soon to include him in the needless sacrifice of five lives.

On arriving at Mountain Cove, or Hanging Rock, on
Catawba Creek, a scene met our gaze that we could not
comprehend. Scattered around in the wood, in the Little
Creek Bottom, were the remains of cannon, caissons,
wagons, etc., the remnants of a battery. Shells and cartridges were lying among the wreck, and the woods being
on fire, they were almost continuously exploding.

I have taken considerable pains to learn the true cause
of this state of affairs, and being an eye witness and parti-
cipant, I shall submit what I believe to be a correct version of this unfortunate affair. When the main force of
Crook and Averell camped at Salem, Colonel Oley was
ordered forward with his brigade to occupy and hold
Catawba Gap, some five or six miles from Salem. When this
force moved out from camp, an officer commanding a battery which had been marching in the rear of Oley's brig-
age, supposing the entire army was moving, broke camp
and followed. The battery was some distance in the rear
of the brigade, and as no force followed after, it was entirely without support, or guard of any kind. No general
officer knew of this state of affairs. The battery marched up
Catawba creek about one mile in the rear of Oley's force.

When they reached Mountain Cove, a narrow defile where a small stream falls into Catawba Creek, a little band of Confederates, about sixty men, supposed to be McNeal's Rangers, were concealed near this defile, watching for some opportunity to inflict injury on the "invaders." They saw Oley's brigade pass, and soon the battery came in sight, winding up the creek road. From his position the officer could see nothing following, and the wily ranger saw a prize within his grasp, and was quick to act. With a wild rebel yell they swooped down on the defenceless battery, capturing the entire outfit. Some of the artillery men escaped to the woods, but most of them were taken prisoners. The few minutes spent on that spot by the rebel rangers was time enough to wipe the battery completely out of existence. Horses were cut out and taken away, carriage wheels cut down, and everything rendered useless. They then withdrew, and, owing to the nature of the country, were virtually free from pursuit. Some of Colonel Oley's men heard the noise, and returning were the first to view the destruction. The escaped artillery men then set fire to the woods and the wreck.

While Crook's infantry was passing a guard was placed to prevent the men going into unnecessary danger, and Colonel Powell also placed a guard for the same purpose.

At sight of the wrecked artillery, the major in command of the rear guard seemed to completely "lose his head," for with loud and angry oaths he led his little band a zig-zag route through and among the burning wreck. I distinctly remember having ridden over some capped shells, which would have easily exploded if struck by a horse's hoof. However, we got safely through, and formed in line, face to the rear, The ground was rough, yet the major insisted on having the line straight.

Lieutenant J. W. Ricker was in command of Company H, and after the line had been formed, he was ordered to dismount half his company, the dismounted men numbering about fifteen. This little squad of men was led back to the wrecked artillery, by the major. A wagon was pointed out to Lieut. Ricker, who was ordered to take his squad and destroy a considerable quantity of powder that was in a wagon. The Lieutenant rode up to the wagon, viewed the situation, and informed the major that it was a most hazardous undertaking, as there was fire all around, and the powder would evidently soon be exploded. The major said it must be destroyed at once. The lieutenant led his band up to the wagon, directing Mr. Thomas Warman, who was the eldest of the party, to get in the wagon and hand the packages of powder to the men, who would carry it to the creek near by and throw it in. While this was being done the men protested against the dangerous employment, to which the major replied by calling them cowards. He then withdrew from the immediate scene.

In a few minutes a fearful explosion occurred on the ground, and a few seconds later the powder in the wagon exploded with fearful effect, killing and wounding over half the guard.

The killed were Scott Gard, Benjamin Prim, William Garvin, Isaac Moore, of Company H, and Marion McMillin, of Company C, who was on duty with Company H. A number were wounded, some having their clothes blown almost wholly from their bodies. Lieutenant Ricker, who was sitting on his horse near by, had a thrilling experience. His hat was blown away so it was not found, his saber scabbard hanging at his side was shattered, his head was adorned with its first gray hairs, and he was otherwise so shaken up that he has not completely recovered to this day. His faithful horse dropped dead after carrying his master to camp that night. Mr. Warman, who was in the wagon, was blown across the dead body of the lead horse of the team, and was picked up in an insensible condition. The circumstances surrounding the death of young Marion McMillin were most distressing. Mr. William R. McMillin lived near Buckeye Furnace, Jackson county, Ohio. He had a family of six boys, and at the breaking out of the war those who were of proper age promptly volunteered.

When the Second West Virginia Cavalry was recruited, three of the boys, Andrew, Murray and Emerson, enlisted in Company H. Later in the war two more, Milton and Harvey, also volunteered in the regiment, and when Marion, the youngest, was old enough he, too, enlisted, and Company H already having its share of recruits, he was assigned to Company C. During the perilous times of the Lynchburg raid he was permitted, at his own request, to march with company H, that he might be near his brothers. He was called the "baby" of the McMillin family, and it was with almost broken hearts that two of his brothers, Emerson and Murray, looked upon the dead body of their idolized Marion. But even the boon of looking upon the dead body of my near and dear friend and relation was to me denied.

This occurred on Tuesday, June 21, 1864. Since the war Major E. S. Morgan has stated that he positively refused to execute the orders of Maj. Carman to destroy the powder; and if the accident had not occurred as it did, in all probability he would have been called to answer the charge.

From this point we marched via Newcastle, Sweet Springs, White Sulphur Springs, to Meadow Bluff. From there the march was continued in easy stages until we reached Charleston, about July 1st. At or near Dogwood Gap, between Sewell and Gauley we met supplies. The one hundred days men who had charge of the supplies asserted that we were the hardest looking body of soldiers they had ever seen. Thus ended the ill-fated Lynchburg raid.

Who was to blame? Certainly not the rank and file.

The losses of Generals Hunter, Crook and Averell, after leaving Staunton, in killed, wounded and missing, was a total of 940. The loss of the Second West Virginia since May 13th, was thirteen killed, thirty-three wounded and twenty-one missing. J. J. Harding, who was General Duffie's orderly, was killed June 26th, as the following letter and telegram will explain:

Telegram:—

Gauley Bridge, June 28th, 1864.

To Davis Mackley, Jackson, Ohio:—Killed by gunpowder explosion, Scott Gard, Benjamin Prim and three others, near Salem, June 22. Joseph Harding killed by bushwhackers Sunday morning, 26th, just this side of Lewisburg. All of Co. H.   J. J. HOFFMAN,
Maj. Com'g 2nd Va. Cav.

Letter:—

Charleston, W. Va., July 1st, 1864.

Mrs. Harding, Jackson, Ohio:—I telegraphed you from Gauley Bridge, June 28th, announcing to you the sad and painful news of the death of your son, Joseph. I crossed Brushy Ridge, some six miles from Lewisburg, Saturday night last, and while resting my command at the foot of Little Sewell Mountain on Sunday, June 26, Gen. Duffie, with a portion of his staff rode up and told me that he had been bushwhacked while crossing the ridge that morning, and that his private orderly, Joseph Harding had been killed. His death was caused by a shot in the back fired from a small rifle, and he died instantly; that he had buried him, he did not say where. The general was much attached to Joseph, and grieved much over his death. He was a faithful orderly and a brave soldier, honorable, upright and reliable, and could always be depended upon in time of need. Having been with us in the field since 1861, and knowing him as we did, his death is to us a very great loss. Loved and respected as he was by both officers and men, we can freely sympathize with you in this your hour of affliction. While we sincerely regret his death, yet we are pleased to know he was a member of our regiment. His purse, revolver and letters I send you as given me by the general. His papers I will have made out as soon as it can be done, and forward them to you.

Yours very truly,
J. J. HOFFMAN,
Maj. Comd'g 2nd Va. Cav.

As we were passing a little group of houses just beyond Salem on our return, a lady was observed standing in the doorway of one of the dwellings, watching the column march by. One of our men ventured to ask her the name of the place. To his inquiry the lady politely replied, "Little Lick Springs." Then to show off smart be-

fore his companions, he said, "How far is it to Big Lick?"
To this the lady quickly and innocently replied, "About
four miles this side of Lynchburg." The laugh that followed, as we all saw the point, was shared in by the
lady herself.

There was one well known member of the regiment
noted for his ungainly appearance. He was over six feet
tall, raw boned and awkward looking to the last degree. A
full government ration was not sufficient to keep his stomach in first class condition. As the poet says:

"And when with savage-gleaming knife and fork,
　He brought himself down seriously to work,
　And marched through every dish in conquering glory,
　And ravaged all the adjacent territory,
　Making the table for some distance round
　Look like a fiercely, hard fought battle ground,
　A smile upon his placid face would fall,
　As if life wasn't a failure after all."

While on the return march he became dismounted,
and being a poor walker, he soon became footsore and
weary. To add to his misery, his capacious stomach had
been comparatively empty for several hours. In this condition, one evening, he overtook a portion of the hospital
corps, just as they were beginning to eat a bountiful supper
of "slap-jacks," fried ham and coffee, which commodities
they had procured during the day. Our dismounted
man took his seat on the ground a few feet from the diners,
and with nearly tearful eyes watched the ham and slap-
jacks disappear. Then with a heavy sigh, he said, apparently to himself, "I wish I was Lazarus." One of the company said to him, "Why do you wish that?" "Well," said
he, "the bible tells us that Lazarus ate the crumbs that fell
from the rich man's table; but those slap-jacks don't crumb
worth a d———n."

It is needless to say that after the laugh subsided, the
slap-jacks did crumb, much to his satisfaction.

CHAPTER XIII.

IN THE SHENANDOAH VALLEY.

On Friday, July 8th, Powell's brigade left Charleston for Parkersburg, which point was reached on the 12th, and the command went into camp near the city at "Camp Wood." While here we drew a number of horses, and the brigade was fairly well mounted. On the 16th we embarked on the B. & O. R. R. for Martinsburg, W. Va. reaching that place about the 19th. The brigade was not fully collected until about the 23rd. General Averell had preceded us, and with detachments of regiments had advanced to the front beyond Martinsburg. On the 20th occurred the battle of Stephenson's Depot, or Carter's Farm, four miles north of Winchester. This was one of the most brilliant and quickly executed victories of the war. Our force consisted of Col. I. H. Duval's brigade of infantry, consisting of the 9th West Virginia, 14th West Virginia, 34th and 91st O. V. I., in all, 1,400 infantry, and about 500 cavalry under command of General Averell. In this brilliant achievement a largely superior force under General Ramseur was utterly routed and their artillery captured, together with 154 prisoners. The following official documents will explain themselves. It has, however, been claimed that General I. H. Duval and the infantry are entitled to the fruits of the victory, as the cavalry were so few in number, (less than half what General Averell reports) that they were unable to reap the fruits of the victory, other than stampeding the two rebel regiments mentioned in General Rode's letter. I make these statements in justice to all concerned. Some have said that there were not over 100 cavalry present, and that there was no casualties in that arm of the body. This is a mistake, and does injustice to the troopers, who, the writer knows, were there and participated as described ; and the casualties are to be found in the report of the Adjutant General of West Virginia. It was a glorious victory, and immortalized the name of General Duval and his brigade.

REPORT OF GENERAL AVERELL.

(Official.)

July 28, 1864.

Being informed during the night of the 18th that the enemy had reached Berryville from Maryland by way of Snicker's Gap, I marched on the morning of the 19th with Col. Duval's brigade of infantry 1350 strong, and 1000 cavalry, viz., First and Third Virginia and Fourteenth Pennsylvania cavalry, together with the First Virginia and First Ohio batteries, to within four miles of Winchester, driving the enemy's cavalry under Jackson before me. During the evening of the 19th information was received that Early had arrived at Berryville and divided his command into two columns, one then moving via Millwood toward Strasburg, and the other going toward Winchester (Early himself being with the latter,) and that Crook's division and the Sixth corps were at Snicker's Gap. I endeavored to communicate with General Wright, advising him to attack the column on the Millwood road, but subsequently learned that instead of attacking he retired toward Washington. On the morning of the 20th, I advanced toward Winchester, and being apprised by my scouts of the presence of the enemy in some force about three miles north of the place, I formed in line of battle before arriving in his view. In the morning 200 of the 14th Penn. Cavalry were sent out on the Gerrardstown road to approach Winchester from the west, the balance of the regiment being sent to attack at Berryville. About 300 of the Second Virginia Cavalry joined me at this time from Martinsburg. Placing a regiment of infantry in line of battle on each side of the road with skirmishers in front, and a regiment of infantry in colomn in rear of the right and left flanks, artillery in the center and a regiment of cavalry on each flank, I advanced in this order vigorously to the attack. After marching nearly two miles through a country almost entirely open, with the center upon the pike, the enemy announced his position by opening a rapid fire from four guns concealed in the timber which stands upon Carter's farm, three miles north of Winchester. He at the same time made some demonstrations with a cavalry brigade upon each flank. My artillery was placed in position, the infantry regiments in column were thrown forward into line, cavalry skirmishers occupying my entire front were quickly withdrawn to the flanks, the concentrated fire of .the twelve guns were opened upon the enemy's center, and the infantry .advanced and became hotly engaged, while the cavalry entered into a fierce struggle on each flank. My right being imminently threatened, I sent the Second Virginia Cavalry to assist the Third in its attack, leaving not a man in reserve or any support to my batteries. The enemy, unprepared for such an onset, after a short but determined resistance were thrown into confusion, driven from the woods and along the road toward Winchester, leaving four guns, seventy-three killed, and one hundred and fifty wounded on the field. Seventeen officers and two hundred and fifty men were captured. Our loss was fifty-three killed, one hundred and fifty-five wounded and six missing. Advancing my cavalry and artillery I pressed the pursuit, but soon found that I could not venture with the force at my command to inflict further injury upon the enemy without running an imminent risk of loosing all we had gained. I therefore maintained my position until dark, constantly threatening the enemy with a renewal of the attack until the cannon, prisoners and wounded were sent to Martinsburg. The enemy's force engaged was a division of infantry commanded by General Ramseur and the cavalry of Vaugn, in all about 4,500 strong.

W. W. AVERELL, Brigadier General.

Report of Major General Robert E. Rodes, C. S. army, of engagement at Stephenson's depot:

(Rebel.)

Stephenson's Depot, September 12, 1864.

My Dear General:—From what I can gather from all sources I am afraid that officers at Richmond, and the department officers especially, and perhaps you, have taken an incorrect view of Ramseur's affair, near Winchester, last July. The facts are these, as can be sustained by ample testimony. Ramseur went out to chastise a small force which Vaugn had reported as one regiment of infantry and one of cavalry. He thought at first he would only take a portion of his command, but concluded to take all as a measure of perfect safety. He formed his force with two brigades in the front line, skirmishers out— brigades deployed. Behind this line Pegram's line was deployed. The enemy advanced upon him suddenly, was repulsed by Johnson, and at first by Hoke's brigade, but Ramseur's left being overlapped by Averell, Hoke's two left regiments broke and ran, behaving very badly, as General Lewis himself said.

Ramseur was on the right near Johnson's brigade; thought everything was going on finely until he saw this panic on the left. He immediately endeavored to restore the line by advancing Pegram's brigade, but it being embarrassed by Hoke's panic-stricken men, became so itself, broke and fled, as did the balance of Hoke's brigade, and finally Johnson's.

Now, sir, this result would not occur one time in a hundred with these same troops under the same circumstances, and ought never to have occurred with old troops at all. Ramseur acted most heroically, as usual exposed himself recklessly, but could do nothing with the men; they were under the influence of panic.

I do not hesitate to record my belief that the cause of the disaster was the conduct of the men, and the prime cause was the breaking of the two left regiments of Hoke's brigade. Of course, if Ramseur had put Pegram's brigade in the front line, the disaster might have been averted, but who knows? * * *   R. E. RODES.

Immediately following the battle of Carter's farm, the regiment with the brigade under Colonel Powell, advanced up the valley to Newtown where the enemy was encountered.

An amusing incident occurred here which might have ended disastrously, and which illustrated the fact that the men in the ranks, at least, had not fully comprehended the difference between an action in this valley and one in the mountains of West Virginia. It also thoroughly demonstrated the fact that Colonel Powell was alive to the importance and requirements of the hour. On this occasion the Second West Virginia was in line in advance, with skirmishers deployed a short distance ahead. Soon the enemy fired on us from a piece of woods in our front, and before the sound of the shots had died away, the entire regiment was on a run to the front, with no semblance of a line. Every man rushed madly on, endeavoring to be the first in at the capture. This new mode of warfare so scared the enemy that they hastily fled from their position. The bugles sounded the recall, orderlies hastened to the front, and finally the regiment was again in line. Colonel Powell came forward and formed us in a hollow square. He then mounted a stump, while our hearts beat high at the expected compliment. We did not doubt but that we had done the proper thing. The first words dashed our hopes to the ground. "Second Virginia Cavalry, I am ashamed of you. Your conduct is disgraceful in the extreme. You are not fighting an enemy that requires horse racing to catch, but an active, vigilant and brave foe. Scattered as you were a short time ago, a well drilled squadron would cut you to pieces. Another repetition of such conduct, and I will dismount yon. Remember, you are confronting veterans of the army of Northern Virginia, and I am confident, if you will act here as you have on other occasions, presenting a solid front to the enemy, I will never have occasion to censure you again. Now your officers will take charge of you, and place you in the front."

We fully realized the justice of the colonel's remarks and never gave him occasion to refer to the matter again.

On the 22nd the brigade was engaged in developing the enemys position, and gradually pushed their way to near Middletown. On the 23rd, the position of the army was about as follows: The main infantry force under command of General Crook occupied a position a few miles south of Winchester; Averell's division of cavalry was camped some distance to the front of the infantry. The main force of the enemy occupied a position near Strasburg and Fisher's Hill. On the afternoon of the 23rd, Captain Davidson, with about 20 men detailed from companies E and H, was sent to the front to locate the rebel pickets. They were found occupying a strong position on the main pike. Captain Davidson attempted to drive them from their position, but they seemed disposed to stay where they were. Thereupon our officer sent back to the brigade for another detail. While waiting for this re-enforcement the rebel picket was also strengthened. Soon our little force was increased to two hundred, and a charge was made on the rebel outpost, and they were driven several miles onto their main force. Our body was deployed as skirmishers, and, while resting in this position, we suddenly saw a heavy force of rebel cavalry advancing in line. It was a grand sight to see that fine body of horsemen as they came forward, completely enveloping our right and left with ten times our number. Realizing the gravity of the situation, in that we had stirred up a hornet's nest, our little force at once began to fall back. For five miles we fought to keep from being surrounded. At Kearnstown some of the enemy had gotten completely in our rear, but by vigorous use of revolver and saber they were driven out of the way. This was one of the most thrilling experiences the writer encountered during the war. We were frequently ordered to surrender, but true to the old rule that no cavalry man should surrender while he is mounted, we reached the division, and the advance of the jubilant enemy was checked.

On the 24th occurred Crook's battle of Winchester. Early had received large re-enforcements, and promptly moved out from Fisher's Hill to give battle. In the meantime Colonel Powell's brigade had been moved to a position on the Front Royal and Winchester pike, on the left of Crook's line. It is unnecessary to describe this battle in detail. Sufficient to say that the Union forces were completely defeated. The Second Virginia made a charge on a body of rebel infantry; and swinging round

their immediate flank, forced them back quite a distance.
In this charge Sergeant Major E. A. Thomas, of Company
B, and Lieut. J. D. Barber, of Company E, were killed.
They were two brave and efficient officers. Captain Davidson, of Company E, was so badly wounded that he was
left for dead. As the Confederates were passing him, Captain Davidson heard them say, "There's another poor fellow done for." After the enemy had passed on in pursuit,
the resolute captain crawled to a house near by, and was
concealed and taken care of by the inmates until our return in September.

Toward evening the entire army was in retreat toward the Potomac. Just north of Winchester the Confederate cavalry cut off a portion of the 36th O. V. I. who
had taken refuge in an orchard; then, seeing our brigade,
they (the rebels) turned in our direction and came on in a
charge, cheering like mad. Colonel Powell gave the order
to face about, draw saber and charge. Every man seemed
to be inspired with one desire—to whip that body of cavalry. And it was done most effectually, as they were
driven in utter route until artillery posted on Winchester
Heights compelled our withdrawal. General Averell witnessed this charge, and expressed the utmost satisfaction at
the result. During this time the isolated portion of the
36th O. V. I. made its escape.

General George Crook, in speaking of the cavalry of
the Army of West Virginia, says:—"Averell's division
was much disorganized, worn out by long marches, poorly
equipped, wretchedly mounted, and armed with inferior
weapons, was almost worthless. Exceptions, however,
should be made to Colonel Powell's brigade of Averell's
division, but this brigade owed its efficiency solely to the
skill, energy and courage of its commander." (See General Crook's War Record, page 802, Ohio in the war.)

The night of the 24th the brigade camped south of
Martinsburg. On the 25th the cavalry held a line just
south of Martinsburg, Powell's brigade on the right.
About noon we were attacked by a heavy force of infantry

LT. JAS. W. RICKER.

See page 133.

GENERAL SHERIDAN'S Headquarters,
AT CEDAR CREEK.

and artillery. The Second West Virginia occupied a
position in a corn field, where they received a terrible
shelling from a confederate battery. The regiment, with
the brigade, remained at their post until after General
Duffie's division had retired from the field. That night we
crossed the Patomac at Williamsport, and once more that
race ground, the "the valley of humiliation," was in the
hands of the enemy. Averell's division took a position
near Hagerstown, the Second West Virginia camping and
holding a line near Sheperdstown. A few days of com-
parative inactivity followed, other than attempts to de-
velop the intentions of the enemy.

Great excitement prevailed in Maryland and Pennsylvania, and in fact, all over the north. A formidable invasion was dreaded, but no infantry crossed the Potomac
on this second "invasion." A special session of the Pennsylvania legislature was called to meet on the 9th of
August, to take such action as the occasion might require.

CHAPTER XIV.

BURNING OF CHAMBERSBURG.

Gen. Couch was in the neighborhood of Chambersburg with a force of state militia. On the 30th a rebel cavalry force under command of Gen. John McCausland burned the little city of Chambersburg, Pennsylvania, involving the destruction of about two hundred and fifty buildings, with an estimated loss of one million dollars. Some space will be devoted to an account of this Chambersburg raid, from July 30th to August 7th, including the Moorefield affair, also a statement from the rebel General McCausland, furnished for this work.

On the morning of July 30th, General Averell learned that a considerable body of rebel cavalry had crossed the Potomac above Williamsport, and gone in the direction of Chambersburg, Pa. As soon as practicable, pursuit was begun, our force consisting of about 2,000 cavalry and two pieces of artillery. We were about twelve hours behind the raiders, marching as rapidly as possible. We passed through Hagerstown, and were soon on northern soil. As we passed through this beautiful southern part of Pennsylvania, with its fields of ripening grain, and with abundant evidences of thrift and happiness everywhere, we felt sure that should the foe be overtaken here, they would be roughly handled. The stars and stripes were waving from every house, something we had not before witnessed. On Saturday evening, July 30th, we entered what had been the beautiful city of Chambersburg, but now a mass of smoking ruins. We learned that it had been burned that morning at 9 o'clock by order of General McCausland. As we beheld the destruction, and saw whole families standing around their homes destroyed, one general cry went up from the whole command to be led against that vandal foe. The rebel officer, to whom was given the execution of the order to burn the place, says: "I felt more like weeping over Chambersburg, although the people covered me with reproaches, which all who know me will readily believe I felt hard to digest; yet my pity was highly excited in behalf of these poor· unfortunates, who were made to suffer for acts perpetrated by the officers of their own government. The day was bright and intensely hot. The conflagration seemed to spring from one vast build- ing. Dense clouds of smoke rose to the zenith, and hov- ered over the dark plain. At night it would have been a grand but terrible object to behold. How piteous the sight of those beautiful green meadows—groups of women and children exposed to the rays of a burning sun, hover- ing over the few articles they had saved, most of them ringing their hands, and with wild gesticulations bemoan- ing their ruined homes. We passed rapidly through the place in pursuit, the march being kept up all the night of the 30th.

All along the road the raiders had left marks of their passage by burning barns that had already received the fruit of the harvest. On Sunday morning we entered a little town at the base of the mountains. The inhabitants had retired late, after the raiders had passed through, and were still slumbering. The boys began calling to them to get up, the rebels had come back, and wanted breakfast. The wildest consternation prevailed among them until they learned we were Union soldiers, and then they went nearly wild with joy. Having recovered from the chaotic state into which they had been innocently thrown by our unlooked for arrival, they were only too glad to feed as many of the boys as would stop. That Sunday march through Pennsylvania was indeed a memorable one. The greatest enthusiasm was manifested by the inhabitants as we rapidly pursued the fleeing rebel column. All along the route we were greeted by the smiling faces of friends, by waving flags, by proffers of food, and with such other acts of kindness as we had not been accustomed to receive. Usually, on our marches, we had been greeted with scowling faces and insulting words, while nearly every tree concealed an enemy, and the sharp crack of the squirrel rifle was a common sound. All day Sunday the farmers erected impromptu tables near their dwellings, and kept them well supplied with cooked food, while some member of the family would stand by and invite the hungry to eat.

The enemy being in advance and able to supply themselves with fresh horses, escaped across the Potomac at Hancock, Maryland. We had a sharp skirmish at that place with the rebel rear guard, and there was some artillery firing.

Owing to the condition of our horses, General Averell was compelled to cease pursuit, and we went into camp and rested four days. This rest proved to be a very fortunate thing for us, and made the Moorefield affair possible of accomplishment. McCausland continued the march to the south branch of the Potomac until near Moorefield, where there was an abundance of grass. He knew that General Averell had gone into camp near Hancock, Maryland, and there being nearly sixty miles between them, the confederate commander went into camp also. The south branch of the Potomac separated the rebel commands, General Bradley T. Johnson, with one brigade and four pieces of artillery camping on the north side of the river, while General McCausland, with the other brigade, occupied a position on the south side. The enemy kept the country well scouted while in camp.

About the 5th of August General Averell received orders from Washington to pursue the rebel raiders until overtaken, and then fight them as long as there was a fighting man left. Under these instructions we broke camp, crossed the Potomac, and were once more on the soil of Virginia, marching in the direction of Moorefield. On the night of the fifth we camped north of Romney. We passed through Romney in the afternoon, and learned that a rebel scouting party had been there during the day. The horses were unsaddled and rested an hour in the evening, and then the march was resumed through the night. Averell's scouts, dressed in Confederate uniform, were in the advance, carefully feeling for the rebel pickets. This caused frequent haults, and the men would lie down by the road side, and with bridle rein in hand, snatch a few minutes sleep. Then, clanking sabers would warn them that the column was in motion, they would partially arouse themselves and pursue the silent march.

About 2:30 a. m. of the 7th of August the rebel pickets were encountered. "Halt!" was the command that came from the Johnnies accompanied by the usual "who comes there?" Our daring scouts promptly responded "Friends." "Advance one, and give the countersign." Two men were on this outpost, and instead of one only, two of our men approached and told the pickets that they were a scouting party of McCausland's command, and had gone out of camp on another road in the afternoon and did not have the countersign. After asking a few questions to which the scouts gave ready answers, the Johnnies seemed to be satisfied. While this parley was going on our heroes had dismounted, tightened their saddle girths, and, acting in a careless manner, walked up to the pickets. At a given signal they each seized a bridle rein, and with cocked revolvers took the two outposts prisoners. From them it was learned that the picket post was half a mile distant, and that there were seven men there. These men were found asleep, the sentinel sitting on a low fence. He, like the others, was awakened to find pistols in their faces. The reserve picket of fifty men was also captured, and thus the way to the rebel camp was clear. It was three miles distant. The column was closed up, and just at break of day, with wild cheers and cries of "Remember Chambersburg," we dashed into Bradley Johnson's camp, capturing four pieces of artillery while the gunners were attempting to get them into position. Over five hundred prisoners, including several officers, were secured, several hundred horses, six or eight hundred stands of arms, and the entire camp of the enemy. McCausland's brigade was one mile distant on the south side of the river, and owing to the firing and cheering in Johnson's camp, this brigade was quickly formed, and part of the force sent to defend the ford. But our brigade, elated by the capture of Johnson's camp, and remembering the enemy's devastation in Pennsylvania, plunged into the water, fiercely charged the enemy, killed and captured many, and cut them off from their main force. A line was again formed, which charged McCausland's brigade, cutting it completely in two. A running fight was then kept up for four miles, when the enemy became so scattered that there was nothing to follow. A large amount of private property, including horses and buggies, was recoverd and subsequently returned to the owners. The loss to the enemy in killed, wounded and captured was near eight hundred. The rebels stated that they expected to be very severely dealt with, and so when we struck the camp they made desperate efforts to escape. Some time after the war the confederate colonel Jenkins' bugler told the writer that with four companions he had escaped across the river on one bare-back horse, one holding to the animal's tail, and permitting himself to be dragged through the water. Our loss was forty-one killed and wounded. Colonel Conger, of the Third, was among the killed. A large amount of greenbacks was found scattered over the camp, the prisoners being afraid to be found with it on their persons. Considerable money was picked up by the men. Most of it was found secreted in the saddle pockets. The men who were so fortunate as to find the treasure were not in the fight, but those whose privilege it was to follow in the rear; owing to the secrecy maintained by the "finders" it was impossible to ascertain anything like the amount recovered from the Chambersburg raiders. One man of the regiment expressed a package home from New Creek station, and after the war he bought a good farm. When the officers learned that money was being found about the camp, the provost guard, under direction of some officers, searched the camp faithfully. While performing this duty, a young soldier, unknown to any of the searchers, was observed transferring gold coins from a pair of saddle pockets to his own pockets. He was called upon to halt, but being well mounted he put spurs to his horse and continued transferring the money until he was in possession of all of it, crossed the river and was lost to the guard.

While all this had been going on Company E had been on picket on the Potomac, and when McCausland crossed in the night they were cut off from the command. They at once followed on the flank of the Confederates, and on the way they fell in with a squadron of Cole's Maryland Cavalry. They arrived at Chambersburg at nearly the same time the rebels did, capturing their picket at the toll-gate on the Gettysburg pike. They joined the command on Sunday morning.

The prisoners, artillery and property were safely delivered to the proper authorities at New Creek Station, on the 10th day of August. The garrison at this post fired an artillery salute on our arrival, and went nearly wild with joy at the capture of the Chambersburg raiders. The following is a copy of the original report on file in the war department:

Official.   Harrisburg, Pa., Aug. 9, 1864.

Major:—I have the honor to report relating to the late invasion by the rebels in Chambersburg, Pa., on the morning of July 30, 1864. Being on detached duty at headquarters of the department at that place, and being unavoidably detained there, I was present both on the entering and departure of their force, and was an eye witness of the following:

The rebels entered the town with a force of—I do not think—over 500 mounted men. They were under the command of General's McCausland and Bradley T. Johnson. The main body of this force was camped at the fair grounds one and a half miles out of town, on the Pittsburg pike. Before entering they fired two shells into town. They then entered by every street and alley, the main force coming up in the rear. On their arrival in town I met General McCausland, who said to me. that if I had any self interest at stake, it would be well for me to listen to the order he would read, and to get the municipal author-ties together, and comply with the demands contained therein. The order was placed in my hands and read, and was in substance as follows:

That in retaliation for the depredations of General Hunter of the United States forces, committed during his recent Lynchburg raid, it is ordered that the citizens of Chambersburg, Pa., pay to the Confederate States of America, by General McCausland, the sum of $100,000 in gold, or in lieu thereof $500,000 in greenbacks or national currency, and if not paid within three hours, the town would be burned. The order was signed by General Jubal A. Early.

After reading this document I started out to find members of the town council. Meeting one of them, I in-formed him of the demands. He replied that he would not pay them five cents. I then returned to the hotel. The rebels had dismounted, and were breaking into stores and dwellings, and pillaging the same. When they entered town it was 5:30 a. m., from which time I was in company with both Generals McCausland and Johnson. I being in citizens clothes, they did not know I was a Federal soldier. At 9 o'clock McCausland ordered the town burned. In a few minutes the commissary store house was in flames, while General McCausland and Col-onel Harry Gilmore were riding through the street, notify-ing citizens, as they pointed to the flames, that they would carry the order into execution if the demands were not complied with. General McCausland then returned to the Franklin Hotel, when I heard him say that General Av-erell was within four miles of the place with 2,000 cavalry. Said he, "We will now burn the place and retreat." In a few moments the court house and town hall were in flames, and almost simultaneously fires broke out on most of the streets. I repaired to the hotel and found the rebels were ransacking the rooms and trunks of the boarders, and don-ning the clothes contained therein. * * † * About this time—near noon—the rebels had nearly all left town, except a rear guard. When they left most of them were so intoxicated they were hardly capable of sitting on their horses. I have the honor, Major, to be your obedient servant, WILL S. KOCHERSPERGER,
Serg't Co. L, 20th Pa. Cavalry.

Con. Gen. JOHN McCAUSLAND,

See page 146 to 158,

STATEMENT OF GENERAL MCCAUSLAND.

Dear Sir:—Yours of February 15th, 1892 received· The burning of Chambersburg was done in accordance with the written instructions of General Early. His instructions accompanying the order were explicit: To proceed ·to Chambersburg and levy a contribution on the place, to re-imburse citizens of Virginia, viz. Andrew Hunter, A. R. Botelar, John Letcher and others for the wanton destruction of their property by General Hunter, a federal commander. The route was even indicated, and if the money was not paid to burn the town as an act of retaliation. The order also directed me to go to Cumberland, Maryland, and do the same thing. Also to collect all the cattle and other supplies that I could in the western counties of Virginia and Maryland. I crossed the Potomac above Martinsburg and by a night march reached Chambersburg at daylight. I left a part of my force on the heights overlooking the valley and then entered the place. I tried to assemble the burgesses or city council to submit my orders to them, none, not one, could be found. I then posted notices on the court house door and other places, and after waiting several hours the burning began, and ended in the destruction of most of the place. This matter has all been gone over many times, and the citizens of Chambersburg have been paid their losses by the state of Pennsylvania and the United States government. My connection with the matter was that of an officer obeying orders, and I did not then, nor have I since, ever discussed the merits, or the demerits ,of the same. The affair at Moorefield was caused by the surprise of Johnson's brigade.

I had notice from my spy, Kuykendall, of Moorefield, of the approach of Averell, and as far as I was concerned, the necessary orders were issued to meet the case. These orders were not executed, and there ends my responsibility.

Any other matter pertaining to the case will be cheerfully given you. Enclosed, find photo. It is of an older man than I was in the war. Yours, etc.

(Signed) JOHN MCCAUSLAND
Grimes Landing, W. Va.
Feb. 17, 1892.

To J. J. SUTTON,
Portsmouth, O.

McCausland's and Johnson's brigades never recovered from the effects of the Moorefield affair. So said General

Early is a report written to the rebel secretary of war some time in the winter of 1864.

After the Moorefield affair, having returned to Martinsburg, the regiment with the brigade under Colonel Powell, was constantly in the saddle, enjoying spirited engagements with the rebel cavalry under Imboden and Vaughan. Averell's division soon learned how to handle these forces, and although there was no severe fighting for several days, it was a good school for the regiment, and learned it many new lessons in the art of war. We had been newly armed with the Spencer carbine, which was a splendid cavalry arm, and capable of rapid and accurate firing. This new gun greatly surprised the enemy, and some of the prisoners avowed that during our absence from the valleys we had been loading.

A new era was inaugurated in the valley dating from the 7th of August, when Major General Philip H. Sheridan assumed command. The presence of this commander inspired all with new hope and courage. Hunter's forces were badly scattered, and that general himself did not know where to find the enemy. He had been so embarrassed by orders from Washington, moving him first one way and then another, that he lost all trace of Early. To afford a "peep behind the scenes," as it were, of this Washington interference with the army movements, the following documents are given.

General Grant wrote General Halleck, August 1st, as follows:

"I am sending General Sheridan for temporary duty, whilst the enemy is being expelled from the border. Unless General Hunter is in the field in person, I want Sheridan put in command of all the troops in the field, with instructions to put himself south of the enemy, and follow him to the death. Wherever the enemy goes, there let our troops go also. Once started up the valley, they ought to be followed until we get possession of the Virginia Central railroad. If General Hunter is in the field, give Sheridan command of the Sixth Corps, and the Cavalry Division. All the cavalry will reach Washington in the course of to-morrow.

U. S. GRANT.

This letter was read by President Lincoln, and he thereupon sent Grant the following remarkable dispatch:

Lieutenant General Grant:—I have seen your dispatch in which you say "I want Sheridan put in command of all the troops in the field, with instructions to put himself south of the enemy, and follow him to the death," etc. This is, I think, exactly right as to how our forces should move. But please look over the dispatches you may have received from here, even since you made that order, and discover if you can, that there is an idea in the head of any one here putting our army south of the enemy, or of following him to the death in any direction. I repeat to you it will neither be done or attempted, unless you watch it every day and hour, and force it.   A. LINCOLN.

Grant's reply was characteristic of the man. He answered: "I start for Washington in two hours."

U. S. GRANT.

The Lieutenant General came on to Monocacy without even stopping at Washington, and himself directed the army to move to Halltown, four miles above Harper's Ferry, feeling sure that Early would soon be in front of our troops moving south. General Hunter now asked to be relieved from command. This was at once granted, and General Grant telegraphed to Sheridan to report immediately at Monocacy. He came, and General Grant met him at the little station, telling him what had been done and what there was to do.

Sheridan, in a general order to his troops, assumed command. I quote from one of our war historians: "Sheridan's first grand opportunity had come. He was about thirty-two years old, and in command of 30,000 men, the flower of our army. Included in this was 8,000 of the finest cavalry in the world, under such commanders as Averell, Torbett, Custer, Merritt and Gregg. Against him was Early with an equal force, including Stonewall Jackson's veterans and Rosser's and Wickham's rebel cavalry. The valley was a familiar battlefield to their forces, and eminently adapted to the offensive-defensive operations which distinguished the entire history of Lee's struggle in Virginia."

On the morning of August 10th the march up the valley was begun. Early was at, or near Winchester Our army consisted of the Sixth Corps, the Nineteenth Corps, Crook's Division of West Virginia infantry, and Averell's, Torbett's and Wilson's divisions of cavalry, which included such noted brigade commanders as Custer, Devin, Merrit and Powell. As our army advanced, the enemy fell back, and there was skirmishing only, until Strasburg was reached, on the 13th. At this point word was received from the capital that a rebel force was marching through Culpepper county, with the evident intention of striking our rear. The authorities at Washington become alarmed, and on the 15th sent a dispatch informing Sheridan of this new danger. This caused the new commander to fall rapidly back to Halltown, and take a strong position near that place, the regiment, with Averell's division, occupying its old place near Martinsburg. Of course the enemy followed. Shirmishing again commenced, Bunker Hill being the scene of several brisk engagements. On one of these occasions the Second West Virginia drove the rebel cavalry beyond Bunker Hill, capturing a rebel supply train. In this affair Company G, Captain Ankrom particularly distinguished itself by bringing off the train and driving off the force that tried to recapture it. The activity of Averell's division kept the confederates on the Martinsburg pike, in a state of unrest. There was a fight every day, and when the rebel cavalry—under Imboden and Vaugn—attempted to stop Powell's brigade, they would soon be scattered and chased, until infantry and artillery, in large numbers, would be encountered.

On one of these occasions, a rebel force attempted to stop our progress at Bunker Hill, and after they had been dislodged from the four or five empty houses that comprised the place, they were chased toward Winchester, until a battery of artillery began firing at long range.

The Second Virginia was marching in double column near the pike. The rebel battery was throwing solid shot into a piece of timber, near our right flank, and the men were carefully watching the course and effect of the shot. One ball cut the top out of a tree in our front, after which it struck the ground, bounced like a gum ball, and richocheted off down through a field. This ball cut such antics, and looked so innocent, and harmless that a young man who had only recently enlisted quickly jumped from his horse, remarking, "watch me catch the darn thing," and actually started in pursuit of the deadly missile. The shouts of derision that greeted his actions caused him to remount his horse, looking for all the world like he had made a fool of himself.

The division remained in this position until evening, then returned to camp. This kind of warfare was kept up until about the 15th when the division under command of General Averell drove everything before it to near Carter's farm, where Kershaw's divison of confederate infantry was encountered. The enemy was strongly posted, and as a heavy rain was falling, and the fields being very soft horses could not be ridden out of a walk. Under these disadvantages, and after several attempts to break our line had been made, the cavalry quietly withdrew. In the action Lieutenant Boyd, of Company C, was killed. In the war records General Early says that Averell became so troublesome on the Martinsburg pike, that he detached Kershaw and sent him to strenghen their force on that road.

CHAPTER XV.

BATTLES OF WINCHESTER AND FISHER'S HILL.

Sheridan says, "Finding Early's right weakened, I determined to go in and crush him." On the evening of tha 18th we were informed by official orders that there would be a general engagement on the morrow. This news was received by the regiment with the greatest satisfaction, for constant skirmishing without apparent result was getting to be monotonous, and we were quite willing to settle the matter by whipping the enemy, or getting whipped in the attempt.

The reading of orders telling of a battle "to-morrow" was a new experience in our war life; and on that memorable Sabbath evening, gathered about the bivouac fires, the deliberate contemplation of "battle to-morrow" was not unmixed with serious thoughts. The silent preparations were made with many a heartache, many tender memories of home and loved ones. It may be that a tear may steal down the cheek of some old warrior as these recollections rowd upon him. "The bravest are the tenderest, the loving are the true." How many will answer the next roll call? As the night passes and the sentry paces his beat, the camp-fires growing dim in the distance seem to him jack-o-lanterns; his faithful horse shares his watch, while these thoughts flit over his mind, until his quick ear detects the approach of the relief guard, and his mind is freed from the strain of the last hours. The younger soldier is not troubled with these thoughts, he does not think of consequences, as with flashing eye he pictures the conflict of to-morrow. He does not dream of defeat; and as he sits by the fire writing to some fair-haired Northern maiden, his words tell of victory already won and he the sharer in that victory.

It is not purposed to describe these Shenandoah battles in detail, but the narrative will be confined more particularly to the operations of the cavalry of which the regiment was a part. The cavalry movements just now beginning under Sheridan were so gigantic and so audacious that they gave the world a new conception of such warfare. The dash, vigor and boldness displayed at all times startled the Confederate commanders. They recognized that this was a "new departure" and the abler ones saw that the end was not far off. It would require the pen of a poet and the brush of a painter, made red with the blasonry of battle, to describe the tone, color and movement of these events. It is simply impossible. It is glorious to have lived and participated in them.

At break of day, on Monday, the 19th of September, the advance began, and soon the little white puffs of smoke plainly told us that the skirmishers were at work. Near Bunker Hill a considerablr body of cavalry, supported by artillery, was encountered, but they were quickly driven away. The boom of cannon to our left indicated that the battle was on, and through that day, as the sounds grew louder and nearer, we knew the enemy was disputing every inch of the way. The fighting on our left was desperate, with charge and counter charge, until about 4 o'clock in the afternoon, when Crook, with his division of West Virginia infantry and Torbett's cavalry, joined Averell on the Uuion right, and boldly charged the rebel left. An historian, speaking of this, says: "The sight was inspiriting, and at once the Union lines moved solidly forward on the rebel right and center. The cavalry and Crook's infantry repeatedly charged the retreating Confederates, following them to their fortified heights."

About the time Averell formed a junction with Torbett and Crook, a portion of the Second West Virginia was sent a short distance to the left in a wood. Here they ran into a brigade of rebel cavalry in line faced the other way. The seven shooters were brought into play, the enemy became panic stricken, and was followed in flank by our little band, which, with wild shouts of victory, apparently drove them from the field. The regiment bore an important part in the charge with the brigade under Colonel Powell, capturing eighty prisoners and two cannon on Winchester Heights. In this rout, which sent Early whirling up the valley, the regiment occupied the right; and when crossing Winchester Heights in the evening, we had a panoramic view of Early's panic stricken army, pursued by our victorous troopers.

The night of the 19th the regiment camped a few miles to the south and west of Winchester.

The result of the battle is well known. Sheridan captured 2,500 prisoners, nine battle flags and five pieces of artillery. The enemy left 3,000 wounded in Winchester. Our loss was also heavy, the killed, wounded and missing aggregating 4,500.

A critic in writing of this battle, has said:—"The battle of the Opequan was fought with the precision of clock work, and was the first one of the war in which cavalry, artillery and infantry were all used concurrently and to the best possible advantage, each according to its own nature and traditions."

The overthrow of the enemy was absolute and complete. The country was electrified, and the gloom which had hung over it was dispelled as if by magic. Gold took such a tumble as it had not received since the outbreak of the rebellion, and from that time forth no one doubted the triumph of our arms or the re-establishment of the Union.

Early on the morning of the 20th the march was again taken up, and soon the Second West Virginia was deployed as skimishers. The rebel cavalry was soon driven away, and we were confronted by infantry skirmishers, who gradually gave way all day.

GENERAL JUBAL A. EARLY,

From a Photo. since the war.

On the 21st the same tactics were followed, the enemy making some bold stands, but they were dislodged and forced back. On this day, while our skirmishers had halted to receive ammunition, a red fox trotted along our front, making for North mountain, but when firing again commenced, some trooper may have halted him with a shot from his carbine.

On the morning of the 22d we dismounted and skirmished as infantry, owing to the nature of the country. About noon the Confederates had all been driven into their works at Fisher's Hill, their left resting on North Mountain. Our skirmishers had worked their way to within one hundred yards of the rebel works, and a desultory firing was kept up. Crook, with his infantry marched in the rear of our line, and gained North Mountain. At 5 p. m. this gallant commander charged the rebel left, doubling up their line; then the infantry on our left charged, and the entire rebel position was carried. Through this gap made by Crook, Colonel Powell, with the brigade, charged the broken masses until nine o'clock at night. Many prisoners were taken in this chase. One thousand men and sixteen guns were taken at Fisher's Hill. Sheridan's biographer says that all that saved Early's army from destruction as an organization was the stubborn fight made against Torbett at Milford, in the Luray valley by the confederate cavalry under General Wickham, who at Front Royal the day before (Sept. 21st) had fought Wilson most vigorously. On the 22d, Torbett was held in check all day at Milford, finally at sundown, driving Wickham before him. Both were splendid and well matched cavalry battles, in which the advantage finally rested with us, but the stubborn fighting of the confederate troops saved their army, nevertheless.

On Sept. 23d, while in the face of the enemy, General Averell was relieved from his command, and for the gallant conduct of the Second brigade, Colonel Powell was assigned to the command of the Second Cavalry Division. This was a responsible position for Colonel Powell, assuming command of so large a body of mounted men and in the face of the enemy. General Sheridan reposed great confidence in Colonel Powell, and subsequently expressed his satisfaction with the choice he had made. Colonel Powell handled the division with good judgment, and for this efficiency was finally commissioned as brigadier general of volunteers.

On the 24th, the pursuit was renewed, Powell's division taking the back road several miles to the right of the valley pike. About 9 o'clock in the morning a determined body of rebel cavalry was found posted on a hill in a small town, prepared to resist our advance. Lieut. J. W. Ricker's squadron of the Second Virginia was sent forward, and boldly charged the Confederates, taking them in flank, and driving them upon their main column, capturing a number of prisoners. The ground on the left of the road admitted of mounted men riding at good speed, and while the advance in the road time and again charged the rebel rear, our little force rode along their column and poured a withering fire into them at short range. This wild fight was kept up all day, our enthusiastic pursuers not permitting them to form a line to protect their column; for every time this was attempted, the flankers were there with a deadly cross fire from their seven shooters. The whole division was coming rapidly up, full of that electric fervor of victory which makes the soldier forget fatigue and hunger, and making him to feel as if the world was akin to his mood, as the passion of victory with which he is animated beating in his breast with rythmic jubilance.

The main infantry force was camped near Harrisonburg, the division under Powell continuing to Brown's Gap, on the 26th, and Meyer's cave on the 27th, where the Confederate cavalry was encountered. Of this affair General Powell, in his paper on "Sheridan in the Shenandoah" published in the Indianapolis American Tribune, April 17, 1891, says: "The disposition of my line had but barely been made and executed, when Gen. Wickham, commanding Fifth Hugh Lee's cavalary, having moved around the south end of the Meyer's cave ridge, attacked my right, opening the engagement with artillery. I immediately ordered Lieut. Weir with a section of the 5th U. S. Artillery to change position, and bear upon the advancing line of the enemy on my right. I then assumed command of my old regiment, the Second West Virginia Cavalry, and by a vigorous fire from my guns, skillfully and energetically executed by Lieut. Weir, and a determined charge by the Second Cavalry, that I must say here, never failed me in an emergency, Wickham's dashing cavalry were driven back in confusion, utterly routed, and they did not again disturb my right."

The cavalry under Torbett went as far as Waynesboro, and on their return, laid waste the valley. The army then quietly returned to Strasburg. Of this destruction in the valley, General Sheridan says: "In moving back to this point, the whole country from the Blue Ridge to the North Mountain was made untenable for a rebel army. I have destroyed over two thousand barns filled with wheat, hay and farming implements, and over seventy mills filled with wheat and flour; have driven in front of this army over four thousand head of stock, and have killed and issued to the troops over three thousand sheep. Since I entered the valley from Harper's Ferry, every train, every small party, and every straggler has been bush-whacked by the people, many of whom have protection papers. Lieutenant Meigs and his engineer were murdered near Dayton. For this atrocious act all houses within an area of five miles were burned." About the 25th or 26th, Companies H and I, under command of Lieut. J. W. Ricker, were ordered to report to General Sheridan's headquarters at Harrisonburg. Soon after arriving there they were sent with the headquarters signal corps to Massanutten Mountain, six miles east of Harrisonburg. The signal corps established itself on a spur of the mountain, and with their powerful field glasses commanded a view of the valley for miles in nearly every direction. They signaled to Sheridan's headquarters, detailing all that came

within scope of their observation. It was nearly two
miles from the base of the mountain to the top; and while
the weather was warm in the valley, large fires were kept
burning on the top. The first duty performed, and that
after night, was to clear away the brush and timber so there
was an unobstructed view of General Sheridan's headquarters, six miles distant. The first dispatch signaled by
the torches was, that near the base of the mountain, to the
east of us, there was a large camp of cavalry supposed to
be Torbett, as his route had been up the Luray valley.
The answer was returned "O. K." The next morning the
cavalry named broke camp early; but to our surprise they
went in the direction of Early's position, and proved to be
General Wickham with Fitz Hugh Lee's division of rebel
cavalry. The signal corps officers were very kind to us,
and frequently allowed us to take a peep through the large
field glasses. Water and provisions had to be carried to
the mountain top, which was very laborious. The squadron camped near the base of the mountain, and as the
country was rich, they lived off the fat of the land. A
water power mill containing plenty of wheat, and a fine
sweet potato patch were found near by. These had been
left by General Early, and were promptly taken charge of
by the squadron. They operated the mill,—or rather
asked the miller to do so; they dug the sweet potatoes, exchanged flour for butter, eggs and honey and other commodities not usually found in the commissary. A few of
the boys were seen carrying their canteens, and otherwise
guarding them carefully. To the uninitiated this did not
mean anything, but to the knowing it told its own story.
There was apple jack in the country. This article was
always regarded as a contraband of war. From the signal
station they had a grand panoramic view of the destruction of the barns, granaries and mills of the valley.
About the 5th of October the squadron was withdrawn
from the mountain, and ordered to report to General Torbett's headquarters, near Harrisonburg. The order was
received late in the evening, so that when they arrived

there, the general and staff had retired. An orderly reported their presence to the general, who directed them to tie up and camp until morning. They were right in the midst of the army, and after some delay found a resting place near General Crook's headquarters. The next morning they drew rations and forage, and, as Colonel Powell had gone down the Luray valley, they were expected to join the division. However, they were held in camp until about ten o'clock, when Lieutenant Ricker received orders to proceed down the valley pike with the squadron as escort to eight or ten ambulances containing two U. S. paymasters, a member of Congress from Michigan, an eastern newspaper correspondent, General Custer's adjutant general, and a few other officers, in all about twenty persons, on their way to Martinsburg. The lieutenant's orders were to proceed down the valley pike, and not to permit himself to be drawn off the road by any demonstrations of the enemy, but to proceed rapidly until a train under escort of a division of infantry which had left camp in the morning, was overtaken, then to turn the ambulances over to them and join the division in the Luray valley. It was expected they would overtake the train by two or three o'clock. The little band, numbering about sixty carbines, with their charge, left camp about 10:30 a. m. Soon after passing the union pickets, squads of the enemy were observed on both flanks, but it was well known that the country below was alive with rebel forces under Mosby and McNeal. The object of the enemy seemed to be to make demonstration with only a few men to induce them to leave the road with a part of their force, when they hoped to stampede the rest and capture the wagons at least. At the little town of Edinburg a citizen told them that the train was just ahead when the fact was the train was more than twelve miles away. One of the men noticed an old colored man, apparently concealed behind a house, making motions as if to attract attention. The trooper went up to him, and learned that the enemy were all around there, that they had destroyed a small bridge north of town after the train had passed, and

that they would have to make a considerable detour to the
west to cross the stream. In making this crossing they
were confronted by a force of rebel cavalry nearly twice
their number, but our boys kept a solid line, with carbines
in position, and beyond a few shots fired by the foe, there
was no disposition shown to attack them. When they
finally regained the pike, their course seemed clearer. It
was now after 5 o'clock, and the train was still far ahead.
In this way they kept on until dark, when all distinctly heard the rattle of the train on the stony pike
ahead, and from every elevation in the road expected to
see the camp fires of the infantry, or at least find their
pickets. So certain were they as the noise indicated that
the train was just ahead, that they somewhat relaxed their
vigilance, and relieved from the anxiety of the afternoon
were chatting and laughing and congratulating themselves
on their escape. From the ambulances came tones
of good cheer, as in the darkness they pursued their way.
At last, from the top of a little hill in front came the
the welcome and expected challenge "halt, who comes
there." "Friends." Advance one." Corporal George
A. Stewart went forward to satisfy the picket as
to who they were. The rest of the party properly remained where they were, awaiting the signal "Come on!"
Just as they were getting impatient at the delay, the welcome summons was borne on the night air in clear and
loud tones, "All right, come ahead." As the little band
neared the top of the hill where the picket was supposed to
be, a heavy fire was poured into their column from an ambuscade scarcely twenty paces away. It was very dark,
and the flash of the enemy's guns seemed right at their feet.
Fortunately, their aim was too low, for not a man was
touched, and only two horses were killed. The persons in
the ambulance hastily sought shelter behind some stone by
the roadside. Quickly recovering from a momentary surprise, the escort opened fire on the now retreating rebels,
shouting to them, calling them bushwhackers and cowards.
Stewart afterward told how the two rebels that had hold of

him said, "Run faster, Yank, or the last one of us will be killed." The corporal said that for once in his life the whiz of bullets was a welcome sound to him, for he had the pleasure of seeing the discomfiture of his captors.

It was near 10 o'clock when they came up with the train where it had gone into camp. The officers in the ambulances were overjoyed at the happy termination of the lively adventure.

After some thrilling experiences, Stewart finally escaped from his captors, and made his way to Winchester, six days after. He informed us that the officer commanding the enemy and three men were killed.

The colonel, commanding the infantry, backed up by the officers they had been escorting, prevailed upon Lieutenant Ricker to accompany the train to Winchester. The squadron deployed on the flanks of the infantry as skirmishers, and proceeded in this manner to Fisher's Hill. The commanding officer at Winchester ordered the squadron on to Martinsburg with the officers under escort. While in this place they drew clothing, of which the entire command was in sore need.

The squadron started for Front Royal, where the division was camped, about the 10th of October. The distance from Martinsburg to Winchester is twenty-four miles; and that morning the weather was very cold. They were accompanied by about an equal number of infantry, and on account of the cold the troopers invited them to ride their horses, they preferring to walk. The footmen were much pleased with the change, it being new to them, and they sat on the horses until they became numbed with cold. They reminded us of the story of the boy on horseback whom a stranger met, and observing that the boy was very cold, asked him why he did not walk and warm himself. To this inquiry the boy replied, "Stranger, this is a b-b-borrowed horse, and I'll ride him if I f-f-freeze."

At that time the election for state officers in Ohio was held on the second Tuesday in October, and a law had been passed permitting soldier voters in the field to cast their ballots. The squadron proceeded to Ceder Creek, and exercised the right of suffrage by voting at the polls of the 36th O. V. I. They then joined the division at Front Royal.

Picketing, scouting and foraging kept the regiment quite busy. A strong line of videttes had to be kept in front, and it was common to see rebel troopers come in sight, take a look at the situation of the outposts, and then retire.

On one occasion a detail of about six hundred from the division under command of an officer of the Second Virginia, went out on a four day's picket duty. Colonel Powell had sent word to this officer that all citizens from whom property of any kind had been taken for use of the army were entitled to a hearing in their own behalf. During the time mentioned Major Morgan had gone out with a large foraging party of the regiment. It is said that a good soldier will make a "good forager," implying that a good soldier knows where foraging leaves off and pillage begins. The major belonged to this class, for when he came into camp he was laden with everything eatable, from a potato to a beef, and following in his wake were all kinds of citizens, from the butternut clad mountaineer to the lady in her carriage. To the officer on picket they all began to pour out their tale of woe, and that officer was so torn with emotion between pity and duty, that he sent the entire party to Colonel Powell. The Colonel was so impressed by their appeals that thereafter officers commanding such expeditions were given authority to pass upon pleas for compensation.

Thus the time passed until the 18th of October. At this time the division occupied a strong position on a low ridge overlooking the plain in front, and the town of Front Royal. On our right the ground was quite rough, and covered with a heavy growth of small timber, thick with underbrush. While the division remained at Front Royal the rebel cavalry occupied a position at Milford. They were constantly driven from their camps and kept in a

MURRAY McMILLIN.

LT. EMERSON McMILLIN.
See page 213.

MARION McMILLIN.
See page 145.

The Six McMillin Brothers.

ANDREW McMILLIN.

J. H. McMILLIN.

LT. MILTON McMILLIN.

The Six McMillin Brothers.

state of unrest.   Between the position of our right, and the left of the infantry at Cedar Creek, for several miles, no troops were placed.   Before Sheridan left for Washington on the 17th, he directed that a junction be formed between these commands.   For some reason this was not done.   In this gap the confederates made their attack.

CHAPTER XVI.

BATTLE OF CEDAR CREEK.

Early on the morning of the 19th we listened to the noise of battle on our right, and some time after daylight our pickets were drawn in, as the increasing noise of battle clearly indicated that our army was falling back. Later in the morning the enemy appeared in our front, but did not make any attempt to attack. The division, or most of it, now marched in the direction of Newtown, and arrived on the Valley pike just as General Sheridan passed on his way from Winchester. We witnessed the movements of the cavalry under Merritt and Custer, but was not called into action there, but just before the final charge that won the battle of Cedar Creek, we advanced in the direction of Front Royal, driving the rebel cavalry under Lomax, and camping in our old position that night. While the division was only slightly engaged in this battle, yet the Confederates had anticipated throwing a force in the rear of our army by the Front Royal road, and the bold stand taken and maintained by Colonel Powell prevented the carrying out of their plans. For this generalship, and the gallantry displayed by Colonel Powell successively as regimental, brigade, and division commander, he was promoted to the position of Brigadier General of Volunteers.

In this promotion the regiment took a pride, and felt, instinctively, that all had a share in the glittering "star" that adorned the shoulders of the old captain of Co. B. As so much has been written and said about the battle of Cedar Creek, I have selected a few sketches from facts already published. The following interview with John B. Gordon, a Confederate general, was published in the Boston Globe in 1888. In response to the remark that had his (Gordon's) suggestions been carried out by Early, even Sheridan could not have "saved the day" on that memorable 19th of October, 1864, at Cedar Creek, the ex-Confederate General said, after remarking that he was a corps commander under Early: "Yes, the plan was mine wholly, and so was the conduct of the fight up to a certain point. If my plan had been carried out there would never have been any 'Sheridan's Ride.'

"We felt the vast importance of success and started in to win it. We had good men, and in most respects we were well organized and equipped. In the Shenandoah Valley we were among as good friends as the southern cause could boast.

"We swept down the valley and whipped Lew Wallace on the Monocacy, and were only a little too late for capturing Washington, while a great career seemed opened to our army. As we moved off from Washington two splendid corps were immediately put under Sheridan. We had a good deal of confidence in ourselves, with a clear field, and the army was in good spirits. Across the Potomac we stopped to rest and to gather forage and food. We also did some recruiting. Sheridan attacked us at Winchester, and we were routed. It was the first battle in the valley. Indeed, before that we had not even had a check of any kind, having been able to live off the country, and even to forward supplies to Richmond.

"When Sheridan came up the valley our troops were very much scattered. This, of course, because it was more convenient to feed them in that way, and we had not gotten well in line when we were plunged into the midst of battle. The federal assault was confident and impetuous, especially that of the Nineteenth corps, and we were in no condition to resist it. One division after another broke, and when the sun went down on the evening of the 19th of September, the federal victory was complete. We

had been beaten in detail. The attack was too sudden to
enable us to consolidate our forces and use them to the
best advantage, and we were shattered and demoralized.

"Dejected and broken we marched down the valley to
Fisher's Hill, where we had a very strong position. There
we stopped and recruited, and tried to repair the damage
which had been done. Our soldiers were very much disheartened, however. The transformation from a hopeful
and advancing army to a beaten and retreating one, was too
great. Three days later we were again attacked in our
position and again defeated.

"For nearly a month there was a respite, and then
came Cedar Creek. For the time being we won one of the
greatest victories of the war. Every detail of the movement was carefully planned, and for twelve hours it was
supremely successful. I had gone the day before, October
18th, to the top of what is called Massanutten Mountain,
where we had a signal corps stationed, and had taken ob-
servations through the field-glasses. There was a magnificent bird's eye view. The Shenandoah was the silver bar
between us. On the opposite side of the river I could distinctly see the red-cuffs of the artillerists. Why, I had so
good a view that I could see the sore spots on the horses'
backs in your camp. In front of Belle Grove Mansion I
could see members of Sheridan's staff coming and going. I
could not imagine a better opportunity for making out an
enemy's position and strength. I could even count the
men who were there. The camp was splendidly exposed
to me. I marked the position of the guards and the pickets walking to and fro, and observed where the cavalry
was placed.

"It flashed upon me instantly that General Sheridan
expected that we would attack him on his right, which was
the only place supposed possible for the advance of an
army. His left was protected by the Shenandoah at this
point and the river ran around it. There was no road at
all, and the point was guarded only by a mere cavalry
picket.

"I saw our opportunity in an instant, and I told the officer present that if General Early would permit me to move my corps (I was then commanding Ewell's corps) down to this point, I could get around the mountain. Both sides believed this was impossible, but I felt sure that it could be done. My plan was to dismount our cavalry, attack Sheridan's cavalry when dismounted, and keep them from moving. I knew if we could do this, we would gain a great victory.

"None of my brother officers at first had any confidence in the plan. When I was on Massanutten, the members of General Early's staff who were with me were utterly incredulous. I told them that if I was allowed to carry out my plan we could annihilate Sheridan's army, and drive him pell-mell out of the valley, and raise the spirits of our people beyond measure.

"There was a back road running from our position on Fisher's Hill to the Federal right, where the cavalry was posted. I expected to deceive the Federals by Lomax's attack. It would be dark still, and they could not distinguish our dismounted cavalry from infantry, and would believe that our main attack was there on their right. This would leave us free to operate their left.

"General Early acted promptly after he understood the project. The plan was submitted, talked over, and finally substantially agreed upon. I took my command, having ordered them to leave their canteens, sabres, and everything that could make a noise behind. I knew that our only dependence was in absolute secrecy and in a complete surprise. After inspecting things with my staff I found I could get my men around the mountain by putting them in single file. I discovered still another place where the horses could be led, although the venture would be exceedingly dangerous. Still the expedition was one of great peril, and more or less danger was of little consequence.

"Sharp men often leave a loop-hole; and as Sheridan, or Wright, of the Sixth corps, who was in actual command, had never through their scouts discovered this narrow

country road, or did not deem it possible to move an army
by it, we were left to complete our surprise unmolested. The
event was taking things as they were, not only possible but
actual, and we did what none of your people dreamed of
as possible. Early in the night I began to move my men
around the mountain. My object was to have them all
ready for an attack before daylight in the morning. The
movement took all night. All through the hours of darkness the silent figures moved to their positions near the
sleeping enemy. An entire brigade of cavalry was moved
in this way, and reached the point in about one and a half
hours in advance of the men. I instructed the cavalry
that as soon as I got ready to move they were to proceed
in my front, rush across the river, open on the cavalry
pickets, and capture them if possible. If they could not
do this, they were to put their horses to full speed, ride
right through the federal camp, firing their pistols to the
right and to the left as they passed through, and make
directly for Sheridan's headquarters and capture him.

"At that time I did not know that Sheridan was absent
and Wright in command. I had selected his house from
the flags which floated from it and the couriers who were
constantly going in and out. My orders were: 'Go right
through the Federal camp with your command before daylight and directly to General Sheridan's headquarters.
Capture him.' I told them not to take any prisoners, not
to mind anything, but every mounted man was to press
toward Belle Grove. We, with the infantry, would take
care of what was behind. I knew very well that the little
fighting or capturing they could do would be of little account compared with the prize they were expected to get.

"My signal was obeyed exactly. On the morning of
of the 19th, just about daylight, we fired three or four
shots. Away the Federal pickets went, with our cavalry
brigade after them. I rushed across, wading the river
with my whole corps of infantry. We went with a rush
and double-quick. Before starting I had selected the
house on the road at which the head of my column should

stop. It was a white house at the turn of the road, farther
down toward the river, and was on the flank of the enemy's
line. As soon as I got there I was in position, and I had
nothing to do but to close up in front and move.
Dashing forward with one brigade, we plunged into the
enemy's camp and found the men asleep. Many of them
never awoke in this world. We went right through them
and shot every one in sight. The cavalry had reached
head-quarters and General Wright barely escaped, leaving
his papers behind him, and they fell into our hands. We
killed and wounded between seven and eight thousand of
the panic-stricken Federals and broke two corps entirely
to pieces. The loss in my command was only about two
hundred. By sunrise we occupied the breast-works. The
enemy's cavalry was compelled to retreat before Rosser,
although superior in numbers. We did not press our advance. The enemy still had the Sixth Corps in reserve,
but we drove it back and captured a few of its pieces.
That was a complete victory.

"To show that this was true, let me remind you that the
eighth corps was scattered to the winds. The Nineteenth
Corps, after hard fighting, was routed and driven entirely
out of their works, and we had possession of the entire
Federal position except a part of that held by the Sixth
Corps. This corps had filed out by the left toward the
pike, and we had driven them back and forced them to a
ridge just west of Middletown. We had the pike away
along up to the edge of Middletown, and our position was
admirable every way.

"What was the real cause of the halt in our progress?
There has been a great deal of misunderstanding on this
point. I saw that the enemy had a strong position,
but that it was the last one they could hold.
We had one of the finest positions for porting artillery I
ever saw, right on the highest point of the pike south
of Middletown, and east and above Sheridan's headquarters. I called for Colonel Carter, the chief of artillery, and wanted thirty guns planted right there, and we

would have battered that federal line all to pieces, demoralized an already beaten army, and sent it in utter panic down the valley. Let me tell you the real cause of our failure to get the artillery effectually at work. We did get a few guns—enough to break the line—but herein comes the lamentable feature of that day's business. You know that Early says that the final defeat was caused by the demoralization of his own men in plundering the federal camp and of gorging on sutler's supplies there captured. There isn't a word of truth in it. There never was less straggling or plundering among any troops than there was among ours that morning. I had them well in hand, and had issued the strictest orders that any soldier falling out for plunder should be shot instantly.

"That whole statement is false. The real trouble was here. I was making every effort to get a mass of artillery in position when General Early rode up. He was wild with joy. I exclaimed, General Early, give me thirty pieces of artillery right here and we will destroy that army and send its fragments over the Potomac. I knew the supreme moment had come.

" 'No, no,' he said. 'We've won a great victory ; we've done enough for one day ; we will stop here.'

"But, I said, let us finish the job. It it true we have won a great victory ; let us complete it. We can do it in an hour, and so destroy that army that it will never show its head in the valley again.

"But General Early said no ; that the men had seen fighting enough, and that we had won glory enough for one day.

"Very well, sir, I replied, then I will return to my command.

"Until then I had entire charge of the movements on the right. I did return to my corps, and General Early carried on the battle. We followed up the Federals as they retreated. Our men were too much elated with their victory." As to Early's own conduct on the field, General

SHERIDAN'S RIDE.

"But there is a road from Winchester town,
A good broad highway leading down;
And there through the flush of the morning light,
A steed as black as the steeds of night
Was seen to pass, as with eagle flight.

Gordon permitted himself to say nothing. He describes himself vividly how the battle changed:

"Everybody knows about how Sheridan reached the field in the nick of time, and how he came thundering down from Winchester. He found his men scattered along the road in terror-stricken confusion, and he compelled them to turn about and follow him. He was a fury on horseback, dashing here and there among the flying soldiers and beating them back to the field of death which they had quitted. Meanwhile, the men who were retreating from the front had been brought to some sort of order. Then followed one of the most extraordinary reversals in the history of any war. As soon as Sheridan reached the field he reformed his lines and practiced upon us precisely the same movement which had demoralized his own forces in the morning. He just moved around our flank, swept down it and whipped us out of existence. He broke our line all to fragments, and routed the whole army most absolutely. It was as thorough a defeat as I ever saw. The day had dawned upon victory and exultation. It closed upon utter disaster and dejection. Two distinct battles had been fought, and in the last we lost all we had gained in the first one, and all that we had before. The reaction was dramatic in its suddenness and completeness, and when we left the fied that evening, the Confederacy had retired from the Shenandoah. It was our last real fight in the valley."

In regard to the number killed and wounded on the Union side, General Gordon overstates the facts. In the four battles we fought and won our loss was, killed 1938, wounded 11,893, missing 3121, total 16,952. These figures include all skirmishes and cavalry fights during a period of seven months. General Sheridan's historian says: "General Gordon's statement is, however, a most noteworthy one. The character of its author is a clear guarantee of its truthfulness, so far as he was able to know the facts in their completeness."

The roster of the Confederate army under Gen. Early

on the 30th of Sept 1864 was composed of five divisions of infantry, comprising eighteen brigades of ninety-seven regiments; fifteen batteries of artillery; two divisions of cavalry composed of seven brigades, representing thirty regiments.

Wickham's brigade of Lee's division of cavalry was composed of the First Virginia, Colonel Carter; Second Virginia, Colonel Mumford; Third Virginia, Colonel Owen; Fourth Virginia, Colonel Payne.

Sheridan's ride which is here appended was composed under the following circumstances: There was to be a gathering at Pike's opera house in Cincinnati, Ohio, soon after the battle of Cedar Creek, in honor of the union victories, and a reception to James C. Murdock, who had helped the "Soldier's Aid Society" in raising funds. Murdock asked T. Buchanan Read to write something on the battle of Cedar Creek that he might read it that night. The famous poem was written in less than five hours and read by the great dramatist that night, with the effect of raising such a storm of enthusiasm as had never been seen in this country.

————‡————

SHERIDAN'S RIDE.

Up from the South at break of day,
Bringing to Winchester fresh dismay,
The affrighted air with a shudder bore,
Like a herald in haste, to the chieftain's door,
The terrible grumble and rumble, and roar,
Telling the battle was on once more,
And Sheridan twenty miles away.

And wider still the billows of war
Thundered along the horizon's bar;
And louder yet into Winchester rolled
The roar of that red sea uncontrolled,
Making the blood of the listener cold,
As he thought of the stake in the fiery fray.
And Sheridan twenty miles away.

But there is a road from Winchester town,
A good, broad highway leading down;
And there, through the flush of the morning light,
A steed as black as the steeds of night,
Was seen to pass, as with eagle flight,
As if he knew the terrible need;
He stretched away with his utmost speed;
Hills rose and fell; but his heart was gay
With Sheridan fifteen miles away.

Still sprung from those swift hoofs thundering south,
The dust like smoke from the cannon's mouth;
Or the trail of a comet, sweeping faster and faster,
Foreboding to traitors the doom of disaster.
The heart of the steed, and the heart of the master,
Were beating like prisoners assaulting their walls,
Impatient to be where the battle-field calls;
Every nerve of the charger was strained to full play
With Sheridan only ten miles away.

Under his spurning feet the road
Like an arrowy Alpine river flowed,
And the landscape sped away behind
Like an ocean flying before the wind,
And the steed like a bark fed with furnace ire,
Swept on, with his wild eye full of fire.
But lo! he is nearing his heart's desire;
He is snuffing the smoke of the roaring fray,
With Sheridan only five miles away.

The first that the general saw were the groups
Of stragglers, and then the retreating troops.
What was done? what to do? a glance told him both;
Then striking his spurs, with a terrible oath,
He dashed down the line mid a storm of huzzas,
And the wave of retreat checked its course there, because
The sight of the master compelled it to pause.
With foam and with dust the black charger was gray;

By the flash of his eye, and his red nostrils' play,
He seemed to the whole great army to say,
"I've brought you Sheridan all the way
From Winchester down to save the day."
Hurrah! hurrah! for Sheridan
Hurrah! hurrah! for horse and man.

And when their statutes are placed on high,
Under the dome of the Union sky,
The American soldiers' temple of fame;
Be it said, in letters both bold and bright;
Here is the steed that saved the day,
By carrying Sheridan into the fight,
From Winchester twenty miles away."

The battle of Cedar Creek ended infantry campaigning in the valley, but the cavalry were very active. There is a marvelous fascination in the life of the cavalryman.

The wondrous activity, the ceaseless daring, the constant danger, the perpetual adventure, the well known companionship of man and horse, the exhilarating experience of open air life,—all combined to give the cavalryman's life a keener zest in the administration of an army. The "tented field" soon became a myth to the soldier on horseback. We might or might not carry the useful "dog tent," but all he wanted was easily carried on his horse. The call to "boot and saddle" found them always ready, and the clear resonant notes of the "charge" tightened every rein, steeled every nerve, and made every man and horse part of a terrible machine of war, and yet an individuality that was full of character and freedom.

Whatever despondency had ever been felt by other portions of the army, there never was a day till the war ended when Sheridan's cavalry did not go forth cheerfully, even gaily, to its appointed tasks. The boom of the enemy's artillery, the stirring notes of the bugle's "to horse," were sufficient in themselves to bring forth cheers from the ranks. This doubtless, was due to the unflinching courage, the watchful care, and the cheerful alacrity, which characterizd the movements of General Sheridan. He was the prince of commanders, and won his way at once to the hearts of his troopers.

Scouting was kept up for a month, several minor engagements occurring with a portion of Mosby's force and Lomax's cavalry. This latter officer made a reconnaisance toward Front Royel about October 26th, but Colonel Powell with the 2nd Virginia and detachments of the 1st and 3rd chased Lomax to Milwood, capturing a few prisoners.

On the day of the presidential election, in 1864, the regiment left camp near Front Royal for Martinsburg. The term of service of the three years men, who had not re-enlisted, having expired, they were to be mustered out. While enroute the command halted near Winchester, the poles were opened, and the voters again exercised the right of suffrage. A special act of congress provided for this manner of holding elections. Judges were appointed and the returns were sent to the respective counties where the voters resided. After the election the regiment proceeded to Martinsburg, and established camp southeast of the place. As soon thereafter as practicable, two hundred and forty officers and men left for Wheeling, West Virginia; where, about the first of December, 1864, they were regularly mustered out of the service. While in camp at this place, a new company, numbering sixty-two men from Jackson county, Ohio, joined the regiment, and were assigned to duty as Co. M. This letter M was only used a few days until the reorganization. Captain Gilmore's company served with the regiment as Company L from July 1863 to August 1864, when they were mustered out; only eleven men of the company re-enlisting. The total enlistments in the regiment during the war were as follows: 1861, or the original enlistments, 862 men; 1862, 70 men; 1863, 118; 1864, 171 men, including the new company. This makes a total of 1221 men. At the time of reorganization the losses by deaths, discharges and desertions amounted to about 600 men, leaving an effective force in the regiment of near 500. The command was now consolidated into seven companies as follows: Company A, Capt. Alberto Campbell; Company B, was composed of B and I with Captain Will S. Merrill; Company C was composed of C and H, with Captain E. E. Wilson; Company D, Captain John McNally; Company E, Captain Joseph Ankrom; was composed of Companies G and K; Company F, Captain, Henry F. Swentzel; Company G, Captain, Jasper A.

Smith, was composed of the new Company M. Other transfers had been made, but the above constitutes the principal changes. The field and staff were as follows: James Allen, Lieutenant Colonel, who so ably commanded the regiment until the final muster out; Edwin S. Morgan, Major; Adjutant, Abijah B. Farmer. The lieutenants of the companies under this new deal were: Company A, Elihu D. Robinson and Emerson McMillin; Company B, Edwin A. Rosser and Martin Kramer; Company C, Abijah B. Farmer (acting Adjutant) and George Freeman; Company D, Samuel McVey and W. S. McClanahan; Company E, James W. Hicks and John M. Corns; Company F, Charles C. Clise and Elisha T. Fisher; Company G, Milton McMillin and Wm. J. Kirkendall.

About this time General Powell left the service. His military career had been a most creditable one, having served in all the grades from captain to general; as captain of Company B, from the 8th of November 1861, to August 19th, 1862; as major until December 5th, 1862; as lieutenant colonel until May 18th, 1863; as colonel and brigade and division commander until October 19th, 1864; as brigadier general until the foregoing muster out. General Powell is now living at Belleville, Illinois. Since the war he has written a number of valuable war articles, and in no instance has he ever forgotten to honorably mention his own regiment.

While under his care the regiment had attained a proficiency and effectiveness that was second to none. Among the records of West Virginia troops appears the following: —"No regiment in the service from any state has performed more arduous duty than the Second Regiment of West Virginia Cavalry, and none have better deserved the compliments and praise it has received."

All this must have been exceedingly gratifying to the general, who had led the command in its most trying times; and it was intensely gratifying to the rank and file of the regiment, who, soon after, while serving under that prince of cavalry leaders, General Philip H. Sheridan, saw that

their old colonel had been justly honored with the star of
a brigadier general, thus ·proving the possibilities of the
American citizen soldier.

After the completion of the re-organization the regiment repaired to a position a few miles north-east of Winchester, and with the brigade established winter quarters
in what was known as Camp Averell. Very comfortable
log houses were built and covered with the ever useful
"dog tent." The bodies of stables were also built but
were not covered, owing, probably, to the lack of the
proper material. The portion of the winter spent here was
very pleasant to the troopers. The ground was covered
with a deep snow which was more preferable than the mud
we had been used to in the Kanawha Valley. The camp
was established in an open wood, so that fuel was easily
obtained. A soldier is naturally an inventive genius, but
this is owing to the fact of so many persons being together,
and the necessities likely to arise cause their minds to devise various ways to help themselves out of seeming diffi-
culties. To exemplify this: While in quarters here a set
of harness was improvised as follows: A half blanket
was passed over the back of a horse, another piece around
his breast, held in place by the "back piece," made a very
good substitute for a collar; and to this ropes were tied for
tugs. With this arrangement a horse could pull a very
good load of wood. Sometimes this would be placed on a
horse that had never been learned to work, but this was
only fun for the boys. Another thing that perhaps may
not be generally known was the soldier's way of clearing a
chicken of its feathers when they have no boiling water at
hand: Wring the fowl's head off over a stream of water,
letting it drop into the water, and what feathers it does
not kick off can be easily removed. In this connection I
will describe what constituted a "ration." A ration is the
established daily allowance of food for one person. For
the U. S. army it was composed as follows: Twelve
ounces of pork or bacon, or one pound and four ounces of
salt or fresh beef; one pound and six ounces of soft bread

or flour, or one pound of hard bread, or one pound and four ounces of meal; and to every one hundred rations, fifteen pounds of beans or peas, and ten pounds of rice or hominy; ten pounds of green coffee, or eight pounds of roasted or roasted and ground coffee, or one pound and eight ounces of tea; fifteen pounds of sugar; four quarts of vinegar; one pound and four ounces of adamantine, or star candles; four pounds of soap; three pounds and twelve ounces of salt; four ounces of pepper; thirty pounds of potatoes when practicable, and one quart of molasses. Dessicated compressed potatoes, or dessicated compressed mixed vegetables, at the rate of one ounce and a half of the former and one ounce of the latter to the ration, may be substituted for beans, peas, rice, hominy or fresh potatoes. The forage ration was fourteen pounds of hay and twelve pounds of corn, oats or barley. A full ration was more than an ordinary man could eat. There was but one known exception to this rule in the regiment, and that person is still living. If he should read this sentence it is hoped he will recognize himself. While in camp here the good people of New York City sent a large consignment of turkeys and chickens to General Sheridan's army, as a gift for a thanksgiving dinner. Although our style of cooking these delicacies was not such as might have been done at our homes, yet the camp kettles and mess pans enabled us to cook the fowls in such a manner as to afford an enjoyable meal, and I am sure it tasted better and sweeter because they were the gifts of our loving friends of the north. It is hardly proper to call the above article delicacy, for the taste of the delicate flesh of the barnyard fowls were not entirely unknown to the average cavalryman, for on many of the little scouts of the horsemen, while in the valley, the shrill notes of the chanticleer or the warning voice of the mother hen have been suddenly hushed, and on returning to camp the mess-pans and camp-kettles were again called into special service. During the month of December, while in Camp Averell, the troopers did not remain idle, but were constantly on the move, picketing and scouting. Much of the latter was performed during the night time. Some of these little forays often bordered on the romantic and the tragic. The surroundings and conditions of these night marches will never fade from the memory of the living participants. The pale moon, casting its bright silvery rays over the surrounding mountains and valleys, sparkling and shimmering on the snow covered earth; the crisp, frost-laden air; the silent troopers with poised carbines or pistols; the steady jingle of the srbres; the grinding sound of the horses feet in the frozen snow; the farm houses, standing like sentinels, dark and silent, all combined to impress upon us a feeling of awe.

These surroundings would hardly indicate that the little band pursuing these lonely marches was on other missions than those of love and mercy. And yet, while these thoughts are in the troopers minds, the snow, now so white and beautiful, may soon be crimsoned with the life-blood of some boy in blue. In that country, every tree might conceal an enemy, and even the innocent children were taught to hate us. This winter in the Shenandoah Valley was a delightful one to us, and all enjoyed the best of health and spirits. The entire command was placed in the best possible condition, the horses were improving so that they would be able to endure the hardships of a severe campaign.

About the 18th of December General Torbert with 5,000 cavalry, including our own brigade, started on an expedition through Upshur, Culpepper and Madison counties to the Rapidan river. The object of the expedition was never quite clear to us. On this march the regiment experienced some thrilling times, but no engagement of consequence took place. Major Farribee, of the First Virginia, with a portion of the brigade, destroyed a bridge over the Rapidan river. The country through Culpepper and Madison counties consists of high table-lands, The turnpike, which at the time was covered with a deep snow; under the tramp of the union horsemen, soon became a sheet of ice, and fortunate indeed were those who

were riding sharp shod horses, for they had no difficulty
in keeping in the smooth roadway. The others had to
seek the fields and woods where they were not in danger of
life and limb, from their horses slipping and falling on
them. A portion of the regiment had captured quite a
number of beef cattle, and these were being driven along.
One night they seemingly became tired of standing in the
cold and snow without anything to eat; near midnight
while the tired troopers were sleeping on the bare ground
and without tents, the entire drove of cattle stampeded
through the camp. The guards commenced yelling, whoa!
whoa! This warning and significant sound speedily
aroused the sleeping soldiers, who, instinctively sought
refuge from the panic-stricken cattle by getting behind
trees, wagons, or anything that afforded protection. A
snow had fallen during the night, covering the sleeping
men, and when they were so rudely awakened, the covering of snow was shaken into their beds. After the cattle
had tramped over some of them, they were in a sorry
plight. But there was ludicrous incidents enough connected with the scare, to keep all in a good humor. During the rest of the night some one was continually shouting, Whoa! Whoa! The return march was made by way
of Warrenton; and about December 26th all were again in
winter quarters. Picketing had become quite hazardous in the vicinity of Camp Averell. Mosby's command
was well acquainted in the neighborhood and thoroughly
understood the topography of the country. They would
dress in the uniform of the Union soldier, and often, under
the pretence of giving the countersign, murder the sentinel. Such precautions were soon adopted as to put a stop
to this dishonorable warfare.

Some time in January, 1865, the brigade officers gave
what was called the "officers ball." To obtain the ladies
necessary for the occasion, invitations were sent to all the
ladies living within a radius of three miles of Camp Averell, to attend the party. A cavalry guard and ambulances were to be sent around in the evening to bring in

all who would attend. The invitations were accompanied with the assurance of protection, and a safe return under escort after the close of the festivities. This was all carried out, and on the evening of the party, a picket of the regiment northeast of Winchester admitted a small detachment of cavalry, having in charge an ambulance load of young ladies, enroute to the ball. The outer picket above mentioned consisted of two men, or rather boys. During the night these boys talked of the ball and thought what fun it would be if the ambulance was to return by that road, and the escort would not have the countersign. Each gave the other a significant look, but no more was said on the subject at the time. One of the sentinels was so amused at something that was running through his mind that he dismounted and ran around through the snow. The other picket seemed to divine his friend's thoughts, and he became suffused with laughter.

About three o'clock in the morning the sentinels heard wheels grinding in the frozen snow, and soon the ambulance came in sight, under escort of four men of the First Virginia Cavalry. At the proper distance the party was halted. In answer to the challenge of "Who comes there?" they gave the proper answer: "Friends." "Advance one with the countersign!" Said the spokesman; "We neglected to get the countersign, but are only taking these ladies home from the party, and you know we are all right." The pickets again exchanged glances, when one nodded an assent to the other. Said he, "You can not pass this post without giving the countersign, and you will save time by sending back to camp and getting it." With that two of the escort returned to Winchester. The ladies accepted the situation very gracefully, one of them remarking "that the Yankees had captured them." During the hour and a quarter they remained there, they talked and laughed about the ball, and seemed to enjoy the novelty of this last episode, as much as any of the events of the gay night they had spent within our lines. The balance of the winter spent in Camp Averell was uneventful.

CHAPTER XVII.

PREPARING FOR THE FINAL STROKE.

In volume two of Grant's Memoirs he says: "On the 8th of February I ordered Sheridan, who was in the valley of Virginia, to push forward as soon as the weather would permit and strike the canal west of Richmond at or about Lynchburg; and on the 20th I made the order to go to Lynchburg as soon as the roads would permit, saying: As soon as it is possible to travel, I think you will have no difficulty about reaching Lynchburg with a cavalry force alone. From there you could destroy the railroad and canal in every direction, so as to be of no further use to the rebellion. * * * * I would advise you to overcome great obstacles to accomplish this." Sheridan's historian says: "Winter quarters in the valley had been, on the whole, of an attractive character for our cavalry. The six weeks of needed rest preceding this, the last of Sheridan's extended raids, had been spent in the crisp, cold winter days of that delightful region. Veteran troopers still speak of their last winter in that field with pleasurable associations. Men and horses were alike in good condition, both well fed, and the men well clothed, and prepared for a severe campaign. The fine clear cold of a Virginia mid-winter vanished before the bugler's "boots and saddles," and it was a cheerless and chilly morning, with a cold and mizzling rain, that greeted the column when Sheridan moved out of Winchester on the 27th of February, 1865."

From memoranda kept at the time, and for this purpose, I submit this account of the final struggle, to the "round up" at Appomattox, and thence to the muster out. About this time the brigade, consisting of the First, Second, and Third West Virginia Cavalry, under command of Colonel Henry Capehart, was attached to the division of General Custer. We were ever after known as the Third Brigade Third Division Cavalry Corps. Sheridan's marching force consisted of the First Division under command of 'Tommy" Deven, the Third Division under General, Custer. General Wesley Merritt accompanied the expedition as chief of staff. The force consisted of about 8,000 men, and, taking this mounted command in all its appointments, it was probably the finest and most efficient cavalry force the world had ever seen. All were in excellent spirits and eager to be led against the enemy, and, with the confidence and enthusiasm inspired by our commanders, felt that we could whip or ride through any force that would dare oppose our progress. The troops had been expecting marching orders for several days, and when, on the evening of the 26th, orders were issued to be ready to break camp on the morrow, all became bustle and hurry. Letters were written to home and to friends, arms and ammunition looked after, and long before bed-time all were ready. Reveille sounded at four o'clock on the 27th and by daylight the column was in motion, passing through Winchester and up the valley pike. After many unavoidable delays, usual in getting so large a column in motion on one road, it was ten o'clock when camp was pitched two miles north of Woodstock, and as it had rained most of the day, considerable difficulty was experienced in getting fires to burn. The mode of going into camp on a march was about as follows: After a brigade had been assigned to its place, the regiments were given their places, then if the nature of the ground would permit, they were thrown into columns of squadrons open order. The latter would then prepare to camp by numbers one and three advancing a few paces. This would give plenty of room for the horses, and in this manner stakes were driven in the ground, and the animals tied to them. Usually the men formed themselves into messes of two. Each man carried a "dog tent," a poncho or gum blanket, and an army blanket. In addition to this, the two between them, carried a smell ax with short handle, a sheet iron frying-pan, and a quart coffee-pot. Each man carried his own rations, and the prudent ones always carried a bunch of matches, carefully tied up in a piece of gum material, and secured about the body where they would be safe from damp. As soon as the order to dismount was given by the company commanders, the men were virtually free. As soon as dismounted one of the two men who were mess-mates would take the two horses in charge, and as soon as possible secure them to stakes. The other would divest himself of carbine and sabre, and start on the run for a load of the dryest rails that might be near. If it was pos-sible to secure hay or straw, this was attended to first. However, the load of fuel was thrown down in front of the horses, and while the first one builds the fire, the other, with canteens and coffee-pot, would go in search of water. Whilst one was getting sup-per, number two put up the "dog-tent" and fed the horses. There are many things that could be thrown into the little tent for a bed. Hay, straw, leaves, weeds, cedar-brush, the soft side of a board pulled from a fence or some build-ing, or even rails, have been used in preference to the wet ground. The troopers adapt themselves to circumstances, and are content with the best that can be obtained. The grumblers are only laughed at. If the cavalry do not get enough sleep in camp on these marches, they can enjoy some of that luxury, at least, while riding.

At four o'clock, on the morning of the 28th, the bugles aroused the drowsy soldiers from their short night's rest, and soon after the last notes of the reveille had sounded, hundreds of camp-fires were burning, casting a flickering light through the damp, misty morning air. Be-fore day had fairly broken, the column was again in mo-tion, passing through Woodstock, Edinburg and Moun

Jackson. Near the latter place the Shenandoah river was found to be so swollen with the recent rains, that fording it proved quite dangerous. The pontoon train came forward and soon one of those "war bridges" was being used by the troopers. The command marched very fast all day, and at 7 o'clock went into camp nine miles north of Harrisonburg. Before nine o'clock all were in bed enjoying needed rest, save the tired sentinels whose duty it was to keep watch over the slumbering camp. At two o'clock a. m., March 1st, the third brigade was aroused by the bugle sounding reveille. The orders were to "prepare to march immediately without getting breakfast, or feeding the horses. All were soon in ranks and moving for the pike, passing through the camp of the first division. We almost envied those sleeping soldiers, yet we felt quite "important" when the clanking of our sabres and the rattle of the camp accessories caused some of them to look out from their beds and ask "What brigade was that?" We were much amused at the actions of a darkey who stood near the column, and as we were passing cried out: "Look out dar, don't ride ober de colonel." The fact soon becomes known to the men that Capehart's brigade was to push forward and drive Rosser, who was reported to be between Harrisonburg and Staunton, out of the way. On the middle fork of the Shenandoah river Rosser was encountered prepared to resist the Union troopers crossing that stream. The covered bridge had been filled with rails for the purpose of being burned. A portion of the brigade was dismounted, and engaged the Confederates at the bridge. Colonel Capehart then sent the First Virginia above to an apology for a ford, yet they succeeded in crossing, and dashing down on the "savior of the valley" (Rosser), putting him and his force to flight, capturing fifty prisoners. The bridge was soon made passable, when a wild and exciting chase ensued between Capehart's brigade and Rosser, the enemy not being permitted to burn a bridge between them and Staunton, nor to annoy the advancing column to any extent. The brigade

went into camp four miles north of Staunton, and soon
were partaking of breakfast, dinner and supper, all in one.
The excitement of the day somewhat relieved the monot-
ony of the march. At sunrise on the second of March,
General Custer, with the remainder of the division, passed
the camp, when the brigade took its place in the column.
Early in the morning it commenced raining, and at the
same time the weather turned cold. Soon the trees,
fences, and even the pouches of the troopers were covered with a coating of ice. The roads were in a miserable
condition, and when we quietly entered the pretty little
city of Staunton the people · saw a mud-bespattered and
sorry looking lot of riders. At this place it was learned
that General Early had left there the day before with 2,500
men for Waynesboro, and that at the latter place he would
fight. It was only eight miles to Early's position. He
had boasted that Sheridan would not get through Rock-
fish Gap.

Custer was given the task of disposing of Early, and
in the afternoon the advance drove in the Confederate
pickets. As the third brigade formed into line on the left
of the road, the Confederate artillery, which was posted on
a rising piece of ground near the railroad, greeted us with
shot and shell. The rebel works extended some distance
to our right. The first brigade of Michiganders dismounted and formed as infantry.

They at once charged the rebel right, gaining the
works in fine style. The dismounted men swept on, doubling up the enemy's line in Fisher's Hill style. At this
juncture our own brigade charged mounted and cut off
over half of Early's force, which was forced to surrender.
Many of the enemy took refuge in houses and other buildings, as it was still raining very hard. They averred
that they could not fight in the rain. General
Early escaped on a train of cars that was
conveniently near. All his headquarter equipments
fell into our hands. The captures consisted of 1700 prisoners and eleven pieces of artillery. It was here the can-

GENERAL GEO. A. CUSTER.

From a war sketch.

non was captured that bore the inscription, "to General Phillip H. Sheridan, in care of General Early." Seventeen battle flags also fell into our hands. The Second Virginia now took the advance of the brigade, and crossed the mountain, capturing a train of two hundred loaded wagons. Early was engaged in gathering supplies for Lee's army. The region east of this place had been free from our raiding parties, and, being rich in produce, the army of northern Virginia had been getting their main supplies from this section. It was estimated that there was nearly a million dollars worth of stores at and near this place destroyed by our forces. This defeat finished General Early as a military commander, and we heard of him no more during the war. This was also the last seen of Rosser and his cavalry, "the savior of the valley." A few years after the war General Early was in Charleston, West Virginia. In the evening he was the central figure in a group of ex-confederate officers and citizens who had called to meet their old soldier friend. (We must admit that the military career of General Early had been a creditable one.) The conversation as was natural turned to the war. General Early gave his experiences in the valley, and among other things said: "The Richmond authorities wanted to know if I could not do something with Sheridan's cavalry. I told them that I did not have enough mounted men to attack the Yankee cavalry, and if they could spare any horsemen to send them along. Soon after this I received a dispatch from Richmond that the celebrated "Laurel Brigade" had been sent me. This was General Rosser and his command. In due time they arrived and reported to me. My men were down-spirited and disheartened with their reverses, and they turned out to view this new command. It was a fine body of cavalry, well equipped, well mounted and well dressed. Each man carried a sprig of laurel on the lapel of his coat. My boys would purposely ask 'What cavalry is that?' The reply would be: 'This is the Laurel Brigade.' 'Can you whip the Yankee cavalry?' 'We always have done so, and can do it again.' I then gave General Rosser all my available cavalry, and ordered him to go on down the road, and he no doubt would find Custer, his old classmate at West Point. The result of that fight is well known. Rosser was the most used up man I ever saw, and when the famous 'Laurel Brigade' came back all torn to fragments, their artillery gone, and all badly demoralized, my boys fairly went wild, at their appearance." And the old general laughed heartily. Just then a gentleman who had not heard all the account said, "why General, did Rosser get whipped?" The general excitedly replied, "whipped, yes, he got h—ll whipped out of him."

The Second Va. continue don to Greenwood station nine miles from Waynesboro. The station house filled with rebel bacon and flour was burned, after which the regiment returned four miles to the brigade camp.

Quite an amusing incident occurred before Greenwood station was reached. A small force of the regiment which was in the advance, came to where the road forked, and at this point a fine brick house occupied a site to the left of the Charlottesville road. A wagon loaded with sacks of wheat was standing by the road, near which a citizen on horseback had been captured. He was at once plied with questions as to where the roads led and which one led to Charlottesville, and so on. Several of the men had jumped from their horses and commenced emptying the wheat, so as to secure the nice, clean sacks. Unnoticed the citizen rode off down the road and had gone quite a little distance before some one called upon him to halt. He then put spurs to his horse, when two or three shots were fired over his head. When the crack of the first carbine sounded, four or five ladies at the house rushed out on the veranda, and wringing their hands, cried, "They will kill Mr. Johnson." One of the troopers rode up to the mansion and assured the screaming beauties that Mr. Johnson was safe.

On the morning of the 3rd the march was resumed on the Charlottesville road, the mud impeding the march so that our progress was slow. The command marched in columns of fours, the horses making great ridges of mud between the files, and number one and four forming a ridge on each side of the road. At three o'clock p. m. we entered the pretty little city of Charlottesville. A deputation of citizens meeting us in advance of our entrance and surrendering the place. Monticello, the old home of Thomas Jefferson, and the University of Virginia, founded by Mr. Jefferson, are at this place. These places were visited by hundreds of the command during our stay. General Sheridan in his memoirs says that it took two days to get his trains from Staunton to this place owing to the mud, and then the animals were so jaded they had to be rested. During the fourth of March the brigade went out a few miles and again destroyed the railroad. Some of the men gathered together a number of negroes and put them to work. When there was a straight piece of track, enough men would arrange themselves on one side and turn over a half mile at a time. Cross ties and fence rails were then placed on the iron, fire applied, which soon rendered the rails worthless. Again on the fifth ten miles of road in the direction of Gordonsville was effectually destroyed. The command was now subsisting off the country, carrying only rations of coffee. An abundance of flour and bacon was found, more than enough to subsist a large army for some time. This raid did certainly cut off a large supply of food that had been going to Richmond. About this time the prices of provisions in Richmond was: flour, fifteen hundred dollars per barrel; tea, one hundred dollars per pound; coffee, fifty dollars; bacon, eighteen dollars, and beef, fifteen dollars per pound. Living there at that time was not only expensive, but very uncertain.

The same day prices in New York City, for the same and other commodities, were: Flour, eight dollars and twenty-five cents per barrel; coffee, thirty-one cents; sugar thirteen cents, and eggs eighteen cents.

The morning of March 6th was clear and warm, and once more the column was in motion, filing down through the streets of Charlottesville with bands playing and colors flying. It marched on the Lynchburg road, and continued the work of destroying the railroad. The road was narrow, rough and muddy, and when in the evening we went into camp near Rock Fish River, the poor horses were almost tired out. The next day the march was continued to Roseland Station, and in the evening the entire command worked on the railroad for three hours. The men were adepts at this kind of work, and they took hold without orders. It was ten o'clock on the 8th when the column was again in motion, taking the road to New Market on the James River. The river was bank full, owing to the recent heavy rains. Just before going into camp near New Market, a violent rain storm set in, and while the men were hastily putting up their little tents, they were ordered on. This change of camp was made three times, when a muddy field was assigned our brigade, and in this unfavorable condition the tents were put up and an attempt made to get supper. Even the rails would not burn, and the language indulged in by the troopers on this occasion was not such as had been learned at Sunday school. Those who did not make use of this kind of talk, experienced a sort of secret satisfaction in the comfort the others seemed to be enjoying. Getting supper had to be abandoned. The rails that would not burn in water were placed in the tents, and on these the men went to bed—angry. The poor horses were tied to stakes in the mud and exposed to the pitiless storm, without hay or a place to lie down.

On the 9th the line of march was near the swollen James River. Eight miles below New Market the column filed onto the tow-path which afforded much better marching. While passing down the river, squads of Confederates were seen on the opposite side watching the column, but no firing was done, owing to the distance. Traveled fast all day and in the evening went into camp near Scottsville, and, the surroundings being more pleasant than those of the night before, all enjoyed a good night's rest; and, like children, forgetting that any one had been out of humor. General Sheridan says that he intended crossing the James River at Duguidsville but the enemy had burned the bridge at that place, and, owing to the swollen condition of the river, his pontoons would not reach much over half way across. He was therefore compelled to choose between returning to Winchester or to pass behind Lee's army to the White House, thence to the army of the Potomac. He chose the latter. On the 10th the column moved in the direction of Richmond. This was a typical March day, alternately raining, snowing and sunshine. At three o'clock we reached the city of Columbia at the junction of the Rivannah with the James River. An abundance of hay was obtained here. One old farmer remarked that if the boys did take all his hay they ought to have left him the fence. March 11th was a day of rest. Large foraging parties were sent out, and returned with plenty of edibles for both man and horse. The country around Columbia was rich and healthy. While here our presence produced a panic in Richmond. A Confederate officer said that the presence of the bold troopers so frightened the Richmond authorities that Secretary Mallory and Postmaster General Reagan were in the saddle, and he further says that Jeff Davis and the Cabinet were ready for flight. General Lee came up from Petersburg to Richmond to confer with Davis in regard to the seeming danger. On the 12th the command was once more on the Richmond road, which was continued to a cross road called Fife's, where the column executed a "column left" and started on the trot for the Virginia Central railroad, which was struck at Tolersville near Frederickshall station. At the latter place a company of Confederate soldiers were enjoying the luxury of snug winter quarters. They escaped but left fires burning, and most of their equipage, which showed that they left in haste. Some time before midnight the regiment was ordered out on picket. Two miles on the Gordonsville road, camp was pitched in a wood, near where more rebel quarters were found. The morning of the

13th revealed to us that the work of destruction was still in progress. Near the picket post two barrels of grape wine had been found at the house of a physician. This was duly seized as contraband of war, and the doctor's good wife seemed to enjoy the eargerness which the soldiers displayed in securing some of this wine. She was even so kind as to loan one of them a bucket to carry some of it to camp. When the vessel was returned she seemed surprised and remarked, "that is more than I expected of a Yankee."

At Fredrickshall Station a large amount of property was destroyed, including the depot, water tank, and a large warehouse filled with tobacco. The burning of the latter so impregnated the air with the fumes of tobacco that many of the horses had to be moved. On the 14th the command moved to Beaver Dam Station along the line of the railroad. At this time there was near 2,000 negroes following the force, who, as they expressed it—wanted to journey to that paradise—the north. After our arrival within the Union lines they were all eventually shipped to Washington. The enemy were entirely deceived as to Sheridan's intentions, he being at so many different places, they could not make proper dispositions to meet him. On the 15th the command again moved rapidly toward Richmond reaching Hanover Junction. The first division encountered the enemy near the South Anna river, but the union horsemen succeeded in destroying an important bridge there. The main command now countermarched to the Fredricksburg road, and at four o'clock reached the north Anna river. It was after night before all had crossed.

At eight o'clock a halt was made, supper cooked and eaten, horses fed, when the march was continued until eleven o'clock. The night was very dark, and fires were built at frequent intervals along the road, which served as beacon lights, and very materially assisted the wagon train in keeping up with the column. On the 16th the troopers were out on the road in column and in motion before breakfast.

At nine o'clock a halt was made at Mongohick church, where the men cooked their meal of "slap-jacks," pork and coffee. Those terrible slap-jacks; even the name is shrouded in mystery. The ingredients for their "construction" were flour, salt and water. This was mixed in a tin cup or any other vessel at hand. A quantity of grease was put into the frying pans, and into this the batter was poured until the bottom was well covered. This was then placed over the fire and baked. Sometimes when the fire was very hot, the pans being thin, the bread would be burned on the outside and somewhat raw in the middle. Many of the men were quite expert at this baking. The handles on the pans were from one to two feet in length, and the bread could be dextorously tossed into the air in such a manner that in descending the cake would turn over and be caught in the pan ready for the fire again. After the meal had been cooked the pan was placed on the fire and all the grease burned from it, after which it was rubbed with a piece of wood, or a bunch of hay or grass, until clean and ready for packing. This bread was not near so wholesome as the army cracker, yet they often filled an "aching void" that but for their presence might have given us trouble. I believe there are some of the old "army crackers" still in existence. Some of those "slap-jacks" ought to have been preserved among the war relics, for aside from the recollections they would call forth, of sleepless nights and horrid night-mares, they would be looked upon by the old veterans with tears of joy, as they gently reposed in all their simplicity and purity. On the 17th the march was over ground made historic by the Army of the Potomac. Silent evidences of the conflict were to be seen on every side, in the way of rude fortifications, trees torn by shot and shell, ruined farms, depopulated towns, and here and there graves of the dead whose rude head-board told of him who slept beneath.

At noon the head of the column reached the Mattapony River at Elliott's warehouse, and continued down that stream to King William C. H. The peculiar name of this river led some of the men to inquire the origin of the name. This was quite simple. The Mat, the Ta, the Po and the Ny rivers unite, forming the Mattapony.

On the morning of the 18th the sun was shining brightly when the column was again in motion. Word had passed along the column that White House would be reached during the day, which would end the raid. Cheerful hearts characterized the march that day, for no doubt all were hoping to hear news of home and friends. There is nothing in the life of the soldier that will so soften the heart and give joy to his life as the reception of a letter. The little silent messenger is eagerly seized, opened, and then the warrior is a boy again. When a column is marching in this manner, it is customary to ask any one seen at the houses, how far it is to some place they may know or suppose to be the destination. On this occasion a very pretty rebel miss was standing in the doorway of a farmhouse, watching the column pass. No doubt she had been asked how far it was to White House a number of times. As our part of the column was passing, the usual question was asked by some one, "How far is it to White House?" The little miss had probably tired of this monotonous question by this time, so in sharp tones she replied: "It is three miles, and I am not going to tell another man." The laugh this raised in the ranks caused the young lady to slam the door and disappear within.

At noon our eyes were greeted with the stars and stripes waving from the shipping on the Pamunkey River at White House Landing. Cheer after cheer rent the air at the inspiriting sight.

We went into camp on the north side of the river and commenced laying plank on the old West Point railroad bridge for the purpose of crossing. On the 19th the entire command crossed the river and went into camp along a line of works erected by General McClellan in 1862. The river presented a picturesque scene, covered with gunboats, transports and other shipping, all sent there to meet the command. Soon rations and forage were issued and all were once more happy. The only disappointment being that our mail had not arrived. Here is the sum total of the raid:

General Badeau says, "Sheridan's loss during the campaign did not exceed one hundred soldiers, and many of these were the men unable to bear the fatigues of the march. Incessant rains, deep and impassable streams, swamps mud and gloom, were the impediments offered by nature to his advance. Seventeen pieces of artillery and seventeen hundred prisoners of war were captured. Forty-six canal locks, five aqueducts, forty canal and road bridges, twenty three railroad bridges, one foundry, one machine shop, twenty-seven warehouses, forty-one miles of railroad, fourteen mills, and immense quantities of ammunition, gray cloth, saddles, horses, grain, and other supplies were taken and destroyed. Sheridan's cavalry had annihalated whatever was between Richmond and Lynchburg, and having completed its work in the Shenandoah valley, was ready to join the army of the Potomac in the struggle to come. It was this raid and its results that made Grant decide on the final movements, ending in the surrender of Lee. General Sheridan says in his final report. The first and third cavalry divisions which belonged to the army of the Shenandoah had marched in midwinter over three hundred miles, in constant rains, over almost impassable roads, and swollen streams, to participate in the final campaign, and were rewarded by the honor of having the flag of the Army of Northern Virginia presented to them on the morning of the surrender.

On the 20th, from appearances, we were to have a little rest, so the camp was made as comfortable as possible. Wood and water had to be carried half a mile and both were poor articles. Everything was being pushed forward to enable the command to resume the offensive. Men and horses were alike in good condition. Clothing was issued at once, and also plenty of ammunition. The most formidable task presented was the shoeing of the horses. Portable shops were placed all over the camp, and, as every

company had one or more blacksmiths, the merry ring of
the anvils were heard in all directions. On the 22nd the
men passed a very uncomfortable day, the wind blowing
furiously, filling the air with sand. Everything was sand
and pine timber. I believe that White House was the old
home of the Custis family, and, when George Washington
came here to woo Mrs. Martha Custis, he must have loved
her well, for there is nothing in the surroundings that
would inspire his soul with tender thoughts. On the 24th
the brigade of infantry which had been at White House
left for the Chickahominy River with our pontoon train.
This was good news to us, as we were anxious to leave
this place. At night no marching orders had been received.

CHAPTER XVIII.

OFF FOR PETERSBURG.

On the 25th reveille sounded unusually early, and the first indication of marching was "boot and saddle." This was greeted with cheers. In a short time all were in ranks, the Second Virginia taking the advance, on the Charles City C. H. road in the direction of Petersburg. At the Chickahominy we found the infantry with the pontoon across that narrow, deep and treacherous looking stream. Near what had once been Charles City C. H. we went into camp and threw out a strong picket on our right. On the 26th the weather was bitter cold and windy, rendering marching very unpleasant. At noon the head of the column commenced crossing the James River at Deep Bottom. A pontoon was used and the crossing was very slow. The bridge had to be opened to permit boats to pass up or down the river. I have the pleasure of saying to those of the boys who became annoyed while waiting on the pontoon for a boat to pass, that on board that vessel was the president of the United States, Abraham Lincoln, and that he was looking at the cavalry; and if the remarks he made respecting them had been heard, their cheeks would have burned with pride.

During the march day fires were built along the road, and every time the column halted, the men would dismount and rush for a fire. At dark all are over the bridge and went into camp near Jones' Landing. On inquiry it was learned that it was only eight miles to Richmond.

On the 27th the command crossed the Appomattox

river, five miles below Petersburg. The crossing was
done rapidly, two pontoons being used. Within a short
time after crossing the river, we reached the right of the
lines of the army of the Potomac. A shotted salute of one
hundred guns was given in honor of our recent achievements. They turned out enmasse in rear of their
works and greeted us with prolonged cheers. Our line of
march lay immediately in the rear of General Grant's lines.
This gave us a full view of their works, also a fair view of
the Confederate works. While we were passing, some
shelling took place between the forces. The works were
closer than we expected to see, and both looked quite formidable. Went into camp near the old Norfolk railroad.
On the 28th we remained in camp, but were permitted to
view the lines in front of Petersburg. John Nunnemaker,
of Co. D, was killed while thus looking on. The place
that most interested us was Fort Steadman, where the
enemy had but recently made a sortie, capturing that fort,
but were repulsed and driven back to their lines.

MARCH 29TH.—THE LAST FIGHTING CAMPAIGN.

This morning the head of the column filed out to the
west in the direction of Rowanty Creek. The force consisted in all of thirty-seven regiments of cavalry and three
batteries of artillery, in all ten thousand men. All dismounted men had been sent to City Point, Va. Custer's
division was in the rear of column in charge of the supply
trains. As soon as the left of the army of the Potomac
was passed, the trains became hopelessly stuck in the mud,
bogs and quicksand. The wagons had to be often un-
loaded and lifted out of the boggy places. We had been
ordered on a big raid by General Grant, to destroy the two
railroads that remained within the Confederate lines.
General Sheridan had disapproved of this move, and had
said to General Grant, "Let's go in and finish the job
right here." Getting stuck in the mud and sand during
these two days, and the fearful rainstorm of the 30th
brought on the battle of Five Forks. General Sheridan
was at Dinwiddie C. H., and he says: "Dinwiddie C. H.,

though a most important point in the campaign, was far from attractive in feature, being made up of a half dozen unsightly houses, a ramshackle tavern propped up on two sides with pine poles, and the weather-beaten building that gave official name to the cross-roads.

We had no tents—there were none in the command—so I took possession of the tavern for shelter for myself and staff, and just as we had finished looking over its primitive interior, a rain storm set in. The wagon containing my mess equipments was back somewhere on the road, hopelessly stuck in the mud, and hence we had nothing to eat except some coffee which two young women, living in the tavern, kindly made for us, a small quantity of the berry being furnished from the haversack of one of my escorts. By the time we got the coffee the rain was falling in sheets, and the evening bade fair to be a most dismal one; but songs and choruses set up by some of my staff—the two young women playing the accompaniments on a battered piano—relieved the situation and enlivened us a little. However, the dreary night brought me one great comfort, for General Grant, who that day had moved out to Gravelly Run, sent me instructions to abandon all idea of the contemplated raid, and directed me to act in concert with the infantry under his immediate command, to turn if possible the right flank of Lee's army. The dispatch made my mind easy, so notwithstanding the suspicions excited by some of my staff concerning the Virginia feather-bed that had been assigned me, I turned in at a late hour and slept soundly."

At dark, of the 29th, we had only gotten seven miles with the train, worked all night, and daylight found us but ten miles from the starting place. Another day and night was spent in getting the train about the same distance, and to add to the discomfiture it rained all day of the 30th, and just after dark it poured down. On the 31st there were rumors of fighting in front. We had been with the train for two days and nights, sleeping only in the saddle, or by lying on the wet ground, using a log for a pillow, and this but a few moments at a time. Shortly after noon of the 31st we were relieved from caring for the train, and ordered to the front. We passed down the narrow road rapidly, the other cavalry giving way by crowding to either side of the road in the bushes. The firing to our front and right got plainer, indicating that the enemy were getting nearer. Great enthusiasm prevailed among the troops we were passing at sight of the Virginia brigade (as they term us) going to the front. Soon we halted in column and dismounted, forming on the left of the lead horses. We then double quicked and went into position near a battery in an old field. The boys quickly concluded that if they had to fight as infantry they must do as the latter, so a lot of convenient fence rails were soon transformed into temporary works. Just as these were finished, General Sheridan rode along our line, telling us to hold our position. Just then the enemy came in sight in the woods. When our carbines turned loose on the gray-backs they suddenly halted. Barrett, the historian, says of this affair: "On the 31st General Ayers division (of infantry) was sent by Warren to dislodge the enemy on the White Oak road. Ayers was repulsed and driven back upon Crawford, whose division in turn broke, and both retreated in some confusion upon the position occupied by Griffin. The enemy then ceased pursuit and rapidly turned upon Sheridan at Dinwiddie Court House. A battle followed in which the enemy's entire cavalry force and two divisions of infantry were kept in check by Sheridan's cavalry." General Sheridan in his official report says: "I determined to defend Dinwiddie C. H. and selected a place about three-fourths of a mile north-west of the cross-roads, and, Custer coming up with Capehart's brigade, took position on the left of the road to Five Forks in some open ground along the crest of a gentle ridge. Custer got Capehart into place just in time to lend a helping hand to Smith, who, severely pressed, came back on us here from his retreat along Chamberlain 'bed,' the vernacular for a woody swamp such as that through which Smith retired. A little later the brigades of Grigg and Gibbs falling to the rear slowly and steadily, took up a line some distance to the right of Capehart, the intervening gap to be filled by Pennington's brigade. It was now near sunset, and the enemy's cavalry thinking the day was theirs, made a dash at Smith, but just as the assailants appeared in the open fields, Capehart's men opened so suddenly on their left flank as to cause it to recoil in astonishment, which permitted Smith to connect his brigade with Custer's unmolested." This ended the fighting for the day, but we remained in this position all night. General Sheridan's headquarters were in a tent just in the rear of the position of the Second Virginia. A war historian says: "Early in the week, when the Confederates became aware of the extension of Grant's lines, they added a division of infantry to the force encamped on our flank line. These were directed to avoid an infantry fight, but to seek out the cavalry, and, by getting it at a disadvantage, rid the region both of the harmfulness of Sheridan and that prestige of his name so terrifying to the Virginia housewife. So long as Sheridan remained upon the far left, the Southside road was unsafe, and the rapidity with which his command could be transferred from point to point rendered it a formidable balance of power. The Confederates knew the country well, and the peculiar course of the highways gave them every advantage.

THE BATTLE OF FIVE FORKS.

Five Forks is a point where five good roads meet in the edge of a dry, high, well watered forest, three of them radiating to the railway, and their tributaries unlocking all the country. The Confederates fortified this place as if it had been their capital. Upon the principal road—the White Oak road—they had breastworks of logs and earth reaching east and west three miles. All the roads were well picketed and a desperate intention to hold it averred. Five Forks is eight miles from Dinwiddie C. H., four miles from the Southside railroad, and eighteen miles from

Humphrey Station, the nearest of our military railway stations. A little stream called Gravelly Run gives name to a little Methodist church about one mile from the cross-roads.

The morning of Saturday, April 1st, opened bright and clear, when we left our position and dismounted, advanced into the deep pine forest. Soon after starting the clear resonant notes of a rebel bugle, far to our front, was borne upon the air, and we readily recognized the sound "to horse." Cautiously our skirmishers advanced feeling for the enemy. Nearly a mile was covered in this way when the first shots were fired. This was answered by hearty cheers from our side. The enemy fell back slowly, each side increasing the number of skirmishers until there was almost a line of battle. Five thousand dismounted cavalry were in this move and were to ingeniously drive the Confederates into their works. The object of the wily Sheridan was to capture as well as to rout. Our led horses were following at a reasonable distance. A writer in speaking of this affair says: "With their horses within call, the cavalryman in line of battle, stood together like walls of stone, swelling onward like those gradual elevating ridges of which Lyell speaks. All the afternoon the cavalry pushed them hard; and the strife went on uninterruptedly and terrifically. The battle was fought at so close quarters that the Union carbines were never out of range; had this been otherwise, the long rifles of the enemy would have given them every advantage." I will now follow the fortunes of our own brigade and regiment.

It was after five o'clock in the evening when our horses were brought to us, and mounting, we prepared to charge the enemy's left and rear. Away off to our right the battle raged fiercely. With the gallant Custer in the lead we started on a wild ride for the enemy. It was getting late and, though there was no road, only timber, brush and logs, we kept up a trot until considerable cleared land was reached. On an elevation near a house a rebel

CAPT. WILL. S. MERRELL.

One of Gen'l Custer's Staff Officers.

battery was located, and being unable to depress their guns, their shot passed over our heads causing a good many of the boys to unconsciously "duck" their heads. Captain Ankrom with a squadron captured the battery, or rather took the gunners prisoners. Just beyond the battery, a drove of beef cattle being hurriedly driven to the rear by a squad of soldiers, all fell into our hands.

The rebel cavalry skirmishers were met by our brigade and soon put to flight. About this time we gained the top of a low ridge, a stubble field in front. Across this field, stretched away to the right and left, was the nicest line of rebel cavalry we ever beheld. Our cheers were answered by the famous "rebel yell." Our carbines were brought into play as we steadily advanced, but the enemy did the same. The bugles were sounding "trot," the band playing "Hail Columbia," the roar of battle on the right almost drowning the sound of our carbines. The sun was sinking behind the western hills as the two lines of opposing horsemen approached each other. The order to cease firing was passed along the line, when, instinctively it seemed, a thousand sabres were flashing in the air, recalling the words of Tennyson who says:

"Flashed all their sabres bare,
Flashed as they turned in air,
Sab'ring the gunners there."

The opposing lines met near the center of the field, where a ditch or drain ran parallel with the line of battle. The Confederates halted about ten paces from the edge of the ditch, our line going to the drain and also halting. During the brief time this halt was made, the opposing forces eyed each other as if preparing for the deadly hand to hand encounter. Lieutenant Emerson McMillin said: "Boys, this won't do, let's go over." when, putting spurs to his horse, the ditch was cleared, and at the same time the rest of the regiment boldly went over and fell onto the rebel horsemen with sabre. Owing to the position of the lines, nearly all the casualties fell on the Second Virginia, most of the loss being in wounded. In this hand to hand fighting, many of the enemy were killed before they retreated. The regiment followed the enemy until the edge of the field was reached, when we were met by a large force of rebel cavalry, which so overlapped our left that we in turn were forced back a short distance, when the left of our line was re-enforced by the rest of the brigade; then our boys turned, and in a spirited charge drove the enemy from the field, capturing a number of prisoners and twelve Confederate flags. The regiment followed the enemy on the jump for three miles, then returned to near where the main fight had been.

To sum up the important battle of Five Forks, General Sheridan's historian says: "It was seven o'clock before the Confederates came to the conclusion that they were outflanked and whipped. They had been so busily engaged that they were a long time in finding out how desperate were their circumstances; but now, wearied with persistent assaults in front, they fell back to the left, only to see four lines of battle waiting to drive them across the field, decimated. At the right the horsemen charged them in their vain attempt to fight "out," and in the rear, straggling foot and cavalry began also to assemble; slant fire, cross fire, and direct fire, by file and volley, rolled in perpetually, cutting down their bravest officers, and strewing the fields with bleeding men; groans resounded in the intervals of exploding powder, and to add to their terror and despair, their own artillery captured from them, threw into their own ranks from its old position, ungrateful grape and canister, enfilading their breastworks, whizzing and plunging by air line and richochet; and at last bodies of cavalry fairly mounted their entrenchments and charged down the parapet, slashing and trampling them, and producing inexplicable confusion. They had no commanders—at least no orders—and looked in vain for some guiding hand to lead them out of a toil, into which they had fallen so bravely and so blindly. A few more volleys—a new and irresistible charge,— a shrill and warning command to die or surrender, and with a sullen and tearful impulse, five thousand muskets were flung upon the ground, and five thousand exhausted and impotent men were Sheridan's prisoners of war. Those who escaped he ordered the fiery Custer to pursue with brand and vengeance, and they were pursued far into the desolate forest, spent and hungry, many falling by the way of wounds or exhaustion, many pressed down by hoof or sabre-stroke, and many picked up in mercy and sent back to rejoin their brethren in bonds. Thus ended the splendid victory of Five Forks, the least bloody to the union troops, but the most successful, proportionate to numbers engaged, that was fought during the war. One man out of every three took a prisoner. Sheridan captured four cannon, an ambulance train and baggage teams, eight thousand muskets, and twenty-eight battle flags. Sheridan's loss only reached eight hundred. The enemy lost three thousand in killed and wounded. The scene at Gravelly Run meeting house at ten o'clock on Saturday night was one of the most solemn contrasts of the war. A little frame church planted among the pines, and painted white, with cool green window-shutters, held at its foot a gallery for the negroes, and at its head a varnished pulpit. Blood ran in little rills across the floor, and human feet treading in them, made indelible prints in every direction. The pulpit lamps were doing duty, not to shed holy light upon holy pages, but to show the pale and dusty faces of the beseeching; and as they moved in and out, the groans and cursing of the suffering replaced the gush of the peaceful hymns and the deep responses to the preacher's prayers. Federal and Confederate lay together, the bitterness of noon assuaged by the common tribulation of the night, and all the while came in the dripping stretchers, to place in this Golgotha new recruits for death and sorrow outside the portals. The scenes within were reiterated, except that the greatness of a starry night replaced the close and terrible arena of the church. Beneath the trees where the Methodist circuit-rider had tied his horse, and the urchins, during class meeting, had wandered away to cast stones at the squirrels, and measure strength at vaulting and running, the gashed and fevered lay irregularly, some soul going out at each whiff of the breeze in the tree tops; and the teams and surgeons, and straggling soldiers, and galloping orderlies, passed all night beneath the old and gibbeous moon and hushed stars, and by trickle of Gravelly Run, stealing off, afraid. But the wounded had no thought that night, the victory obsorbed all hearts."

While the men were asleep the night of the 1st, Captain Wilson awoke three men of his company and asked them to get up, take some pine torches and go back over the field where the sabre fight occurred and see if they could find any of the wounded of his company. After the torches had been secured and directions had been given, the little band started forth on their mission of love and mercy. The light from the torches looked weird and spectral in the darkness. Arriving at the stubble field the torchmen took distance of about twenty paces so as 'to cover as much ground as possible. Dead and wounded horses were seen by the score, and if there is anything that appeals strongly to human sympathy, it is the dumb, pleading look of a wounded horse.

Looking for the dead and wounded by torchlight is a sad and sepulchral calling. The pale stars glint and glimmer in the awful distance. The hour is pregnant with silence, save when it is broken by the wail or sigh of the dying. When the loved and lost lie at home on beds made soft by loving hands, with heads reposing on pillows moist with the tears of affection, it is sad enough; but, when far from home, with no canopy but the heavens, one searches in the long grass and unyielding stubble for the dead and the dying, it chills the blood and makes the bravest sick at heart. Welcome the sabre charge, the musketry and the cannon. Men look to that, knowing there is a certain chivalry in death, when sought in the smoke and conflict of battle, where brave men meet to submit their differences or the differences of their leaders to the stern arbi-

trament of deadly strife; but after the battle, when the
sun has gone down upon the battlefield, when the only
sound to break the solemn stillness is the moan of the
wounded and dying, it appeals to the higher and holier
impulses of manhood; and, as the flickering torch flashes
on the face of the dead, if it be an enemy, there is a silent
monitor in the heart that is quick to stifle resentment; if it
be a friend, an impulse to mourn the departed, and, remembering the comrade of the tent and field, to turn away
with a heart too full for utterance.

Whether friend or enemy, the causes that led to their
death were not unlike. Each believed himself right.
Men do not throw away their lives in such gallant action
unless they believe they are in the right. Mothers kissed
the sons who wore the gray with as deep affection as the
matrons whose sons put on the blue in their country's defense; and as they passed over the stubbornly contested
ground, with no eye but the All-seeing-eye and the stars,
and looked upon the blue and the gray lying rigid in death,
side by side, they felt that desolate homes in the north
will be no more desolate than the stricken homes in the
south. Men from the north have met foemen worthy of
their steel from the south, and the deadly carbine and the
terrible sabre have caused us to grope by the fitful light of
the torch to find the upturned faces of the northern and
southern dead, ghastly and frightful in the gloom of night,
and the startled cry of the night bird or the hoot of the
owl is their only requiem as they are hurried into the
trenches. The searching party returned without having
found those sought for, but they learned that the hospital
corps had cared for all the wounded. General Porter says:
"Five Forks was one of the most interesting techinal battles of the war; almost perfect in conception, brilliant in
execution, strikingly dramatic in its incidents, and pro-
ductive of immensely important results. General Grant's
headquarters had been moved out to Dabney's mills, where
the news of the victory reached him at nine o'clock p. m.
The General listened to the account of Sheridan's days

work, and, notwithstanding all his staff and escort were
indulging in wild demonstrations of joy, the great commander quietly walked into his tent, wrote a dispatch, sent
it to the wires, and cooly remarked: "I have ordered an
assault all along the lines." It is a well known fact that
the battle of Five Forks caused the evacuation of Richmond and Petersburg, and the surrender of Lee. On the
morning of the 2nd the Cavalry swung to the left, toward
Jetersville, General Sheridan anticipating that General Lee
would evacuate Petersburg and Richmond. The enemy
was not overtaken until near dark, when they were found
strongly intrenched. We went into camp directly in front
of the Confederate works. While going into camp the
enemy threw a few shells among the troopers, killing one
man and two horses. Just as the men were unsaddling
the horses, the brigade mail was brought into camp and
soon distributed. The numerous letters received by nearly
every one caused no little excitement, and soon the grim
veterans were sitting on the ground—tailor fashion—
drinking in the delicious news from home and friends.
While engaged in this pleasant occupation, and almost oblivious to all surroundings, a heavy volley from the Confederate works made the old pine woods ring. Before the
first echoe had died away, saddles were on the horses, and
when the shrill notes of the bugler "to horse" had sounded,
every one was in ranks ready for the foe. However, it
was a false alarm, as the volley was caused by the posting
of our vidette line. Soon all was quiet again. The artillery of the brigade kept up a continuous firing the entire
night. Although the battery was near the regiment, yet I
would be safe in asserting that our boys slept more soundly
than the "Johnnies." Early on the morning of the 3d, a
flanking party was put in motion, but it was soon learned
that the enemy had left. Skirmishing was kept up quite
briskly until Finlicomack Creek was reached, where the
enemy was found posted on the opposite side, and as the
stream was quite deep, two pieces of artillery were brought
forward, and while this was going on, a portion of the sec-

ond brigade secured a crossing above, and in a spirited charge, routed the enemy, capturing many prisoners. Our own brigade now took the advance and engaged in a wild and exciting race until Deep Creek was reached, where the advance ran into an ambuscade, in which Co. B lost one man killed, several wounded, and twelve horses killed. The ford had been blocked with felled trees, while on a low ridge, temporary works had been hastily thrown up. The troopers commenced a rapid fire on the works which prevented the enemy from doing any further damage. By this time the 1st New York—which had been attached to our brigade—succeeded in crossing above the ford, when they charged down on the enemy, capturing sixty prisoners. The New Yorkers did not keep the front long, but gave the road. The second Virginia were exceedingly gratified to once more be permitted to take the front, and enjoy some of the fun the others seemed to be having. Shortly after taking the front they encountered a body of rebel cavalry drawn up in line in a wheat-field, and such a race as the regiment took to get there at that line. They (the enemy) had no time to break into fours, and leave the field with some semblance of order, nor did they ever again form a line, and attempt to stop the union horsemen. Turning the prisoners over to a guard, the regiment kept the front, and at nightfall the entire brigade encountered a considerable body of infantry, posted in a wood and along fences. A portion of the brigade dismounted, and fought as infantry. The regiment advanced mounted, and as usual, the band playing "Hail Columbia." Under the severe fire of the long range guns of the enemy, it was hard to tell what they were playing. The enemy evacuated their position during the night, the brigade camping near where the bands so distinguished themselves by drawing most of the rebel fire. Marched all day of the 4th and went into camp in the evening. After all had retired to rest, orders came from General Sheridan to march with all possible dispatch back to Jetersville, as he had intercepted Lee. Marched all night, reaching Jetersville early on the morning of the 5th. Went into position on the left of the 5th corps. The Army of the Potomac was concentrating here, and as fast as they arrived, were placed in position by Gen. Sheridan, Gen. Meade being quite sick. Gen. Crook who was on the left with his cavalry was quite heavily engaged. This led Sheridan to believe that Lee was endeavoring to escape by his left flank. He therefore was anxious to attack with what force he had, the second and fifth corps and the cavalry. Just then Meade came out and assumed command, and, much to Sheridan's mortification, decided not to attack until the sixth corps arrived. A captured rebel letter was now brought to Sheridan, describing the condition of the Confederate forces. Sheridan sent it to Grant, with the following dispatch :

Jetersville, April 5, 3 p. m.

I send you the enclosed letter, which will give you an idea of the condition of the enemy and their whereabouts. I sent General Davies' brigade this morning around on my left flank. He captured at Paines Cross Roads five pieces of artillery, about 200 wagons, eight or nine battle flags, and a number of prisoners. The Second Army Corps is now coming up. I wish you were here yourself. I feel confident of capturing the army of Northern Virginia if we exert ourselves. I see no escape for Lee. I will put all my cavalry out on my left flank, except McKensie, who is on the right."

After receiving this message General Grant started for Sheridan's headquarters arriving there at midnight. He immediately reversed Meade's plans and ordered an advance at daylight of the 6th. Sheridan with the cavalry was sent west towards Deatonsville. About ten o'clock of the 6th, the first division struck the confederate column at Sailor's Creek, capturing sixteen pieces of artillery, four hundred wagons, and many prisoners. This rebel force proved to be Ewell's corps, and the cavalry at once threw themselves square across the roads, thus forcing them to entrench.

Custer's division went into position across Sailor's

Creek, executing the movement of, "on right into line," then moved forward until within a short distance of the confederate line. After other forces of the sixth corps had been placed in position, and of which we were ignorant at the time, the fiery Custer charged the confederate works. The Second Virginia occupied a position in a field, the rebel works being on the opposite side in the edge of a wood. He was somewhat protected from the direct fire of the enemy, by rising ground in front, although we were within easy carbine range. Our batteries were planted on a ridge across the creek to our rear, and they kept up a heavy fire over our heads, while we were sitting there on our horses, waiting for something, we knew not what.

While going into position considerable cheering had been done, which was always answered by the peculiar "rebel yell." The brigade band was doing good duty now, playing all the national airs. About noon Lieutenant George Freeman caught a rebel ball in his mouth, which knocked out six of that officer's teeth. He secured the ball and ivory, then sought the hospital. Two or three charges were made on the enemy's works on our left by two hundred mounted men, for no other purpose I suppose than to hold them in their works. About three o'clock in the afternoon the enemy had nearly ceased firing. At this juncture General Custer and staff rode through our lines, seemingly for the purpose of viewing the rebel works. As everything was then so silent, such expressions, as "they have evacuated," "skedaddled," and soon, was heard. Just then a volley from the rebels caused Custer's staff to hastily seek the rear, but not so with the golden-haired trooper; waving his sword, he shouted so all could hear, "the whole line charge, FORWARD, TROT, MARCH!" One of the artillerymen afterwards said, "that the grandest sight he ever witnessed was when that long line of cavalry moved forward. The carbines were all loaded with seven shots and when these had been exhansted, half the distance to the works had been covered. Every bugle was sounding forward, officers were shouting, the men cheering, and all were now eager to go on. When the order to cease firing and draw saber, had been given and obeyed, the line was close to the works. In front of the Second Virginia, the works were carried directly in front, the horses leaping over them, thus placing themselves and riders in the rear of the enemy, who were already surrendering. Where the works were too high, the troopers broke through the low places and swept down the rear, capturing—so General Sheridan says—between nine and ten thousand prisoners, including General Ewell and staff, and five other general officers. The prisoners were parked on the ground over which the charge had been made. The sixth corps assisted in hemming in the confederates, but they were off to our right, and at the time we did not know they were there. All camped at Sailor's Creek, and early the next morning a division of infantry took charge of the prisoners, and Sheridan was once more off with the cavalry after Lee. The prisoners were very short of rations, and many of them were supplied from our haversacks. Indeed, this was done to such an extent, as to cause ourselves to be on short rations for several days. On the morning of the 7th while the cavalry was filing out of camp, the route lay near the prisoners. As each band passed they were playing the national airs. The Confederates looked on and most of them seemed to enjoy the sight. Near the line of march a long, lank, mountain Confederate was standing looking on with a sullen appearance. Our brigade band, about this time, struck up the inspiriting air of "Dixie." Instantly the mountaineer gave the "rebel yell" and commenced dancing with all his might. His actions were so ludicrous that all who saw it, both Union and Confederate, enjoyed a hearty laugh, both sides cheering him.

A southern writer says: "And so the retreat rolls on. We are passing abandoned cannon, overturned and wrecked wagons, and their now useless contents belonging to the quartermasters; horses and mules dead or dying in the road. At night our march is lighted by the fires of burning wagons, and the hoarse roar of cannon and the rattle of small arms, before, behind and on our flanks are ever in our ears. The constant marching and fighting, without food or sleep, is rapidly thinning the ranks of this grand old army. Men who have stood by their flag since the beginning af the war now fall out of the ranks and are captured, simply because it is beyond their power of physical endurance to go any further."

General Sheridan, in his memoirs, says, that on the 7th he determined to block Lee's path with the cavalry and also endeavor to capture the rebel supply trains that he (Sheridan) had dispatched for by two of his scouts. The cavalry had swung to the left, leaving the rebel column to pursue their way. It was near midnight when the troopers went into camp. Early on the morning of the 8th Custer's division took the advance, with orders to capture the rebel supply trains before mentioned. It was well understood that the command was now in Lee's front, and in consequence, the men were in fine spirits. General Sheridan rode along the column toward the front, offering words of encouragement, and as stray shots were heard, and the gait increased to a trot, every man was in a high state of expectancy. It was near fiveo' clock in the evening when one of Sheridan's scouts was seen, waving his hat and shouting: "If there is an engineer in the ranks, come to the front." Two men of the First Virginia respond, and soon the shrill locomotive whistles were heard, which created the wildest enthusiasm in the ranks. It was nearly dark when our brigade crossed the railroad near Appomattox Station. In this dash over the railroad the division captured 500 wagons, forty pieces of artillery and 1000 prisoners.

A battery of confederate artillery hurled grape and canister down the road in such a manner that a little column of the regiment, who, under the direction of General Custer, started in a charge, was nearly half unhorsed.

The flashes of the enemy's guns, as reflected against the sky, resembled a furious storm of lightning. But the battery was captured by the brigade, after which camp was established between Lee's army and the captured property. This occurred at Appomattox Station, about fonr miles south of Appomattox village, where the army of General Lee had gone into camp. During the fore part of the night we were somewhat annoyed by a piece of confederate artillery, that kept throwing shells into camp. At each discharge of the piece the old familiar cry of "grab a root" could be heard all over camp.

APRIL 9TH, 1865.

About sunrise this morning the enemy attacked our skirmishers. The first division went to the front, while Custer's division fell back a short distance, and cooked and ate the last breakfast, that was ever eaten within hearing of rebel guns. The sharp and rapid firing of the union car-boniers, caused the humble meal to be hurriedly eaten, and amid much excitement.

But what long blue column was that seen approaching in the gray of that beautiful Sabbath morning. It was General Ord's 24th corps of infantry, and they were rapidly placed in line behind the cavalry screen. Our bugles sound "to horse," and as the division mount and fall into line, the wildest enthusiasm prevails. As they attempt to cross the road the way was blocked by the marching column of infantry, but soon there was a gap sufficient to let all the troopers through, by keeping well closed up, although some of the foot officers tried to stop the cavalry. Every one seemed to feel that the end was near, and we were in high spirts at the prospect of being in at the death of the rebellion. Our direction was toward the left flank of all that remained of the army of northern Virginia.

General Lee's army was not all disposed in battle array. Informed of the situation of affairs, General Custer said to the officer who brought the information, I will charge; show me the way." The entire division had been formed in column of squadron. A writer in the "Life and Deeds of General Grant" says of this occasion: "Custer's command presented a most striking and beautiful effect in color, as also in concentrated power for action. Following the general and his staff, and thrown to the morning breezes, floated not less than forty rebel battle flags captured from the enemy within ten days. These with division, brigade, and regimental colors of the command, made a picture as with flashing sabres they moved into view, at once thrilling and beautiful." As we moved rapidly forward toward the place from where we were to charge the camp, a battery of rebel artillery, paid us compliments with a few shells, but they passed harmlessly over our heads. These were the last rebel cannon we ever heard. Just as a double line had been formed, and the charge had sounded from headquarters, and the long line had started down the slope, three or four horsemen were seen emerging from the woods toward the camp, the leader waving something white over his head. Colonel Briggs, of the seventh Michigan met the party, when they asked for the "general commanding." Custer was pointed out, and the Confederates rode rapidly toward him. General Custer said, "I am not in sole command upon this field, but I will report the request to Gen-Sheridan, and I can only stop the charge upon the announcement of an unconditional surrender." Custer then sent his chief of staff back with the flag of truce party to see if the surrender was all right. Gen. Lee could not be found just then, and the party was directed to General Longstreet and Gordon, who assured the "chief of staff" that an unconditional surrender of the army of Northern Virginia was intended. When the staff officer returned, General Custer at once started for the rebel camp, using the flag of truce the staff officer returned with, and which is now in Mrs. Custer's possession. Custer soon found Longstreet and Gordon, and received from them the assurance that they had surrendered to General Grant. During this exciting period, which occupied at least two hours time, the entire force of Union horsemen were silently awaiting orders. Word had been passed along the line that a surrender was one of the possibilities, but the report

did not obtain much credence in the ranks. The silence
was regarded as ominous, for we were momentarily expecting to move forward. But hark! listen at the cheers to
our left, and now looking that way 'we see the fiery Custer
riding down the line as if mad, his long yellow hair and
red neck-tie streaming in the wind. He was wildly waving his hat, and shouting at the top of his voice: "General
Lee has surrendered his whole army." The change from
anxiety and doubt to a certainty of the result was now
assured. How can I describe the scenes that followed!
Men leap from their horses, toss caps and hats high in air,
shout and cheer until exhausted. Across field and wood
to the right and left resound the mighty joy of the Union
army. Brave men clasp each other, and weep, and sing,
and dance and pray. It was worth our entire term of service to have been there at the death of the rebellion. The
army that was the pride and hope of the Confederacy now
lay helpless at our feet. Victory after victory had followed us in such rapid succession, that to be led against
the enemy was sure to add another laurel to our banners;
but now the gallant army of Northern Virginia was no
more, the rebellion hopelessly crippled, and we knew
that the war was virtually over. As all this comes to the
minds of the men, they again and again break out in cheering, and the grand chorus rolls along the lines. It was
glorious to have been there. The file of the Confederate
army were glad that the war was over, glad they had fired
their last shot, and rejoiced to think they could soon return to their homes. But how different was the return of
the boys in gray and that of the boys in blue. The former were half-starved, poorly clad, no money, homes
ruined, land almost a waste, whipped and conquered on
every side. Verily, they suffered for the sins of their
leaders. How different was the reception of the boys in
blue. Their return was characterized by the firing of
guns, the ringing of bells. Reverberations of cannon were
heard in every city, town and village throughout the land.
Millions of flags danced to the movements of the wind.

But in all our joy there at the time, it was not the mere exultation over a fallen foe. In those ever memorable hours, there was a gentle spirit of clemency diffused among all, that just now became consciously present. The particulars of the formalities of the surrender were about as follows: Grant did not reach Appomattox village until about 1 o'clock p. m. The famous village consisted of less than a dozen dwellings, standing on some rising ground. As the hero of the Union armies came up to the village with his staff, they were met by Sheridan. General Grant said: "How are you, Sheridan?" "First rate, thank you. How are you?" Grant's tone and manner plainly indicated that he was perfectly satisfied with the position of affairs. "Is Lee over there?" asked Grant. "Yes, he is in that brick house," said Sheridan. "Let's go over," and then all started. They went to the house of Wilbur McLean; the only person entering there was General Grant. The others remained in the front yard for awhile, out of consideration for General Lee. Shortly after all were invited in, when the terms of surrender were signed. There were fifteen persons in the room at the time the papers were signed. Frances A. Burr, the historian, says of the occasion: "Sheridan was as marked a figure in face, pose, expression, dress, as was Lee himself. The confederate commander was in full uniform, with sword and equipment, all of which were nearly or quite new. The condition of General Lee's and Colonel Marshall's clothing was explained by the fact that the activity of Sheridan's cavalry in attacking their baggage train had compelled officers to select the most needed articles and leave the rest to be destroyed, rather than have them fall into our hands. Sheridan had fallen unconsciously, as the generals conversed, into a strikingly dramatic attitude. The others sat or lounged with the quiet of intense interest. Sheridan's attitude was that of the soldier who expected to be called suddenly to action. It was that of his mood, for during the whole marvelous pursuit in which he had led the attack and the advance, he had been wrought up to the loftiest

pitch of endurance, courage, foresight, and vital movement.   Indeed, he could almost have stood as a model of
Fate, so alert and unyielding was his attitude.   Cavalry
boots, rusty and soiled, covered half his short, sturdy
limbs.   He wore the full uniform of his rank, with sash,
belt and sword.   His short, broad, sturdy form stood posed
in strength.   The head and face were remarkable.   Beardless, except a close, dark mustache, its striking lines and
forms were seen most clearly.   The expression was that of
set, fixed force and determination.   There was a tremen-
dous degree of vitality in the notable figure—a great
amount of intellectual reserve in the lined countenance.

"With close-cropped head and beardless face the height,
depth and breadth of the general's cranium were felt by
all.   The jaw, strong and well defined, was not heavy.
There was not a gross line to be seen.   The Irish gray eyes
followed searchingly every facial movement of the Confederate leader.   That the brain behind that fixed, impassive
sternness was at work could be understood by one glance.
Standing 'at attention,' with heavy sheathed cavalry sabre
resting on his left arm, Sheridan was indeed the embodied
vigilance of the Union army.   That morning found ample
cause for vigilance.   The bold, ardent, ceaseless pursuit
which had followed Five Forks, and especially marked the
advance from Jettersville, had been rewarded by the securing of the west ridge beyond Lee's position and by the
rapid alignment of infantry across the only road by which
Lee could move.

"The Confederates were enmeshed and knew it.   The
work of disabling guns and destroying military property
was going on.   Custer in the advance was as usual aching
to attack and capture more guns.   His division secured
the last taken by actual combat in Virginia.   It was a
wonderfully picturesque sight, for the topographical fea-
tures permitted a full display of our strengthening and en-
circling lines, as well as the hurried movements of the gallant enemy within the fateful circles forming about them.
Lieutenant General Gordon, with his corps, faced Sheridan

NATHANIEL SISSON.

A Bugler who sounded the last charge at Appomattox

and Ord, fretting with the impatience of valor. It was his desire to cut his way through, and the veterans behind him would at his word have tried it. Lee knew, however, that such sacrifice was useless, and took pains to forward to General Sheridan a copy of his letter to Grant, calling for a conference to arrange the terms of surrender. Sheridan received this at least an hour before Grant did, with information, also, of the short truce allowed by Meade, whose army was steadily pressed to its position. Sheridan at once road down to meet Gordon, accompanied by Merritt, Custer, Irvin and others." How the news was received by the 24th corps can be faintly seen by the following incident. Captain Ricks, a staff officer, was present when the first news of the surrender came to them. The cheering frightened his horse, which dashed off at full speed, heading toward a column of marching infantry. A thought flashed through the riders mind that this would be a good opportunity to carry the news to the rest of the corps; so giving free rein to the excited horse, he rode on. The column opened out for the horse and rider, and he shouted out the news as he sped on. Captain Ricks says: "As I was speeding through one of the regiments, I caught the bright face of a soldier leaning out as far as possible into the road to catch the message that fell from my lips. "What is it? What is it?" he anxiously shouted. "Lee has surrendered his whole army to Grant" was the reply. Clear and loud, above all the voices, and quick as the message fell upon his ear, was his answer: "Great God! you're the man I've been looking for the last four years."

The following little incident is given in the language of General Horace Porter. After the terms of surrender had been signed, and the officers present had been introduced, General Lee said: "I have a thousand or more of your men as prisoners, General Grant, a number of them officers, whom we have required to march along with us for several days. I shall be glad to send them into your lines as soon as it can be arranged, for I have no provisions for them. I have, indeed, nothing for my own men. They have been living for the last few day, principally upon parched corn, and we are badly in need of both rations and forage. I telegraphed to Lynchburg, directing several train loads of rations to be sent on by rail from there, and when they arrive I should be glad to have the present wants of my men supplied from them."

All eyes were now turned upon Sheridan, for he had captured these trains with his cavalry the night before, near Appomattox Station. The cavalry was always there—wherever that might be. After Lee had ridden away from the McLean house, there became a desire among the Union officers to secure some relic of the memorable occasion. Sheridan shared this feeling with the rest, but his desire took a generous turn, for he gave McLean twenty dollars in gold for the little table on which the agreement was written, and at once gave it to Custer, who started to camp bearing it upon his shoulder.

The cavalry remained in line all day, and late in the evening went into camp. On the 10th the return march was commenced, and, strange to relate, the men seemed unusually despondent. But little conversation was indulged in, every one seemed to be busy with his own thoughts. Was it because their grim occupation was gone? Certainly not. As the sombre march of that gloomy, dark and rainy day occurs to my mind, it recalls the words of Shakespeare:

> Oh, farewell!
> Farewell the neighing steed and the shrill trump,
> The spirit-stirring drum, the ear-piercing fife,
> The royal banner; and all quality,
> Pride, pomp, and circumstance of glorious war.
> And O, you mortal engines, whose rude throats
> The immortal Jove's dread clamors counterfeit,
> Farewell."

General Grant and staff marched with us that day, but owing probably to the low spirits of the troopers, no attenion was given the "silent man" although this was the first time the Virginia brigade at least had even seen him. In the evening we camped at Prospect Station, on the Southside railroad. On the 11th the march was continued very slow, and on going into camp the mail was distributed to us, the second received in six weeks. This had the effect of somewhat restoring the "riders" to their normal condition. Soldiers are like children. They can not remain in sullen spirits very long. It was only nine miles to Burkesville Junction which ended our march of the 12th. The roads were again in a miserable condition for marching, and our horses were almost worn out from over exertion. To the noble endurance of these animals may largely be attributed the fact that Lee surrendered when he did, for the wiley Confederate was making desperate efforts to reach Lynchburg. A large ambulance train of wounded, mostly cavalry, came in from the front this evening and were properly cared for. Also a train of supplies and forage came into camp from Petersburg; these were badly needed, for we had been on starvation rations since the fight at Sailor's Creek, and where the Second Virginia, to the writer's knowledge, so generously divided their small stock of rations with the prisoners they guarded that night.

The 13th was another dark and rainy day, and at Nottoway C. H., after a march of only twelve miles, the division again camped for the night. The announcement that we will rest here a few days, was received with general satisfaction. Clothing also reached us at this time, which enabled many of the boys to lay aside their butternut clothes, which, of necessity, they had been compelled to wear. Squads of returning Confederates were passing camp all evening, apparently well satisfied at the turn affairs had taken.

General Custer started for Washington with thirty-seven rebel flags captured by the division within the last eight days. The 14th was to witness the raising of the old flag over Fort Sumpter, and our battery fired two hundred guns in honor of the occasion.

Early on the morning of the fifteenth we were

aroused by the patter of rain on our little tents and as the day of the 14th had been so pleasant, a great many had neglected to cut the essential ditch around the tents, and in listening to the patter of rain upon the roof, the water had been silently and surely working its way under the beds, which were made on the ground. However, the boys consoled themselves with the reasonable conclusion that it might have been worse. During the day the news of the assassination of President Lincoln reached camp, and soon the company streets were thronged by eager crowds discussing the awful tragedy, and all were eager to learn the particulars. So much had occurred within the last two weeks that the mind could scarcely comprehend it all. To again put the boys out of humor, rations had become exceedingly short.

Plenty were within reach, but there seemed to be an over supply of red tape. Semi-starvation does not produce good humor, and the humblest private in the ranks knows that when the rations were in sight, as it were, there was something wrong if they were not issued. Owing to this fact the command remained in camp, with signs of a storm brewing among the troops. On the 17th the rations were issued. On the 18th the column reached Petersburg and camped one mile west of the city, on the ground fought over by the Sixth corps on the second. Several fine residences around this spot had been destroyed, but the beautiful lawns and other outward appearances gave silent evidence of that outward adornment characteristic of Virginia residences.

This day there was given to every officer and enlisted man of General Custer's division, the following order printed in beautiful colors and which to-day adorn the homes of many of the bold riders and their families:

Headquarters Third Cavalry Division, }
Appomattox Court House, Va., April 9, 1865. }
Soldiers of the Third Cavalry Division:—With profound gratitude toward the God of battles, by whose blessings our enemies have been humbled and our arms rendered triumphant, your commanding general avails himself of

this, his first opportunity, to express to you his admiration of the heroic manner in which you have passed through the series of battles which to-day resulted in the surrender of the enemys entire army. The record established by your indomitable courage, is unparalleled in the annals of war. Your prowess has even won for you the respect and admiration of your enemies. During the last six months, although in most instances confronted by superior numbers, you have captured from the enemy in open battel, one hundred and eleven pieces of field artillery, sixty-five battle flags, and upwards of ten thousand prisoners of war, including seven general officers. Within the past ten days and included in the above, you have captured forty-six pieces of artillery and thirty battle flags. You have never lost a gun—never lost a color—and have never been defeated. And notwithstanding the numerous engagements in which you have born a prominent part, including those memorable battles of the Shenandoah, you have captured every piece of artillery the enemy has dared to open upon you. The near approach of peace renders it improbable that you will again be called upon to undergo the fatigues of the toilsome march, or the exposure of the battlefield; but, should the assistance of keen blades, yielded by your sturdy arms, be required to hasten the coming of that glorious peace for which we have been so long contending, the general commanding is proudly confident that in the future, as in the past, every demand will meet with a willing and hearty response.

Let us hope that our work is done, and that, blessed with the comfort of peace, we may soon be permitted to enjoy the pleasure of home and friends. For our comrades who have fallen let us ever cherish a grateful remembrance. To the wounded, and those who languish in southern prisons, let our heartfelt sympathies be tendered. And now speaking for myself alone, when the war is ended, and the task of the historian begins; when those deeds of daring, which have rendered the name and fame of the Third Cavalry Division imperishable, are inscribed on the bright pages of our country's history, I only ask that my name may be written as that of the commander of the Third Cavalry Division,

G. A. CUSTER, Brevet Major General.

A. ADJUTANT GENERAL BARNHARDT.

The few days passed in camp here were pleasant. All the works in and around the city were viewed with much interest. The Confederate works looked quite formidable, but were much defaced by shot and shell. Nearly all the soldier quarters were underground, and from all appearances the Johnnies passed an uncomfortable winter. Several sutlers arrived about this time, and exposed their goods for sale at such exhorbitant prices, that the long pent up wrath of the soldiers toward this enterprising class of merchants was somewhat appeased by the destruction of their tents and the consequent loss of some of their goods. The large majority of the men were opposed to these acts of vandalism, and had nothing to do with them, yet when the raid was made on our own brigade sutler, General Tibbetts then in temporary command, promiscuously arrested every man found on the streets at that hour, 10 p. m. Three such arrests were made from the writer's company, neither of whom had anything to do with the raid. With others, they were hurriedly taken nearly three miles from the camp, and subjected to most inhuman treatment, such as depriving them of food and even water, and being forced to walk until exhausted. I am indebted to Felix J. Baxter, a member of Company H, an educated and refined gentleman, now a resident of Sutton, West Virginia, for the particulars of these unwarranted proceedings of this inhuman officer. The men were kept away thirty-six hours, without the knowledge of either the company officers, or the file. Immediately after this the general had business in Washington.

On the 23d, much to the surprise of the troopers, an order was issued for the arming of all the unarmed men. The general supposition was that we were to march to the rear of General Johnson, who had not yet surrendered. Early on the morning of the 24th the bugles in all directions were sounding "boot and saddle," and the "general call." This meant marching. When a camp near a town is to be broken, hundreds of persons white and black gather there to secure what the soldiers may leave in the way of clothing, etc. On this occasion the camp was thronged, and as the weather had become quite warm they were well repaid. At eight o'clock General Sheridan and staff pass camp, and soon the entire cavalry are in column filing out the Boydton plank road. A halt was made at Dinwiddie C. H., and some of us had the pleasure of visiting the place where we were engaged dismounted on March 31st.

The march was continued, and on the 25th the Nottoway river was crossed on an old and very rickety bridge, and in the evening went into camp near the north fork of the Meherrin river. The next morning that stream was safely forded. The weather was delightful, the road cool and shady, all nature was becomingly dressed in the garb of early spring. Even the grim warriors appreciated the beautiful surroundings, and gathered boquets of rare wild flowers. It is with light hearts and buoyant spirits, at five o'clock in the evening, that the column enters the pretty little village of Boydton. All the bands were playing "Hail Columbia!" The entire population of the village repaired to the main street to view the cavalcade. Went into camp near the college grounds. On the 27th the march was resumed. Great crowds of people, white and black, thronged the road and camp. The joy of the negroes was great, and they afforded considerable amusement for the troopers, who now, more than at any other period of the war, could see fun in almost anything.

At noon the column reached the Staunton river and a temporary bridge was made from boats which had been secured by Major Young and General Sheridan's scouts. On the 28th, marched to near South Boston, on Dan River, not far from the North Carolina line, where intelligence of Johnston's surrender was received. On the 29th the command started on the return march, taking another route, arriving in Petersburg, May 5th. All the houses passed on this return march displayed a white flag in token of surrender. The natives also intended the flag to represent that the days of foraging were over, and that no more chickens were for sale. Remained in camp near

Petersburg until the 10th, when the division started to march to Washington. While in camp here, Gen. Custer's wife visited him. She was a beautiful and accomplished lady and a fine equestrian, and seemed to be a fitting companion for such a brave officer as our idolized commander. Mrs. Custer remained with the division until it was disbanded. General Custer always wore a crimson necktie, which consisted of a strip of red merino goods about six inches wide and one yard long. This was worn around the neck, looped once, and the ends tucked beneath the vest. While at Petersburg Mrs. Custer suggested the idea of the entire division wearing this jaunty affair, and the suggestion was at once concurred in, but the goods could not be secured in Petersburg or Richmond.

During the march to Washington we were much gratified in being permitted to march through the city of Richmond, and many other places made famous by the war, among which might be mentioned Slaughter Mountain, Cedar Grove, Bull Run, and other noted places.

On the 16th the cavalry arrived at Alexandria and camped on Federal Hill in full view of the capital city of the United States. The scene of Colonel Ellsworth's death was visited by about every soldier of the command. The stairs where the Colonel met his death had been nearly cut to pieces by relic hunters. While in camp here, the order appointing the 23rd and 24th days of May for the grand review of all the armies assembling around Washington was issued. A few days after arriving at Alexandria the camp was moved to near the south end of the long bridge, one mile from Washington. While going into camp here, quite an amusing incident occurred which demonstrated the fact that the boys did not know much about the ebb and flow of the tide. Some of them pitched their camp on a beautiful beach near the Potomac River. The tide came up and cut them off from the main camp. When they realized their situation, they hastily shouldered their traps and waded out. This afforded rich amusement for those who witnessed the occurrence. One

of them remarked that was the first time he ever saw a
river run up stream. On Sunday, May 21st, the entire
division marched through Washington to a camp near the
historic village of Bladensburg, six miles from the capital.
While passing through the city General Sheridan was observed standing on the verandah of a house, and was warmly
greeted by the troopers, but while passing down Pennsylvania avenue Gen. Custer viewed the column from Willard's
Hotel, and at sight of him, such cheers were given by each
passing squadron, as fully demonstrated the love and admiration with which the Third Cavalry Division regarded their
commander. Mrs. Custer stood nearthe general and no doubt
very properly thought that some of the cheers were intended for her. Before the review the division was twice
more marched through the city and back again; of course
this was done for display, but by whose orders it does not
appear. In camp great preparations were being made for
the grand review. The red neck-ties had been secured,
clothing was carefully cleaned for the occasion, arms and
equipments brightened, and above all, the horses had been
given the best of care. The event, it was believed, would
be the crowning affair in our soldier lives, for after that
we expected to be mustered out. The only thing needed
to give the troopers the freedom of the city was a pair of
shoulder straps. And as these were quite cheap, the like
of the number of second lieutenants of cavalry was never seen
on the streets of Washington. No more nobler or kinder man
than Lt. Col. Allen ever lived, and, as it was said of Caesar,
"He knew all his men." When the Colonel would meet
dozens of lieutenants of his own regiment whom he knew
had not been promoted, he could do nothing less than
smile and pass on.

Preparations for the review were going forward on a
grand scale within the city. The most beautiful arrangements were the stands arranged for the states. Seats were
erected wherever space would admit. Pennsylvania avenue was one mass of bunting. At length the eventful
day (the 23d) arrived and our division was honored by

being placed at the head of the column. It was not later than nine o'clock, when, with bands playing and colors flying, we marched down Capital Hill in close column, by platoons, and filing up Pennsylvania avenue, the beauty and grandeur of the scene was revealed in all its splendor. Every inch of standing room on the sidewalks and cross streets were packed with people. Verandas and house-tops were at a premium. Two miles of police and patrols were necessary to keep the crowd back. Flags and hand-kerchiefs were waved, clapping of hands, cheering and other demonstrations of the excited throng greeted us on every side. Custer's division of three thousand men, with their crimson ties, received quite an ovation all along the line, and more particularly at the Treasury building and at the Ohio stand, where beautiful flowers were showered into the ranks by fair maidens and children. The review-ing stand was located in front of the president's mansion, and here the crowd was the greatest and the most demon-strative. After passing in review, the cavalry galloped back G street, went to camp, divested themselves of arms and accoutrements, walked back to the city and helped swell the crowd. In the afternoon the army of the Potomac passed in review and the solid tramp of infantry and the rumble of artillery occupied the entire afternoon. This army showed their splendid discipline, by their regular and steady marching, and their straight and compact lines elicited the admiration of all.

On the 24th General Sherman's army of veterans passed in review, and as this was their first appearance in the city, their coming was looked to with much interest. This army more fully exemplified to the people, an army on a march in an enemy's country, as they were accom-panied by the usual accessories, viz: led horses with camp equipage, negroes leading dilapidated mules with their camp goods on their backs, all of which afforded great amusement for the people. A few days after the review—which has gone down in history as one of the grandest affairs of the kind the country ever witnessed—the third cavalry division was called in line to bid farewell to General Custer, who had been ordered to Texas. The general and his wife rode along the front of the line at a gallop, the general waving his hat in token of farewell.

That was the last we ever saw of General Custer, the golden-haired trooper, and one of the most dashing, daring and gallant cavalry leaders, whose genius had been developed by the war. After the great review, and after our leader had left us, we looked anxiously forward to the time when we would be mustered out of service. The enterprising news boys on coming into camp would cry out, "here's your daily, all about mustering out the troops.", This announcement would generally sell the papers,—and "sell" the troopers also. But all things finally come to an end; and when the first few days of balmy June had been added to our term of service, an order was issued for the first Second and Third West Virginia Cavalry, to proceed by the B. & O. R. R. to Wheeling, West Virginia, for the purpose of being mustered out. It was with joyful hearts that the third brigade marched into the capital city and formed on Maryland Avenue, squadron front.

It was late in the evening of the 17th when our horses were all on board, after which another section of train, with a mixture of passengers and box cars, held the men. In due time all arrived safely in Wheeling, horses were saddled, and all marched over the bridge and went into camp on Wheeling Island. Hardly had the command pitched camp when squads were seen going over to Bridgeport, and experienced the proud satisfaction of standing on the soil of our own beloved state of Ohio, or God's country as the boys commonly termed it. While in camp here the writer received from a lady the following poem, which had been clipped from the Pittsburgh Dispatch:

"THE HEROES OF THE CUSTER TIE."

[Dedicated to the Third Cavalry Division.]

The heroes ot the "Custer Tie,"
The lads who love the crimson dye,
　　In all Columbia's glorious land,
　　Where all are brave, there's not one band
Like those who wear the "Custer Tie."

When the fierce charge the trumpets tell,
Their eyes flash fire, their bosoms swell—
　　With rifles cocked and gleaming sword,
　　Like rivers through its outbanks poured,
Rush Custer's lads with deafening yell.

No pause for them when bullets fly,
And battle's clouds obscures the sky ;
　　Some slain, some wounded, fill the dust ;
　　The rest are maddened—onward burst—
And startled foemen fall or fly.

The rider's valor gives new force
In battle's shock to his swift horse—
　　Like eagles sweeping on their prey,
　　Or like the vivid lightning's ray ;
The squadron dashes on its course.

The banners were by proud foes borne,
The guns from field and fortress torn,
　　Where are those flags which once waved high?
　　Where is that dread artillery?
They now those heroes camps adorn.

Well may they shout—well may they brag,
Who never lost one gun, or flag.
　　Who never heard a hostile gun,
　　But quick surrounded, seized and won,
The piece within their lines they drag.

For gallant Custer's boys a cheer,
For honor, will and daring fear,
　　They rushed the bravest, and the first,
　　When at the foemen's ranks they burst,
And spread before them flight and fear.

Famed warriors of the Custer tie,
The time of peace and home is nigh,
   Wont the dear ones you left at home
   With joy and pride around you come
And clasp those with the crimson tie?

Give those for rank and wealth who wear
The pile of gold, the glittering star,
   We'll wear our badge of bravery,
   Our brave divisions crimson tie,
In peace, in war, at home, afar.

And should our country e'er demand
For other wars your veteran band,
   The heroes of the "Custer Tie"
   Prepared to conquer, or to die,
Around the stars and stripes they'll stand.

I had three hundred copies of this poem printed, and sold them over camp. I would usually get a squad around me, read the poem aloud, then offer them for sale. On one occasion when reading it to a squad of the First Virginia, I noticed one man near me who listened to the reading, with interest until I came to the line,

   "And should our country e'er demand
   For other wars our veteran band"—

when with a disgusted look he turned to leave, at the same time remarking,—"I'll be d—d if they get this veteran?" The Jew clothiers of Wheeling reaped quite a harvest in selling clothing to the men. The boys would buy entire suits pack them in a valise, put their names on the valise, and leave them with the merchants until pay day.

These enterprising and grasping people kept open stores all day on one Sabbath, which was contrary to law. For this they gladly paid fifty dollars fine each. They could well afford to do so.

At last, on the fourth day of July, 1865, at 10 o'clock a. m., in one of the streets of Wheeling, our freedom papers were placed in our hand, together with what Uncle Sam owed us, in the way of crisp, new and bright greenbacks. It was very amusing to see the boys walk up to the window as their names were called and receive their final discharges. Several hundred citizens and soldiers were spectators, and as the veterans, who had faced death hundreds of times, realized that they were once more free men, they were so overcome with emotion that many of them, by their ludicrous actions, kept the audience in roars of laughter.

Here let us pause. Near twenty-eight years have passed, with their summers and winters. Dear nature has kissed alike the graves of Union and Confederate, and her robes of verdure or of snow, are the proofs of loving impartiality. But memories live. The boys came home again—but alas! not all of them. As Francis A. Durivage so simply and pathetically sings:

"There hangs a sabre, and there a rein,
With rusty buckle and green curb chain;
A pair of spurs on the old gray wall,
And a moldy saddle—well, that is all.

Come out to the stable, it is not far,
The moss-grown door is hanging ajar;
Look within! there's an empty stall,
Where once stood a charger—and that is all.

The good black steed came riderless home,
Flecked with blood-drops, as well as foam,
Do you see that mound where the dead leaves fall?
The good black horse pined to death—that's all.

All? O, God! it is all I can speak;
Question me not—I am old and weak,
His saddle and sabre hang on the wall,
And his horse pined to death—I have told you all.

A PARTIAL LIST OF ENGAGEMENTS PARTICI-
PATED IN BY THE REGIMENT.

Operated against guerrillras in the Guyandotte and Mud River valleys, December 16th, 1861 to April 28th, 1862; Huntersville, January 4th; Paintsville, Kentucky, January 7th; Dry Fork, January 8th, 1862; Lewisburg, May 10th; near White Sulphur, May 12th; Callahan's Station, May 16th; destruction of bridge over Cow Pasture River, May 17th; Battle Lewisburg, May 23rd. Many minor engagements in the counties of Greenbriar, Fayette, Mercer, Raleigh and Wyoming, during the months of June, July and August, 1862; Barboursville, West Virginia, September 8th; expedition to Greenbriar county, November 9th to 13th; Sinking Creek, November 26th.

1863.

Third action at Lewisburg, May 2nd; Summerville, May 12th; Loup Creek, June 27th; Raleigh C. H., July 4th; Coal River Glades, July 5th; Shady Springs, July 14th; Abbs Valley, July 17th; Wytheville, July 18th; Fayetteville, July 28th; Rocky Gap, August 25th; Millpoint, November 5th; Big Sewell Mountain, December 12th.

1864.

Grassy Lick, May 7th; Abbs Valley, May 8th; Cove Mountain Gap, May 10th; Dublin, May 12th; Jenkins River, May 14th; Salt Pond Mountain Gap, May 18th; Muddy Creek, May 29th; Buffalo Gap, June 9th; Newport, June 10th; near Lexington, June 11th, Buchanan, June 13th; Otter Gap, June 15th; New London, June 16th; Diamond Hill, June 17th a. m.; Lynchburg, June 17th and 18th; Campbell C. H., June 19th; Liberty, June 20th; Bonsack, June 21st; Salem, June 22nd; Mountain Cove on Catawba Creek, June 22nd (evening); near White Sulphur Springs June 23d. Transferred to Shenandoah Valley—Stephenson's Depot, July 20th; Newtown, July 22nd; Kearnstown, July 23rd; Winchester,

July 24th; Bunker Hill, July 25th; Martinsburg, July 25th; Chambersburg, July 30th; Moorefield, August 7th; Williamsport, August 27th: Martinsburg, August 31st; Bucklestown, September 2nd; Bunker Hill, September 3d and 4th; Carter's Farm, September 5th; on Valley Pike each day of September 13, 14, 15, 16, 17, 18th; Opequan or Winchester, September 19th; between Winchester and Fisher's Hill, September 21st; Fisher's Hill, September 22nd; Mount Jackson, September 23rd; Timberville or Broadway, September 24th; Forrest Hill, September 24th p. m.; Weyer's Cave, September 26th and 27th; Cedar Creek, October 19th; Milford, Luray Valley, October 26th; Ninevah, Front Royal Pike, October 12th; Rude's Hill, November 23rd; Liberty Mills, December 22; near Gordonsville, December 23rd.

1865.

Mount Crawford, March 1st; Waynesboro, March 2nd, Dinwiddie C. H., March 31st: Five Forks, April 1st; Deep Creek, April 3rd; Sailor's Creek, April 6th; Appomattox Station, April 8th; APPOMATTOX, APRIL 9TH.

DEATH ROLL.

List of deaths of enlisted men of the Second West Virginia Cavalry Volunteers from the date of organization to the date of muster out, June 30th, 1865:

Edward A. Thomas, Sergeant Major, killed in action at Winchester, Virginia, July 26th, 1864. John R. James, Hospital Stewatt, died September 4th, 1862, at Gauley Bridge, Virginia.

COMPANY A.

Theodore Dunbar, Corporal, killed in action at Deep Creek, Virginia, April 3rd, 1865. Thomas A. Singer, Bugler, killed at Bunker Hill, September, 1864. David C. Bailey, Private, died October, 1863, while undergoing sentence of G. C. M. at Camp Chase, Ohio. Summer F. Chase, Private, killed at Cove Mountain, May 10th, 1864. Thomas B. King, Private, died July, 1864, at Gallipolis, Ohio. J. W. McCormick, Private, killed at Cove Mountain, May 10, 1864. Thomas McMasters, Private, died April 28th, 1865, at Ft. Monroe, Virginia, of wounds received at Five Forks. Charles R. Russell, Private, killed at Deep Creek, April 3rd, 1865. John W. Robertson, Private, killed Front Royal, Nov. 26, '64; Wm. M. Reynolds, Private, killed Shenandoah, Aug. 1864; Joseph Radford, Private, killed by pistol shot at hands of W. H. Crouser, Dec. 28, 1862; Thomas C. Skiles, Private, died Sept. 28, 1862, consumption.

COMPANY B.

John N. Stewart, Commissary Sergeant, died while prisoner of war at Belle Isle, date unknown; Martin Van Every, Sergeant, died April 20, 1862, Charleston, W. Va.; Braxton P. Reeves, Sergeant, killed at Barboursville, W. Va., September 8, 1863; Irwin R. Hailey, Corporal, killed September 5, 1864;

Edward Mitchell, blacksmith, died April 30, 1863, Hospital, Fayetteville, Va.; Thos. H. Tomlinson, Musician, found dead Sept. 1863, Camp Piatt; James H. Butler, Private, drowned, Oct. 11, 1863, Ohio river; E. Blankenship, Private, died Oct. 7, 1862, at Gallipolis, O; Lewis Conway, Private, died Jan. 16, 1864, home of pneumonia; Edmond Davis, Private, died, June 16, 1863, Ironton, O.; Henry H. Henshaw, Private, died from wounds received at Wytheville, Va., July 18, 1863; George Hoffman, Private, died from wounds received at Lewisburg, Va., May 18, 1863; Henry Jones, Private, died from wounds, Sept. 10, 1864; Amos McKee, Private, killed in action at Hager's Hill, Ky., Jan. 7, 1862; Elias Spencer, Private, killed at Deep Creek, Va., April 3, 1865.

COMPANY C.

Enoch L. Dye, Sergeant, killed near Raleigh C, H., July 14, 1863; John W. Swallow, Corporal, died, Jan. 4, 1864, Charleston, W. Va., of typhoid fever; Baldwin Cox, Private, died March 27, 1862 at home of consumption; B. S. Hamilton, Private, died July 15, 1863 of wounds received at Raleigh C. H., July 14, 1863; Hudson Hoskins, Private, killed, Newport, Va. June 20, 1864; Albert W. Leonard, Private, killed on Jennies Creek, Ky, Jan. 7, 1862; Marion McMillin, Private, killed Mountain Cove Va., June 22, 1864; Levi J. Mercer, Private, died April 9, 1865, Frederick, Md.; Saml. M. Stypes, Private, died Dec. 2, 1864, Annapolis, Md.; James H. Shreves, Private, died Sept. 20, 1862, Gallipolis, O.; William Smith, Private, died Jan. 27, 1863, Guyandotte, Va.; Stephen Ullum, Private, died Nov. 14, 1862, Point Pleasant, Va.; Jeremiah M. Boyd, 1st Lieutenant, killed near Carters Farm, Sept. 1864.

COMPANY D.

John Nunnemaker, Sergeant, killed at Petersburg, Va., March 28, 1865; David C. Lowry, Corporal, died March 28, 1863, Camp Piatt, Va.; George F. Black, Private, died July 28, 1862, Vinton county, O.; Granville C. Bobo, Private, died March 23

1863, Charleston, W. Va.; Wm. F. Burgess, Private, died Feb. 15, 1864, Charleston. W. Va.; John Hanning, Private, died of wounds received at Cove Gap, Va., May 10, 1864; Chas. P. Herald, died of wounds received at Cove Gap, Va., May 10, 1864; Granville Jones, Private, died at Andersonville, Ga.; John J. Jackson, killed in action at Branson's Farm, Va., Sept. 5, 1864; Courtney Lowry, Private, died August 12, 1863, Vinton Co. O., of typhoid fever: William Remy, Private, died June 28, 1864 at Loup Creek, Va., of typhoid fever; Benjamin Stephens, Private, died Dec. 9, 1864, at Pleasant Valley, Md., of intermittent fever; Daniel T. Wills, Private, died of wounds received at Five Forks, Va., April 1, 1865.

COMPANY E.

John D. Barber, 1st Lieutenant, killed at Winchester, July 27, 1864; Thomas Lunsford, Sergeant, died January 18, 1865, in hospital at Winchester, Va., from wounds received at the hands of Quince Christian; Alexander Kinneer, Corporal, died January 23, 1865, while prisoner of war at Salsbury, N. C.; William Smith, Corporal, died July 16, 1864, in hospital at Gallipolis, O.; Edward Hempfield, Bugler, died Sept. 9, 1864, from wounds received in action; Silas A. Burdett, Private, died Oct. 15, 1863, at Charleston, W. Va.; John L. Chaplin, Private, died Feb. 1862, Guyandotte, W. Va.; James Cochran, Private, died April 25, 1865, of wounds received in action; Samuel A. Durbin, Private, died July 17, 1862, in hospital at Gauley Bridge, West Virginia; Jackson Elderkin, died November 9, 1864, Washington, D. C.; Wm. H. Filkill, Private, died Sept. 15, 1862, Gallipolis, O.; John Goodfellow, Private, died April 11, 1865, Harper's Ferry; William M. Hartford, Private, killed by bushwhackers on Coal river, July 5, 1863; Justice Irwin, Private, died Belle Isle (prisoner) date unknown; John W. Mullen, Private, died March 20, 1865, White House, Va.; William W. Orr, Private, died of wounds received at Lewisburg, Va., May 2, 1863; George Phillips, Private, killed near Winchester, Va., July 27,

1864; Dennis Sullivan, Private, died April 27, 1865 from wounds received in action, Washington, D. C.; Franklin Worman, Private, died March 1862, Guyandotte, Va.

COMPANY F.

Joseph N. Bolen, Private, reported killed near Giles C. H., May 2, 1863; John Fitzpatrick, Private, died from wounds received at Summerville, date unknown; Isaac Howell, Private, date, cause and place unknown; Alpheus T. Martin, Private, died January 22nd, 1865, Pine Grove, O.; George D. Pyle, Private, killed at Appomattox, April 8, 1865; James W. Perry, Private, date, cause and place unknown; Charles J. Pathers, Private, date, cause and place unknown; Freeman Scott, Private, date, cause and place unknown; Joseph P. Taylor, Private, died May 9th, 1862, lung fever, at Charleston, W. Va.

COMPANY G.

Pressly Lunsford, Sergeant, killed in action at Winchester, Va., July 24, 1864; John Dundan, Sergeant, drowned in Kanawha river, February 26, 1864; James McConnell, Corporal, died August 25, 1864, Cumberland, Md.; Jacob Claybaugh, Bugler, killed at Camp Piatt, June 5, 1864; John Collard, Private, died April 10, 1865 in hospital at City Point, Va., of wounds received in action; George Dunfield, Private, died December 11, 1863, in Libby Prison, Va.; Edward Doran, Private, died March 24, 1862, hospital, Guyandotte, Va.; William Dawson, Private, died April 26, 1865, at Fort Monroe of wounds received in action; W. B. Hutchison, Private, killed at Sailor's Creek, April 6, 1865; Alberto Harvey, Private, killed at Lewisburg, Virginia, May 2, 1863; Matthew Miller, Private, died June 1, 1863, at Camp Piatt, Virginia; E. N. J. Moreland, Private, died May 26, 1865, at Nashville, Tennessee; Griff Zinn, Private, killed at Five Forks, Virginia, April 1, 1865.

COMPANY H.

George W. Shoemaker, Second Lieutenant, killed May 2, 1863, at Lewisburg, Virginia; Wm. H. Burn-

side, Sergeant, died September 4, 1862, at Gallipolis,
Ohio; Scott Gard, Corporal, killed June 22, 1864, near
Salem, Virginia; Joseph M. Baxter, Private, died of
wounds received in action July 24, 1864; William Brooks,
Private, died October 3, 1862, at Gallipolis, Ohio; Samuel
Clare, Private, died April 10, 1863, at Charleston, of
typhoid fever; Cyrenus B. Faires, Private, died April 6,
1863, at Camp Piatt, Virginia; William Garvin, Private,
killed June 22, 1864, near Salem, Virginia; Peter God-
dard, Private, died October 1, 1862, at Gallipolis, Ohio;
George W. Hale, Private, killed at Lewisburg, Virginia,
May 2, 1863; Joseph J. Harding, Private, killed at Brush
Mountain, Virginia, June 26, 1864; John R. James, Pri-
vate, died September 10, 1862; Jacob P. Milhoff, Private,
died February 2, 1862, at Guyandotte, Virginia; Thomas
T. Morton, Private, died of wounds received July 24, 1864;
Isaac Moore, Private, killed near Salem, Virginia, June
22, 1864; Benjamin Prim, Private, killed near Salem,
Virginia, June 22, 1864; George W. Simpson, Private,
killed at Fisher's Hill, September 21, 1864; James H.
Smith, Private, killed at Lewisburg, Virginia, May 2, 1863;
Andrew J. Weed, Private, died from wounds received in
action July 22, 1864; Cornelius Worman, Private, died
September 30, 1863, at Gallipolis, Ohio; James Woodram,
Private, killed at Lynchburg, Virginia, June 17, 1864;

COMPANY I.

George K. Weir, First Lieutenant, killed at Fayetts-
ville, September 12, 1862; John W. Hoover, Corporal,
died May 1, 1862, at Charleston, W. Va.; Thomas O'Brien,
Corporal, drowned in New river, Va. May 11, 1864; My-
ron Packard, Corporal, died March 12, 1864, in rebel
prison; Michael Crantz, Private, died March 12, 1862,
at Camp Piatt, Va; David Dill, Private, died May 1, 1863,
Camp Piatt, Va; Isaac Eggers, Private, died December 4,
1863, in Libby Prison; Cyrus Harris, Private, died February, 1862, Guyandotte, Va.; Casper Hewitt, Private,
died from wounds accidentally received at Meadow Bluff,
July 1862; W. E. M. Roberts, Private, died February,

1864, Tenn; Bryon Roberts, Private, killed at Winchester, September 19, 1864; William Robinson, Private, killed at Wytheville, July 18, 1863; David Sluder, Private, died December 12, 1863, Libby Prison.

COMPANY K.

Jacob A. Myers, Sergeant, killed at Fayetteville, Va., July 4, 1863; Rufus Chamberlain, Private, died, date unknown; John Irwin, Private, died, date unknown; John Javens, Private, died, date unknown; Edward Martin, Private, died, date unknown; Daniel O'Donald, Private, killed on B. & O. R. R., July 19, 1864; James Sweeny, Private, killed at Fayetteville, Va., July 4, 1864.

COMPANY L. (attached)

James W. Nicholson, Quartermaster Sergeant, died Summerville, Virginia, November 7, 1863; Alex. H. Bixler, Sergeant, killed near Raleigh C. H. Va., July 14, 1863; Thomas V. Rush, Corporal, killed at Wytheville, Va., July 18, 1863; John H. Debolt, Private, killed near Bulltown, Va., Aug. 21, 1861; John Elliott, Private, killed at Frederick, Md., Sept. 12, 1862; Daniel G. Higby, Private, died Feb. 19, 1862, at Fayetteville, Va; Jacob McCamm, Private, died of wounds received in action at Raleigh, Va., March 19, 1862; James Noble, Private, killed near Raleigh, Va., March 14, 1862; John Shafer, Private, killed at Wythesville, Va., July 18, 1863; John R. Summers, Private, died Oct. 28, 1861, Summersville, Va.; N. R. Walker, Private, died July 21, 1863, Gallipolis, O.

Total—Deaths, 146; discharges for disability, 109; total deaths and discharges, 255.

The first man killed in the regiment was Amos McKee, of Company B, at Jennies Creek, Kentucky, Jan. 7th, 1862. The last man killed in the regiment was George D. Pyle, of Company F, at Appomattox Station, April 8th, 1865.

It has been found impossible to obtain a full and correct list of the wounded.

A PARTIAL LIST OF THE REGIMENT WHO DIED IN ANDERSONVILLE PRISON.

No. of grave		Co.	Date	Disease
2712	John Golden,	G	July 1, 1864,	diarrhœa
4738	Sam'l Gardner,	G	Aug. 4, 1864,	scorbutus
2969	S. C. Jackson,	E	July 25, 1864,	scorbutus
2734	Wm. Leyshon,	I	July 1, 1864,	anasarca
4463	Adam Steele,	C	Aug. 1, 1864,	scorbutus
6098	Granville Jones	D	Aug. 18, 1864,	diarrhœa
39	Myron Packard,	I	Mar. 13, 1864,	pleuritis
2226	Chris. Stewart,	I	June 20, 1864,	diarrhœa

In Danville, Va. prison, Casey L. Kirker, Co. B, died Dec. 1864, diarrhœa.

At Camp Lawton, Millen, Ga., No. of grave, 255, John Hooley, Co. G, no date.

WE OLD BOYS.

'Twas side by side as comrades dear,
  In the dark days long ago,
We fought the fight without a fear,
  And rendered blow for blow.
In battle, march or prison pen,
  Each unto each was true,
As beardless boys became strong men,
  And braved the long war through.

And tho' thro' all these years of peace,
  We've somewhat older grown,
The spirit of those early days
  We'll ever proudly own.
Our grand old flag is just as fair,
  As in the trying time,
When traitors sought its folds to tear,
  And we suppressed the crime.

What if grim age creeps on apace?
  Our souls shall not grow old;
But we will stand as in the days
  When we were warriors bold.
We stood for right—for our dear land,
  For home, and all that's true,
So firmly clasp hand unto hand,
  And comradeship renew.

———✝———

NAMES AND PRESENT POST-OFFICE ADDRESS OF SURVIVORS OF THE SECOND WEST VIRGINIA CAVALRY.

Brigadier General W. H. Powell, Belleville, Ill.
Lieutenant Colonel J. J. Hoffman, Garnett, Kan.
Major C. E. Hambleton, Chicago, Ill.
Major R. L. Curtis, Marietta, Ohio.
Major E. S. Morgan, Zaleski, Ohio.

COMPANY A.

Robert Merrell, Fayetteville, Arkansas.
R. R. Lyman, Salem Center, Meigs County, Ohio.
G. T. Cartwright, Schuyler, Nebraska.
Joseph W. Grimes, Beatrice, Neb.
John Alkire, Harrisville, Ohio.
Andrew Dye, Harrisville, Ohio.
Henry Davis, Harrisville, Ohio.
Thad. S. Romines, Rutland. Ohio.
Sheffield Russell, Rutland, Ohio.
G. W. Woodard, Rutland, Ohio.
J. C. Rupe, Rutland, Ohio.
Perry Hysell, Pomeroy, Ohio.
Seldon Humphrey, Pomeroy, Ohio.
J. M. Humphrey, Pomeroy, Ohio.
Alex. R. Quickle, Pomeroy, Ohio.
Lieutenant E. D. Robinson, Pomeroy, Ohio.
Clark B. Smith, Pomeroy, Ohio.
David C. Smith, Pomeroy, Ohio.
Geo. P. Stout, Pomeroy, Ohio.
James Garner, Pomeroy, Ohio.
Christopher Ihle, Pomeroy, Ohio.
Geo. W. Fultz, Middleport, Ohio.
T. J. Sprague, Middleport, Ohio.
Joseph H. Gilmore, Bradbury, Ohio.
Nathaniel, Sisson, Marysville, Nottoway Co., Missouri.
Florentine Forrest, Osceola, Iowa.
J. B. Newman, Osceola, Iowa.
B. F. Price, Osceola, Iowa.
W. H. Stevens, Osceola, Iowa.
Freeman Forrest, Burlingham, Ohio.
Ira H. Gilkey, Hemlock Grove, Ohio.
W. G. Saunders, Hemlock Grove, Ohio.
Austin Scott, Hemlock Grove, Ohio.
David Welker, Hemlock Grove, Ohio.
Truman Frost, Hemlock Grove, Ohio.
Alonzo Hunt, Dexter, Ohio.
M. W. Rutherford, Union Ridge, Cabell Co., W. Va.

Thomas C. Hughes, Prospect, Marion Co., Ohio.
Isaac Sansbury, Harrisville, Ohio.
Samuel Welker, Rio Grande, Ohio.
Peter Parr, Tupper's Plains, Ohio.
Ellmore Pierce, Langsville, Ohio.
Harvey McClure, Langsville, Ohio.
A. J. Peck, Hartford City, W. Va.
J. W. Ollum, Proctorsville, Ohio.
W. A. Winters, Cutler, Ohio.
J. L. Waller, Centralia, Ill.
A. R. McIntosh, Hanging Rock, Ohio.
T. J. Calhoun, Coal Grove, Ohio.
W. W. Calhoun, Austin, Tex.
Lewis S. Nease, Antiquity, Ohio.
A. J. Greene, Gallipolis, Ohio.
Stephen Schilling, 433 Homer Av., Indianapolis, Ind.
G. W. Morgan, East Unity, N. H.
B. M. Chappell, Clements, Kansas.
Edward Newsome, Wilkesville, Ohio.
A. T. Biggs, Lincoln Centre, Kansas.
Capt. A.Campbell, 908 e. Capitol St.,Washington, D.C.
Charles Campbell, Washington, D. C.
J. A. Crouser, Racine, Ohio.
Charles McClain, Racine, Ohio.
Geo. M. Krofoot, Syracuse, N. Y.
Peter Gerolman, Chester, Ohio.
Arthur C. Love, Dana, Ind.
S. C. McElhany, Kerr, Gallia County, Ohio.
L. R. Barker, Sioux Falls, S. D.

COMPANY B.

R. M. Monroe, Lexington, Ky.
E. T. Vandervort, Haverhill, Ohio.
D. W. Hopkins, Ironton, Ohio.
Jesse Able, Ironton, Ohio.
J. M. Corns, Ironton, Ohio.
H. G. Hopkins, Ironton, Ohio.
W. G. Hopkins, Ironton, Ohio.
S. P. Gates, Ironton, Ohio.

Thomas James, Ironton, Ohio.
Frank Hafflick, Ironton, Ohio.
Stephen Gates, Ironton, Ohio.
Capt. W. S. Merrill, Ironton, Ohio.
Samuel Clark, Ironton, Ohio.
Robert Mitchell, Ironton, Ohio.
John Carmichael, Portsmouth, Ohio.
John Ridout, Wheelersburg, Ohio.
F. Ginheimer, Wheelersburg, Ohio.
Jacob Messer, Minersville, Ohio.
John Sannders, Pedro, Ohio.
A. W. Starling, Ashland, Ky.
Mills C. Hurn, Ashland, Ky.
J. S. Duke, Plattsmouth, Neb.
Chas. B. Morris, Winfield, W. Va.
Chas. L. Morris, Winfield, W. Va.
John H. Dempsey, Hanging Rock, Ohio.
Mordecia Morgan, National Home, Dayton, Ohio.
Thomas Williams, National Home, Dayton, Ohio.
Jefferson Morris, Campbell, Ohio.
W. L. Caruthers, Pocataligo, W. Va.
Cornelius Carr, Gallipolis, Ohio.
Sydney Brammer, Gallipolis, Ohio.
David Lloyd, Birmingham, Ala.
John Blankenship, Rock Camp, Ohio.
C. P. Bertram, Ohio Center, Kan.
W. W. Furguson, Proctorsville, Ohio.
Evan P. Evans, Holcomb, Ohio.
Alfred McCoy, Columbus, Ohio.
George Kiscadden, Hanging Rock, Ohio.
Eugene Syfield, Farraty, W. Va.

COMPANY C.

Columbus Penn, Browning, Mo.
W. Christopher, 2028 Pine street, Philadelphia, Pa.
Joseph Dodds, Brownsville, Ohio.
John McKaig, Beaver Falls, Pa.
G. C. Barnes, 46 Scott street, Cleveland, Ohio.
Capt. E. E. Wilson, Independence, Kan.

John C. Fields, Atwood, Kan.

James B. Mitchell, Jetmore, Kan.`

Samuel Smith, Thayer, Kan.

Lieutenant William Church, Williamsburg, Kan.

A. J. Hamilton, Williamsburg, Kan.

Capt. Thomas Neal, Pratt, Kan.

S. E. Young, Pratt, Kan.

Lieut. Geo. S. South, 244 Federal St., Alleghany, Pa.

J. M. Wilson, 1172, Santa Fe avenue, Denver, Col.

Alvin Porter, Valparaiso, Neb.

Samuel Ridgeway, Brownsville, Ohio.

Charles Switzer, Brownsville, Ohio.

Elias Stewart, Brownsville, Ohio.

John Brown, Antioch, Ohio.

James W. Brown, Antioch, Ohio.

R. M. Hoffman, Antioch, Ohio.

J. M. Hoffman, Antioch, Ohio.

John M. Burns, Crown Hill, W. Va.

John Coldbaugh, 132 Boyd street, Pittsburg, Pa.

COMPANY D.

A. J. Bobo, Golightly, Alabama.

Morgan Morgan, Zaleski, Ohio.

George Tinkham, Athens, Ohio.

J. S. Shuster, Zaleski, Ohio.

E. A. Johnson, Zaleski, Ohio.

John Kale, Zaleski, Ohio.

James Steele, Wellston, Ohio.

J. F. Tomlinson, McArthur, Ohio.

Pearl Dunkle, McArthur, Ohio.

Frank McDowd, McArthur, Ohio.

John Harbarger, 551 Henry street, Columbus, Ohio.

Lieut. G. W. Snyder, 226 17th St., Columbus, O.

Lieutenant W. S. McClannahan, Creola, Ohio.

Lieutenant J. A. Hoover, Pontiac, Illinois.

B. F. Coulter, Zif, Wayne, County, Illinois.

I. N. Cooper, Caldwell, Kansas.

G. W. Fouts, Ashland, Kentucky.

J. L. Hawks, Loup City, Nebraska.

Z. Chidester, Rock Elm, Wisconsin.

G. F. Black, Remple, Jackson County, Ohio.

Wm. Ervine, Dundas, Ohio.

Joseph W. Andrews, Proctorsville, Ohio.

Dominick O'Donnell, Midland, Missouri.

Capt. John McNally, Pittsburg, Kansas.

J. W. Tatman, Kinderhook, Ohio.

Isaiah Nixon, St. Charles, Iowa.

L. M. McQuaid, Adelphi, Ohio.

Samuel Watkins, Adelphi, Ohio.

John McElhaney, Tennessee City, Tenn.

Emanuel Jones, Walton, Roane County, W. Va.

Robert Workman, Orange, Boone County, W. Va.

Anderson Miller, Orange, Boone County, W. Va.

Edward Soulsby, Hartford City, W. Va.

Sylvester Shry, Columbus, Ohio.

COMPANY E.

Captain Jeremiah Davidson, Ironton, Ohio.

Benjamin Addis, Aid, Lawrence County, Ohio.

I. W. Bunch, Wellston, Ohio.

N. P. Wickersham, Wood River, Neb.

B. F. Fouts, Washington Center, Mo.

Thomas Crisman, Golden, Col.

John L. McMasters, Indianapolis, Ind.

Alex Oliver, Trenton, Mo.

R. L. Coburn, Beverly, Ohio.

R. H. Gilbert, Brooks, Adams County, Ohio.

Archibald Grubb, Waterford, Ohio.

James Burrows, Beverly, Ohio.

Jacob Smith, Rockbridge, Ohio.

Azel S. Vickrey, Sweet Springs, Mo.

A. H. Perry, Fishtown, Ohio.

Elbridge Miller, Watertown, Ohio.

J. M. King, Virginia City, Montana.

G. P. Sanford, Marietta, Ohio.

Martin Eckleberry, Dresden, Ohio.

Solomon Love, 205 North Fourth street, Columbus, O.

W. C. Weir, Columbus, Ohio.

COMPANY F.

Thomas Sharp, Hamlin, W. Va.

Thomas Gray, London, Tenn.

Seneca A. Cowce, Milwaukee, Wis.

Harvey Langley, Milwaukee, Wis.

John Dyer, Goshen, Kan.

John J. McDeid, Zanesville, Ohio.

John A. Goodwin, Zanesville, Ohio.

David Stouts, Zanesville, Ohio.

Hugh S. Hankinson, Zanesville, Ohio.

W. R. Cassell, Zanesville, Ohio.

Paul F. Crouley, National Home, Dayton, Ohio.

Charles V. Dyer, Conroe, Tex.

William McAtee, Dudley, Ohio.

D. J. Morgaradge, New Haven, W. Va.

W. T. Wilson, Keysport, Penn.

John Styers, Beverly, Ohio.

James B. Nichols, Beverly, Ohio.

George W. Rodgers, Parkersburg, W. Va.

John F. Dearner, Parkersburg, W. Va.

Elijah Mains, New Straitsville, W. Va.

Simeon Mains, Patton's Mills, W. Va.

W. H. Rarden, Bartlett, W. Va.

Daniel Ross, Heath, W. Va.

Geo. K. Denny, War Department, Washington, D. C.

COMPANY G.

John Daley, Ironton, Ohio.

James Daley, Ironton, Ohio.

Major John McMahon, Ironton, Ohio.

George Briner, Ironton, Ohio.

Mark King, Ironton, Ohio.

Thomas Barron, Ironton, Ohio.

Richard E. Barron, Ironton, Ohio.

William Doran, Ironton, Ohio.

Levi Lunsford, Ironton, Ohio.

John Harvey, Ironton, Ohio.

James B. Butler, Ironton, Ohio.

Joshua Ashcraft, Ironton, Ohio.

William Woods, Ironton, Ohio.

J. R. Morford, 704 Del avenue, Columbus, Ohio.

Julien R. Morford, Crone, Ohio.

James Barnhart, Coalton, Ohio.

Joseph Jones, Hecla Furnace, Lawrence County, O.

Phillip Riter, Hecla Furnace, Lawrence County, O.

Michael Barrett, Vesuvius F'ce, Lawrence County, O.

C. Waits, Catlettsburg, Ky.

F. J. Zehring, National Home, Dayton, Ohio.

Elam Willey, Hinton, W. Va

John K. Dietz, Charleston, W. Va.

David Todd, Charleston, W. Va.

Granville Sloan, Waverly, Ohio.

George Coates, Wilmington, Del.

COMPANY H.

Emerson McMillin, 40 Wall street, New York.

Martin Cramer, Chillicothe, Ohio.

John Gardner, Hamden Junction, Ohio.

John Radcliff, Buchtel, Ohio.

James Flowers, Portsmouth, Ohio.

Lieutenant Jas. W. Ricker, Portsmouth, Ohio.

Jos. J. Sutton, Portsmouth, Ohio.

Andrew McMillin, Jackson, Ohio.

Jefferson Howe, Jackson, Ohio.

C. H. Willis, Jackson, Ohio.

Nathaniel Hoover, Jackson, Ohio.

Columbus Weed, Jackson, Ohio.

H. H. Marshman, Jackson, Ohio.

John Patton, Jackson, Ohio.

Joseph Meyers, Jackson, Ohio.

Murray McMillin, Marietta, Ohio.

W. E. Tucker, Dundas, Ohio.

James Hutchinson, Wellston, Ohio.

David Bartoe, Wellston, Ohio.

E. G. Kinnison, Oregon avenue, Columbus, Ohio.

S. S. Hawk, Columbus, Ohio.

J. F. Helphenstein, Columbus, Ohio.

R. E. Hull, Cutler, Ohio.

A. J. Louderback, Schell, Ohio.
J. A. Umpleby, Dennison, Ohio.
D. W. Cherrington, Irwin, Ohio.
W. H. Lane, Huntington, W. Va.
Allen Landers, Huntington, W. Va.
G. W. Fullerton, New Cumberland, W. Va.
Felix Baxter, Sutton, W. Va.
J. W. T. Poor, North Vernon, Ind.
G. A. Stewart, Stockton, Kan.
Alonzo Tarr, Thayer, Kan.
M. O. Sutherland, Conway Springs, Kan.
A. A. Grossman, Bosworth, Mo.
Wm. J. McArron, Long Lane, Mo.
A. T. Philley, 6106 S. Tenth street, St. Louis, Mo.
C. W. Branson, Quitman, Mo.
Charles Weed, Kennard, Neb.
P. V. Ellis, Sigourney, Iowa.
Wm. Brunton, Coalton, Ohio.

COMPANY I.

V. S. Hawk, Nelsonville, Ohio.
G. W. Loudon, Nelsonville, Ohio,
Daniel Varran, Nelsonville, Ohio.
L. J. Kline, Nelsonville, Ohio.
J. A. Lowe, Jackson, Ohio.
A. Bowen, Middleport, Ohio.
Edward Thompson, Middleport, Ohio.
William Dawson, Middleport, Ohio.
Lewis Price, Middleport, Ohio.
John H. Lowes, Carbon Hill, Ohio.
John Terrell, Pomeroy, Ohio.
George W. Wiggins, Pomeroy, Ohio.
John C. Carr, Bear Creek, Ohio.
F. M. Bobo, Valley Ford, Ohio.
G. W. Fellows, Long Bottom, Ohio.
James W. Hicks, Hazel, Ohio.
George Humphrey, Harrisville, Ohio.
E. E. Curtis, Garden, Ohio.
J. A. Cowdry, Lyons, Kansas.

Thomas Lax, Longstreth, Ohio.

G. W. Montgomery, 57 Hunt avenue, Columbus, Ohio.

Todd Gilliam, 50 North 4th street, Columbus, Ohio.

Daniel Dudley, Waverly, Ohio.

Gaston Hysell, Henking, Ohio

Wm. Murrah, Ruthland, Ohio.

Henry Crumble, Bridgeport, Ohio.

Wm. Miller, Cheshire, Ohio.

Dorsey Vancleif, Tuppers Plains, Ohio.

Allen Stiff, Wellston, Ohio.

B. F. Miller, White Eye Plains, Ohio.

Wm. Murray, Racine, Ohio.

S. F. Hawk, Ravenwood, W. Va.

Joseph Robson, Malden, Ohio.

Charles Glover, Charleston, W. Va.

Robert House, Fayettte Station, W. Va.

E. L. Gilliam, Leetart, W. Va.

William M. Bone, Logan C. H., W. Va.

David Price, Logan C. H., W. Va.

D. H. Bone, Logan, C. H., W. Va.

H. T. Spicer, Guyandotte, W. Va.

John Warner, Martinsburg, W. Va.

Spencer Saulcer, Point Pleasant, W. Va.

Macon R. Willis, Showners Cross Roads, Tenn.

Moses Price, Showners Cross Roads, Tenn.

Jesse Mahaley, Showners Cross Roads, Tenn.

Wm. Mahaley, Showners Cross Roads, Tenn.

Timothy Roarak, Showners Cross Roads, Tenn.

Jesse Roarak, Showners Cross Roads, Tenn.

Rueben Cornett, Showners Cross Roads, Tenn.

Wm. Price, Showners Cross Roads, Tenn.

Capt. W. S. Fortescue, Leavenworth, Kan.

Lieut. E. A. Rosser, Coffeeville, Kan.

W. H. Fountain, El Dorado, Kan.

Lieut. J. B. Carlisle, El Dorado, Kan.

A. C. Torrence, Ellinwood, Kan.

J. A. Cowdry, Lyndon, Kan.

H. P. Lee, Ingalls, Kan.

W. H. Buckner, Daceta, Minn.
James Stanley, Haldridge, Neb.
G. W. Calvert, Leadville, Col.
John Lamb, Danville, Ill.

COMPANY K.

Lemuel Barr, Culbertson, Ohio.
James McGovern, Wellston, Ohio.
Sanford Stewart, Wellston, Ohio.
S. H. Emmons, Passaic, N. J.
Pleasant Webb, Rock Camp, Ohio.
J. K. Hastings, Sciotoville, Ohio.
J. H. Emmons, Ironton, Ohio.
Abraham Cotheran, Ironton, Ohio.
John Ward, Ironton, Ohio.
Walter Colford, Ironton, Ohio.
Evan Goodman, Ironton, Ohio.
Charles Shelton, Ironton, Ohio.
Major E. S. Morgan, Zaleski, Ohio.

COMPANY M.

A. S. Dempsey, Berlin X Roads, Ohio.
James M. Carrick, Berlin X Roads, Ohio.
Benjamin Kiser, Berlin X Roads, Ohio.
Lieut. W. J. Kirkendall, Dawkins Mills, Ohio.
Isaac Palmer, Dawkins Mills, Ohio.
William Call, Jackson, Ohio.
J. W. Beyron, Jackson, Ohio.
William Montgomery, Wellston, Ohio.
Milton McKinniss, Wellston, Ohio.
J. McLaughlin, Wellston, Ohio.
Wesley Harmon, Wellston, Ohio.
Nathan Lott, Wellston, Ohio.
D. Halderman, Ironton, Ohio.
John Souders, Gallia Furnace, Ohio.
Robert Steele. Athens, Ohio.
George Zinn, Riverton, Ohio.
Joseph Provance, Walsenburg, Col.
Geo. M. Quimby, 877 East Long Street, Columbus, O.

Lightning Source UK Ltd.
Milton Keynes UK
31 August 2010
159207UK00006B/81/P